The
Greatest
Horse Stories
Ever Told

The
Greatest
Horse Stories
Ever Told

EDITED AND WITH AN INTRODUCTION BY
STEVEN D. PRICE

THE LYONS PRESS
Guilford, Connecticut
An imprint of The Globe Pequot Press

The Lyons Press is an imprint of The Globe Pequot Press

10 9 8 7 6 5

Printed in the United States of America

Designed by Compset, Inc.

ISBN 1-59228-011-0 (paperback edition)

The Library of Congress has cataloged an earlier hardcover edition as follows:

The greatest horse stories ever told / edited and with an introduction by Steven D. Price.
     Viii, 257 p. ; 24 cm.
     Essays and articles originally published in various journals and books.
     ISBN 1-58574-237-6
1. Horses—Anecdotes. 2. Horsemanship—Anecdotes. I. Price, Steven D.

SF301.G72 2001
636.1—dc21

                           2001038117

Contents

General Introduction

Reading an anthology of short fiction, essays and articles about horses may be an entertainment, but compiling one is a real education.

As someone who has spent literally the better part of his life delving into equestrian literature, and doing so with the interest and enthusiasm that approach that of being around horses, I had no reluctance to take on the task. A plethora of writing was out there, I knew. However, what I hadn't realized was the number of selections from which to draw. The easy part of the job was locating and then reading the candidates; making the choices was the hard part.

In the course of compiling this volume, I discovered that a disproportionate number of candidates, both fiction and nonfiction, dealt with thoroughbred racing and foxhunting. The reason would at first blush appear to have to do with the British sporting tradition, since both pursuits trace their origins to the British Isles.

However, success in racing and hunting also involves huge amounts of uncertainty—some would call it luck—which is the stuff of which high drama and low comedy and every other kind of literature in between are made.

By the same token, I was surprised by the rarity of good writing about another sport with British connections, polo. Although Kipling's "The Maltese Cat" is a notable exception, that story appears in so many other equestrian anthologies that to omit it here was an easy decision to make. Perhaps sometime soon writers will rectify the lack of good polo stories; the sport certainly provides ample fodder.

The selections reveal a wide range of activities in which horses take part. That was entirely intentional. In addition to racing and hunting are dressage, cutting, draft horses, western ranch work, show jumping, driving, and several aspects of pleasure riding and of training the horse and rider. It was also my intention that readers who are involved in one of these disciplines or perhaps in one that has not been included will find something of value in all the selections.

The variety of styles and purposes will help in that regard. You will find humor in the selections by Cooky McClung and Damon Runyon, inspiration in the ones by Gene Smith and Ellie Phayer, nostalgia in Clarence Day and Ben Green, instructiveness in Tom McGuane and Colonel Podhajsky, lyricism in Felix Salten and James Herriott, and pure emotion in Esther Forbes and William Nack. Indeed, something for everyone.

Despite the diversity of subject matter and style, there is, I would suggest, a certain commonality. Joseph Conrad saw the writer's task as "by the power of the written word, to make you hear, to make you feel—that is, before all, to make you see." By sharing their experiences with and insights into horses, all the authors allow us take part in competitive victories and losses, training advances and frustrations, companionship, exhilaration and sadness, self-realizations, life and death. Through the perceptions and narrative power of these writers, we are able to view and, in no small way, to understand horses just as clearly as we see them in works by Stubbs, Remington, Munnings or any other great sporting artist.

And, as if looking into a mirror held up to life, we come to see not only horses but ourselves in relation to the animal we prize above all others.

—Steven D. Price

The
Greatest
Horse Stories
Ever Told

Mr. T.'s Heart

BY JANE SMILEY

J ane Smiley, who won the 1992 Pulitzer Prize for fiction for *A Thousand Acres,* is an accomplished equestrienne. Articles on a variety of subjects involving horses and riding, such as this one, have appeared in *Practical Horseman* and other magazines.

I always suspected Mr. T. had one of those large economy-size thoroughbred hearts: maybe not Secretariat size (twenty-two pounds) or Mill Reef size (seventeen pounds), but larger and stronger than average (seven pounds). The horse was a fitness machine.

In five years of riding and eventing, I had never tired him out. He was always ready for more, even if I was nearly falling off him from the exertion.

Every year at his well-horse checkup, the vet would comment on his dropped beats—he could drop two or even three (five seconds between two heartbeats seems like a very long time when the horse is standing before you, apparently alive and well)—and attribute it to the residual effect of a great deal of exercise early in life. (He was a racehorse for eight years and had fifty-two starts.) Thus it was that I wasn't too worried when this year, Mr. T.'s twenty-first, the vet detected what he called arrhythmia. As I was taking another horse up to the vet clinic at UC Davis anyway, I packed Mr. T. along.

The results weren't good. On the one hand, the senior cardiologist shook my hand and thanked me for bringing him a big, lean thoroughbred with a heart that was so efficient and powerful that through the stethoscope it was nearly deafening. On the other hand, that arrhythmia had a name. It was "atrial fibrillation"; and it wasn't just a quirk, it was a potentially dangerous condition. The horse could drop dead at any moment.

I was impressed in spite of myself (and in spite of my conviction that Mr. T. was going to live forever) and agreed to have him "converted"—that is, to allow the cardiologist to administer a powerful and toxic drug, quinidine, that might or might not convert his chaotic heart rhythm to a normal or "sinous" rhythm. It was an in-patient procedure. I left him there and brought my other horse home.

Mr. T. was a very bad patient. He wouldn't eat, wouldn't relax, would hardly drink. His separation anxiety was so great that the cardiologist actually feared for his survival. He did, however, "convert"—his heart rhythm returned to normal, without any dropped beats—and stayed converted.

The bad news was that the dose it had taken to convert him was very close to toxic. There would be no trying this again. And the quinidine took maybe twice as long to clear his system as usual, putting him at risk in other ways.

I tried not to pay attention to the cardiologist's other remark—that the longer the heart had been arrhythmic, the less likely a permanent conversion. Those dropped beats we had always heard—I wasn't going to admit the possibility that his heart had been arrhythmic as long as I had known him.

As some readers of this magazine may know, Mr. T. (profiled in November 1998's "Why I Can't Find a New Horse") had stopped being a jumper—age, an eye injury, and timidity on my part. But not long after I wrote about him, he started jumping again, and he was great at it, as he had once been—energetic, fast, and full of thrust. And there was no changing his go-for-it style. I'd tried that, and it had just made him confused and anxious. You couldn't parse a fence or a combination or a course and try to get him to jump in a relaxed, easy style. You had to sit up, hold on, and let him do it. It was hugely exciting.

Anyway, two weeks after the conversion, Mike, my local vet, took another EKG. Tick Tock Tick Tock (that was the horse's real name), everything was perfect. I began conditioning Mr. T. for an event at the end of June.

I was well organized in my training, for once. I had him entered in a schooling show, in a couple of jumper classes, and I was galloping him at a local training track once a week. At the beginning of June, I took him over to the track, a half-mile oval. As soon as we entered the gate, he picked up a huge, even, ground-covering trot on very light contact. He trotted happily, his ears pricked, for two miles. Then I walked him half a mile and asked for the canter. For a mile, it was collected, even, easy, a perfect joy. Then I walked him again.

At the last, I gave in to impulse. After he had caught his breath, I turned him, bridged my reins, and assumed galloping position. I said, out loud,

"Pick your own pace," and he did. He took hold and shot forward, switching leads and going faster about every eighth of a mile, exactly like a racehorse. But then, he was always a racehorse. The other stuff was just for fun.

For me, the "breeze" was both frightening and exhilarating—as fast as I had ever gone on a horse, but incredibly stable. Yes, I was not in control, but he was, and I never doubted that he knew exactly where each foot was at every stride. More important, all this exercise was effortless. He was hardly blowing after we had gone half a mile and I managed to bring him down. It took him the usual ten minutes to cool out.

Three days later, we went to the show. He warmed up and jumped around perfectly, won a couple of ribbons, seemed happy.

Thus it was that I couldn't believe it, four days after that, when Mike told me that his atrial fibrillation was back, and possibly worse. His heart rhythm was chaotic. We took another EKG, sent it off to Davis, discussed it more than necessary with lots of vets. The cardiologist's recommendation was discouraging—walking around, maybe a little trotting from time to time. But, I said. But. But when I galloped him on the track, the work was effortless for him.

The answer to the riddle was in his large, strong heart. He had enough overcapacity to give himself some leeway, to oxygenate himself thoroughly almost all of the time. The danger, to me as well as to him, was that his overcapacity was unpredictable. He could literally be doing fine one moment and drop dead the next. And, the cardiologist suggested, in accordance with the no-free-lunch principle, greater-than-average heart size often went with arrhythmia. His recommendation stayed the same—walking, a little jogging from time to time.

I stopped riding the horse. I'm not sure why, except that I was confused and ambivalent. One day I decided to ignore the cardiologist's advice, the next day I decided to heed it. Mr. T. and I were used to working, and working pretty hard. If we weren't allowed to work hard together, then what? I didn't know. I let him hang out in the pasture with his broodmare friend.

Not too long ago, I decided to pretty much ignore the cardiologist. I wouldn't be stupid and run Mr. T. cross-country or "breeze" him again, but I would do dressage and jump and treat him like a normal horse.

That very day, I went out to give him a carrot, and he was standing in the shade, pawing the ground. I put him in a stall with lots of water and no food—he'd been colicky before. By bedtime, he had manured three or four times.

In the morning he seemed right as rain, so I began introducing a bit of hay. He continued to seem fine. After noon, I let him out. An hour later, he was pawing and looking at his flanks. I called Mike, who was engaged but promised to come ASAP.

Half an hour later, the horse was eating manure. My heart sank. Even though Mike and another vet I asked said this meant nothing with regard to colic, I knew differently. I had never seen him do such a thing, and I thought it was an act of equine desperation.

The rest of the day was a losing battle. No matter how much painkiller of whatever kind we gave him, the pain could not be alleviated. And his atrial fibrillation meant that he could not tolerate surgery. The impaction, which may or may not have been a torsion, was out of reach and would not dissolve. At 10:00 P.M., I said to Mike, "Are you telling me now's the time?"

He said, "Yes."

I led Mr. T. out of the lighted stall where we had been trying to treat him. He moved, but his head was down and he was hardly conscious of me. We went out into the grassy pasture where he had wandered at large every day of the spring. I knelt down in front of my horse's lowered head, and I told him what a wonderful horse he was, perfect from top to toe every minute. Then Mike gave him the two big shots of barbiturates that would cause him to arrest.

Arrest what?

His heart.

It didn't take more than a second or two. Mike held the lead rope. The collapse of a horse is always earth-shaking. His haunches drop backward, his head flies up, his knees buckle, he fells to the side. We flocked around him, petting and talking to him, but he was gone already.

After everyone left, my boyfriend and I covered him with blankets and went in the house.

I slept fitfully, unable to grasp the suddenness and enormity of the death of my dear friend and constant companion. Each time I woke up, I dreaded going out there at daybreak—what would he look like? How would the mare be acting? What would I do next with a thirteen-hundred-pound body?

When it was finally time to get up, my boyfriend got up with me, and we went out. The mare was in her stall, quiet. I fed her. Then we approached the mound. Fermentation from the impacted food had already begun—under the blanket, my horse's belly was beginning visibly to swell.

I folded back the cover, expecting something horrible, but Mr. T.'s eyes were closed—a kindness my boyfriend had done me the night before. I can't express how important this was. It was not that I had ever seen his eyes closed before. I had not—he was too alert to sleep in my presence. Rather, it was that, looking familiarly asleep, he looked uniquely at peace.

We sat down next to his head and stroked and petted him and talked. I admired, once again, his well-shaped ears, his beautiful head and throatlatch, his open nostrils, his silky coat, his textbook front legs that raced fifty-two times, in addition to every other sort of equine athletic activity, and were as clean at twenty years old as the day he was born. I admired his big, round, hard feet.

But we didn't just talk to him and about him. We relaxed next to him, stroking and petting, and talking about other things, too. We felt the coolness of his flesh, and it was pleasant, not gruesome. We stayed with him long enough to recognize that he was not there, that this body was like a car he had driven and now had gotten out of. The mare watched us, but she, too, was calm.

Later, when I spoke to the manager of my other mares and foals, she told me that when a foal dies, you always leave it with the mare for a while—long enough for her to realize fully that it is not going to get up again, and to come to terms with that. I thought then that this is true of people, too. We have to experience the absence of life in order to accept it.

My friends know that I adored Mr. T. to a boring and sometimes embarrassing degree. I would *kvell* at the drop of a riding helmet about his every quirk and personal quality. He was a good, sturdy, handsome horse, and a stakes winner, but not a horse of unusual accomplishment or exceptional beauty. He was never unkind and never unwilling—those were his special qualities. Nevertheless, I watched him and doted over him and appreciated him day after day for almost six years.

The result is a surprising one. I miss him less, rather than more. Having loved him in detail (for example, the feel of his right hind leg stepping under me, then his left hind, then his right hind again . . . for example, the sight of his ears pricking as he caught sight of me over his stall door . . . for example, the sight of him strolling across his paddock . . . for example, the feel in my hands of him taking hold and coming under as we approached a fence . . . for example, the sound of his nicker), I have thousands of clear images of him right with me. I think I miss him less than I thought I would because I don't feel him to be absent.

There is no way to tell non-horsey people that the companionship of a horse is not like that of a dog, or a cat, or a person. Perhaps the closest two consciousnesses can ever come is the wordless simultaneity of horse and rider focusing together on a jump or a finish line or a canter pirouette, and then executing what they have intended together. What two bodies are in such continuous, prolonged closeness as those of a horse and rider completing a hundred-mile endurance ride or a three-day event? I have a friend who characterizes riding as "one nervous system taking over another." I often wonder—which is doing the taking over, and which is being taken over?

I never expected to be writing this article. Rather, I intended, in twenty years, to write, "Oldest Known Equine Is Seventeen-Hand Ex-Racehorse." But I see it is time to take my own advice, the advice I gave my daughter when she got her first real boyfriend. I told her that no matter what happened with this boyfriend, once she had experienced the joys of a happy and close relationship, she would always know how to have that again, and would always have that again. And the truth is, that works for horses, too.

The Lady Who Rides to Hounds

From *Hunting Sketches*

BY ANTHONY TROLLOPE

The nineteenth-century British author Anthony Trollope, best known for his Barchester novels, was a passionate horseman. For example, whenever he traveled around Ireland in his capacity of postal inspector, he rode one horse and led another; when he encountered a foxhunt in progress, he tied his hack to a tree and set off on his hunter to join in. At the end of the hunt, he simply changed mounts and continued about his business.

This selection provides a droll analysis of foxhunting and the men and women who ride to hounds.

Among those who hunt there are two classes of hunting people who always like it, and these people are hunting parsons and hunting ladies. That it should be so is natural enough. In the life and habits of parsons and ladies there is much that is antagonistic to hunting, and they who suppress this antagonism do so because they are Nimrods at heart. But the riding of these horsemen under difficulties—horsemen and horsewomen—leaves a strong impression on the casual observer of hunting; for to such an one it seems that the hardest riding is forthcoming exactly where no hard riding should be expected. On the present occasion I will, if you please, confine myself to the lady who rides to hounds, and will begin with an assertion, which will not be contradicted, that the number of such ladies is very much on the increase.

Women who ride, as a rule, ride better than men. They, the women, have always been instructed; whereas men have usually come to ride without any instruction. They are put upon ponies when they are all boys, and put

themselves upon their fathers' horses as they become hobbledehoys: and thus
they obtain the power of sticking on to the animal while he gallops and
jumps—and even while he kicks and shies; and, so progressing, they achieve an
amount of horsemanship which answers the purposes of life. But they do not
acquire the art of riding with exactness, as women do, and rarely have such
hands as a woman has on a horse's mouth. The consequence of this is that
women fall less often than men, and the field is not often thrown into the horror which would arise were a lady known to be in a ditch with a horse lying
on her.

I own that I like to see three or four ladies out in a field, and I like it
the better if I am happy enough to count one or more of them among my own
acquaintances. Their presence tends to take off from hunting that character of
horseyness—of both fast horseyness and slow horseyness—which has become,
not unnaturally, attached to it, and to bring it within the category of gentle
sports. There used to prevail an idea that the hunting man was of necessity loud
and rough, given to strong drinks, ill adapted for the poetries of life, and perhaps a little prone to make money out of his softer friend. It may now be said
that this idea is going out of vogue, and that hunting men are supposed to have
that same feeling with regard to their horses—the same and no more—which
ladies have for their carriage or soldiers for their swords. Horses are valued
simply for the services that they can render, and are only valued highly when
they are known to be good servants. That a man may hunt without drinking or
swearing, and may possess a nag or two without any propensity to sell it or
them for double their value, is now beginning to be understood. The oftener
that women are to be seen "out," the more will such improved feelings prevail
as to hunting, and the pleasanter will be the field to men who are not horsey,
but who may nevertheless be good horsemen. There are two classes of women
who ride to hounds, or rather, among many possible classifications, there are
two to which I will now call attention. There is the lady who rides, and demands assistance; and there is the lady who rides, and demands none. Each always—I may say always—receives all the assistance that she may require; but
the difference between the two, to the men who ride with them, is very great.
It will, of course, be understood that, as to both these samples of female Nimrods, I speak of ladies who really ride—not of those who grace the coverts
with, and disappear under the auspices of, their papas or their grooms when
the work begins.

The lady who rides and demands assistance in truth becomes a nuisance before the run is over, let her beauty be ever so transcendent, her horsemanship ever-so perfect, and her battery of general feminine artillery ever so

powerful. She is like the American woman, who is always wanting your place in a railway carriage—and demanding it, too, without the slightest idea of paying you for it with thanks; whose study it is to treat you as though she ignored your existence while she is appropriating your services. The hunting lady who demands assistance is very particular about her gates, requiring that aid shall be given to her with instant speed, but that the man who gives it shall never allow himself to be hurried as he renders it. And she soon becomes reproachful—oh, so soon! It is marvellous to watch the manner in which a hunting lady will become exacting, troublesome, and at last imperious—deceived and spoilt by the attention which she receives. She teaches herself to think at last that a man is a brute who does not ride as though he were riding as her servant, and that it becomes her to assume indignation if every motion around her is not made with some reference to her safety, to her comfort, or to her success. I have seen women look as Furies look, and heard them speak as Furies are supposed to speak, because men before them could not bury themselves and their horses out of their way at a moment's notice, or because some pulling animal would still assert himself while they were there, and not sink into submission and dog-like obedience for their behoof.

I have now before my eyes one who was pretty, brave, and a good horse-woman; but how men did hate her! When you were in a line with her there was no shaking her off. Indeed, you were like enough to be shaken off yourself, and to be rid of her after that fashion. But while you were with her you never escaped her at a single fence, and always felt that you were held to be trespassing against her in some manner. I shall never forget her voice—"Pray, take care of that gate." And yet it was a pretty voice, and elsewhere she was not given to domineering more than is common to pretty women in general; but she had been taught badly from the beginning, and she was a pest. It was the same at every gap. "Might I ask you not to come too near me?" And yet it was impossible to escape her. Men could not ride wide of her, for she would not ride wide of them. She had always some male escort with her, who did not ride as she rode, and consequently, as she chose to have the advantage of an escort—of various escorts—she was always in the company of some who did not feel as much joy in the presence of a pretty young woman as men should do under all circumstances. "Might I ask you not to come too near me?" If she could only have heard the remarks to which this constant little request of hers gave rise. She is now the mother of children, and her hunting days are gone, and probably she never makes that little request. Doubtless that look, made up partly of offence and partly of female dignity, no longer clouds her brow. But I fancy that they who knew her of old in the hunting field never approach her now without fancying that they hear those reproachful words, and see that powerful look of injured feminine weakness.

But there is the hunting lady who rides hard and never asks for assistance. Perhaps I may be allowed to explain to embryo Dianas—to the growing huntresses of the present age—that she who rides and makes no demand receives attention as close as it ever given to her more imperious sister. And how welcome she is! What a grace she lends to the day's sport! How pleasant it is to see her in her pride of place, achieving her mastery over the difficulties in her way by her own wit—as all men, and all women also, must really do who intend to ride to hounds; and doing it all without any sign that the difficulties are too great for her!

The lady who rides like this is in truth seldom in the way. I have heard men declare that they would never wish to see a side-saddle in the field because women are troublesome, and because they must be treated with attention lest the press of the moment be ever so instant. From this I dissent altogether. The small amount of courtesy that is needed is more than atoned for by the grace of her presence, and in fact produces no more impediment in the hunting-field than in other scenes of life. But in the hunting-field, as in other scenes, let assistance never be demanded by a woman. If the lady finds that she cannot keep a place in the first flight without such demands on the patience of those around her, let her acknowledge to herself that the attempt is not in her line, and that it should be abandoned. If it be the ambition of a hunting lady to ride straight—and women have very much of this ambition—let her use her eyes but never her voice; and let her ever have a smile for those who help her in her little difficulties. Let her never ask any one "to take care of that gate," or look as though she expected the profane crowd to keep aloof from her. So shall she win the hearts of those around her, and go safely through brake and brier, over ditch and dyke, and meet with a score of knights around her who will be willing and able to give her eager aid should the chance of any moment require it.

There are two accusations which the more demure portion of the world is apt to advance against hunting ladies—or, as I should better say, against hunting as an amusement for ladies. It leads to flirting, they say—to flirting of a sort which mothers would not approve; and it leads to fast habits—to ways and thoughts which are of the horse horsey—and of the stable, strongly tinged with the rack and manger. The first of these accusations is, I think, simply made in ignorance. As girls are brought up among us now-a-days, they may all flirt, if they have a mind to do so; and opportunities for flirting are much better and much more commodious in the ball-room, in the drawing-room, or in the park, than they are in the hunting-field. Nor is the work in hand of a nature to create flirting tendencies—as, it must be admitted, is the nature of the work in hand when the floors are waxed and the fiddles are going. And this error has sprung from, or forms part of, another, which is wonderfully common among non-hunting folk. It is very widely thought by many, who do not, as a rule, put themselves in opposition to the amusements of the world, that hunting in itself is a wicked thing; that hunting men are fast, given to unclean living and bad ways of life; that they usually go to bed drunk, and that they go about the world roaring hunting cries, and disturbing the peace of the innocent generally. With such men, who could wish that wife, sister, or daughter should associate? But I venture to say that this opinion, which I believe to be common, is erroneous, and that men who hunt are not more iniquitous than men who go out fishing, or play dominoes, or dig in their gardens. Maxima debetur pueris reverentia, and still more to damsels; but if boys and girls will never go where they will hear more to injure them than they will usually do amidst the ordinary conversation of a hunting field, the maxima reverentia will have been attained.

As to that other charge, let it be at once admitted that the young lady who has become of the horse horsey has made a fearful, almost a fatal mistake. And so also has the young man who falls into the same error. I hardly know to which such phase of character may be most injurious. It is a pernicious vice, that of succumbing to the beast that carries you, and making yourself, as it were, his servant, instead of keeping him ever as yours. I will not deny that I have known a lady to fall into this vice from hunting; but so also have I known ladies to marry their music-masters and to fall in love with their footmen. But not on that account are we to have no music-masters and no footmen.

Let the hunting lady, however, avoid any touch of this blemish, remembering that no man ever likes a woman to know as much about a horse as he thinks he knows himself.

Pure Heart

BY WILLIAM NACK

I had the unusual opportunity to watch Secretariat's Belmont States triumph on the television set in the jockey's room at Hollywood Park race track. When the horse cantered home by 32 lengths, everyone in the room—and those jocks, valets and others were as unsentimental a group of veteran hardboots as ever gathered under one roof—stood up and applauded.

Published in *Sports Illustrated*, William Nack's tribute to Secretariat movingly captures the universal appeal of that great horse.

Just before noon the horse was led haltingly into a van next to the stallion barn, and there a concentrated barbiturate was injected into his jugular. Forty-five seconds later there was a crash as the stallion collapsed. His body was trucked immediately to Lexington, Ky., where Dr. Thomas Swerczek, a professor of veterinary science at the University of Kentucky, performed the necropsy. All of the horse's vital organs were normal in size except for the heart.

"We were all shocked," Swerczek said. "I've seen and done thousands of autopsies on horses, and nothing I'd ever seen compared to it. The heart of the average horse weighs about nine pounds. This was almost twice the average size, and a third larger than any equine heart I'd ever seen. And it wasn't pathologically enlarged. All the chambers and the valves were normal. It was just larger. I think it told us why he was able to do what he did."

In the late afternoon of Monday, Oct. 2, 1989, as I headed my car from the driveway of Arthur Hancock's Stone Farm onto Winchester Road outside Paris, Ky., I was seized by an impulse as beckoning as the wind that strums through the trees down there, mingling the scents of new grass and old history.

For reasons as obscure to me then as now, I felt compelled to see Lawrence Robinson. For almost 30 years, until he suffered a stroke in March 1983, Robinson was the head caretaker of stallions at Claiborne Farm. I had not seen him since his illness, but I knew he still lived on the farm, in a small white frame house set on a hill overlooking the lush stallion paddocks and the main stallion barn. In the first stall of that barn, in the same place that was once home to the great Bold Ruler, lived Secretariat, Bold Ruler's greatest son.

It was through Secretariat that I had met Robinson. On the bright, cold afternoon of Nov. 12, 1973, Robinson was one of several hundred people gathered at Blue Grass Airport in Lexington to greet Secretariat after his flight from New York into retirement in Kentucky. I flew with the horse that day, and as the plane banked over the field, a voice from the tower crackled over the airplane radio: "There's more people out here to meet Secretariat than there was to greet the governor."

"Well, he's won more races than the governor," pilot Dan Neff replied.

An hour later, after a ran ride out the Paris Pike behind a police escort with blue lights flashing, Robinson led Secretariat onto a ramp at Claiborne and toward his sire's old stall—out of racing and into history. For me, that final walk beneath a grove of trees, with the colt slanting like a buck through the autumn gloaming, brought to a melancholy close the richest, grandest, damnedest, most exhilarating time of my life. For eight months, first as the racing writer for *Newsday* of Long Island, N.Y., and then as the designated chronicler of Secretariat's career, I had a daily front-row seat to watch the colt. I was at the barn in the morning and the racetrack in the afternoon for what turned out to be the year's greatest show in sports, at the heart of which lay a Triple Crown performance unmatched in the history of American racing.

Sixteen years had come and gone since then, and I had never attended a Kentucky Derby or a yearling sale at Keeneland without driving out to Claiborne to visit Secretariat, often in the company of friends who had never seen him. On the long ride from Louisville, I would regale my friends with stories about the horse—how on that early morning in March '73 he had materialized out of the quickening blue darkness in the upper stretch at Belmont Park, his ears pinned back, running as fast as horses run; how he had lost the Wood Memorial and won the Derby, and how he had been bothered by a pigeon feather at Pimlico on the eve of the Preakness (at the end of this tale I would pluck the delicate, mashed feather out of my wallet, like a picture of my kids, to pass around the car); how on the morning of the Belmont Stakes he had burst from the barn like a stud horse going to the breeding shed and had walked around the outdoor ring on his hind legs, pawing at the sky; how he had once grabbed my notebook and refused to give it back, and how he had seized a rake in his teeth and begun raking the shed; and, finally, I told about that magical, unforgettable instant, frozen now in time, when he turned for home, appearing out of a dark drizzle at Woodbine, near Toronto, in the last race of his career, 12 lengths in front and steam puffing from his nostrils as from a factory whistle, bounding like some mythical beast of Greek lore.

Oh, I knew all the stories, knew them well, had crushed and rolled them in my hand until their quaint musk lay in the saddle of my palm. Knew them as I knew the stories of my children. Knew them as I knew the stories of my own life. Told them at dinner parties, swapped them with horseplayers as if they were trading cards, argued over them with old men and blind fools who had seen the show but missed the message. Dreamed them and turned them over like pillows in my rubbery sleep. Woke up with them, brushed my aging teeth with them, grinned at them in the mirror. Horses have a way of getting inside you, and so it was that Secretariat became like a fifth child in our house, the older boy who was off at school and never around but who was as loved and true a part of the family as Muffin, our shaggy, epileptic dog.

The story I now tell begins on that Monday afternoon last October on the macadam outside Stone Farm. I had never been to Paris, Ky., in the early fall, and I only happened to be there that day to begin an article about the Hancock family, the owners of Claiborne and Stone farms. There wasn't a soul on the road to point the way to Robinson's place, so I swung in and out of several empty driveways until I saw a man on a tractor cutting the lawn in front of Marchmont, Dell Hancock's mansion. He yelled back to me: "Take a right out the drive. Go down to Claiborne House. Then a right at the driveway across that road. Go up a hill to the big black barn. Turn left and go down to the end. Lawrence had a stroke a few years back, y'know."

The house was right where he said. I knocked on the front door, then walked behind and knocked on the back and called through a side window into a room where music was playing. No one answered. But I had time to kill, so I wandered over to the stallion paddock, just a few yards from the house. The stud Ogygian, a son of Damascus, lifted his head inquiringly. He started walking toward me, and I put my elbows on the top of the fence and looked down the gentle slope toward the stallion barn.

And suddenly there he was, Secretariat, standing outside the barn and grazing at the end of a lead shank held by groom Bobby Anderson, who was sitting on a bucket in the sun. Even from a hundred yards away, the horse appeared lighter than I had seen him in years. It struck me as curious that he was not running free in his paddock—why was Bobby grazing him?—but his bronze coat reflected the October light, and it never occurred to me that something might be wrong. But something was terribly wrong. On Labor Day, Secretariat had come down with laminitis, a life-threatening hoof disease, and here, a month later, he was still suffering from its aftershocks.

Secretariat was dying. In fact, he would be gone within 48 hours.

I briefly considered slipping around Ogygian's paddock and dropping down to visit, but I had never entered Claiborne through the backdoor, so I thought better of it. Instead, for a full half hour, I stood by the paddock waiting for Robinson and gazing at Secretariat. The gift of reverie is a blessing divine, and it is conferred most abundantly on those who lie in hammocks or drive alone in cars. Or lean on hillside fences in Kentucky. The mind swims, binding itself to whatever flotsam comes along, to old driftwood faces and voices of the past, to places and scenes once visited, to things not seen or done but only dreamed.

It was July 4, 1972, and I was sitting in the press box at Aqueduct with Clem Florio, a former prizefighter turned Baltimore handicapper, when I glanced at the *Daily Racing Form*'s past performances for the second race, a 5½-furlong buzz for maiden 2-year-olds. As I scanned the pedigrees, three names leaped out: by Bold Ruler–Somethingroyal, by Princequillo. Bold Ruler was the nation's preeminent sire, and Somethingroyal was the dam of several stakes winners, including the fleet Sir Gaylord. It was a match of royalty. Even the baby's name seemed faintly familiar: Secretariat. Where had I heard it before? But of course! Lucien Laurin was training the colt at Belmont Park for Penny Chenery Tweedy's Meadow Stable, making Secretariat a stablemate of that year's Kentucky Derby and Belmont Stakes winner, Riva Ridge.

I had seen Secretariat just a week before. I had been at the Meadow Stable barn one morning, checking on Riva Ridge, when exercise rider Jimmy Gaffney took me aside and said, "You wanna see the best-lookin' 2-year-old you've ever seen?"

We padded up the shed to the colt's stall. Gaffney stepped inside. "What do you think?" he asked. The horse looked magnificent, to be sure, a bright red chestnut with three white feet and a tapered white marking down his face. "He's gettin' ready," Gaffney said. "Don't forget the name: Secretariat. He can run." And then, conspiratorially, Gaffney whispered, "Don't quote me, but this horse will make them all forget Riva Ridge."

So that is where I had first seen him, and here he was in the second at Aqueduct. I rarely bet in those days, but Secretariat was 3–1, so I put $10 on his nose. Florio and I fixed our binoculars on him and watched it all. Watched him as he was shoved sideways at the break, dropping almost to his knees, when a colt named Quebec turned left out of the gate and crashed into him. Saw him blocked in traffic down the back side and shut off again on the turn for home. Saw him cut off a second time deep in the stretch as he was making a final run. Saw him finish fourth, obviously much the best horse, beaten by only 1¼ lengths after really running but an eighth of a mile.

You should have seen Clem. Smashing his binoculars down on his desk, he leaped to his feet, banged his chair against the wall behind him, threw a few punches in the air and bellowed, "Secretariat! That's my Derby horse for next year!"

Two weeks later, when the colt raced to his first victory by six, Florio announced to all the world, "Secretariat will win the Triple Crown next year." He nearly got into a fistfight in the Aqueduct press box that day when Mannie Kalish, a New York handicapper, chided him for making such an outrageously bold assertion: "Ah, you Maryland guys, you come to New York and see a horse break his maiden and think he's another Citation. We see horses like Secretariat all the time. I bet he don't even *run* in the Derby." Stung by the put-down "you Maryland guys," Florio came forward and stuck his finger into Kalish's chest, but two writers jumped between them, and they never came to blows.

The Secretariat phenomenon, with all the theater and passion that would attend it, had begun. Florio was right, of course, and by the end of Secretariat's 2-year-old season, everyone else who had seen him perform knew it. All you had to do was watch the Hopeful Stakes at Saratoga. I was at the races that August afternoon with Arthur Kennedy, an old-time racetracker and handicapper who had been around the horses since the 1920s, and even he had never seen anything quite like it. Dropping back to dead last out of the gate, Secretariat trailed eight horses into the far turn, where jockey Ron Turcotte swung him to the outside. Three jumps past the half-mile pole the colt exploded. "Now he's runnin'!" Kennedy said.

You could see the blue-and-white silks as they disappeared behind one horse, reappeared in a gap between horses, dropped out of sight again and finally reemerged as Secretariat powered to the lead off the turn. He dashed from last to first in 290 yards, blazing through a quarter in :22, and galloped home in a laugher to win by six. It was a performance with style, touched by art. "I've never seen a 2-year-old do that," Kennedy said quietly. "He looked like a 4-year-old out there."

So that was when I knew. The rest of Secretariat's 2-year-old campaign—in which he lost only once, in the Champagne Stakes, when he was disqualified from first to second after bumping Stop the Music at the top of the stretch—was simply a mopping-up operation. At year's end, so dominant had he been that he became the first 2-year-old to be unanimously voted Horse of the Year.

Secretariat wintered at Hialeah, preparing for the Triple Crown, while I shoveled snow in Huntington, N.Y., waiting for him to race again. In February, 23-year-old Seth Hancock, the new president of Claiborne Farm, announced that he had syndicated the colt as a future breeding stallion for $6.08 million, then a world record, in 32 shares at $190,000 a share, making the 1,154-pound horse worth more than three times his weight in gold. (Bullion was selling at the time for $90 an ounce.) Like everyone else, I thought Secretariat would surely begin his campaign in Florida, and I did not expect to see him again until the week before the Kentucky Derby. I was browsing through a newspaper over breakfast one day when I saw a news dispatch whose message went through me like a current. Secretariat would be arriving soon to begin his Triple Crown campaign by the way of the three New York prep races: the Bay Shore, the Gotham and the Wood Memorial Stakes.

"Hot damn!" I blurted to my family. "Secretariat is coming to New York!"

At the time I had in mind doing a diary about the horse, a chronicle of the adventures of a Triple Crown contender, which I thought might one day make a magazine piece. The colt arrived at Belmont Park on March 10, and the next day I was there at 7 A.M., scribbling notes in a pad. For the next 40 days, in what became a routine, I would fall out of bed at 6 A.M., make a cup of instant coffee, climb into my rattling green Toyota and drive the 20 miles to Belmont Park. I had gotten to know the Meadow Stable family—Tweedy, Laurin, Gaffney, groom Eddie Sweat, assistant trainer Henny Hoeffner—in my tracking of Riva Ridge the year before, and I had come to feel at home around Belmont's Barn 5, particularly around stall 7, Secretariat's place. I took no days off, except one morning to hide Easter eggs, and I spent hours sitting on the dusty floor outside Secretariat's stall, talking to Sweat as he turned a rub rag on the colt, filled his water bucket, bedded his stall with straw, kept him in hay and oats. I took notes compulsively, endlessly, feeling for the texture of the life around the horse.

A typical page of scribblings went like this: "Sweat talks to colt . . . easy, Red, I'm comin' in here now . . . stop it, Red! You behave now. . . . Sweat moves around colt. Brush in hand. Flicks off dust. Secretariat sidesteps and pushes Sweat. Blue Sky. Henny comes up, 'How's he doin', Eddie?' 'He's gettin' edgy.' . . . Easy Sunday morning."

Secretariat was an amiable, gentlemanly colt, with a poised and playful nature that at times made him seem as much a pet as the stable dog was. I was standing in front of his stall one morning, writing, when he reached out, grabbed my notebook in his teeth and sank back inside, looking to see what I would do. "Give the man his notebook back!" yelled Sweat. As the groom dipped under the webbing, Secretariat dropped the notebook on the bed of straw.

Another time, after raking the shed, Sweat leaned the handle of the rake against the stall webbing and turned to walk away. Secretariat seized the handle in his mouth and began pushing and pulling it across the floor. "Look at him rakin' the shed!" cried Sweat. All up and down the barn, laughter fluttered like the pigeons in the stable eaves as the colt did a passable imitation of his own groom.

By his personality and temperament, Secretariat became the most engaging character in the barn. His own stable pony, a roan named Billy Silver, began an unrequited love affair with him. "He loves Secretariat, but Secretariat don't pay any attention to him," Sweat said one day. "If Billy sees you grazin' Secretariat, he'll go to hollerin' until you bring him out. Secretariat just ignores him. Kind of sad, really." One morning, I was walking beside Hoeffner through the shed, with Gaffney and Secretariat ahead of us, when Billy stuck his head out of his jerry-built stall and nuzzled the colt as he went by.

Hoeffner did a double take. "Jimmy!" he yelled. "Is that pony botherin' the big horse?"

"Nah," said Jimmy. "He's just smellin' him a little."

Hoeffner's eyes widened. Spinning around on his heels, jabbing a finger in the air, he bellowed, "Get the pony out of here! I don't want him smellin' the big horse."

Leaning on his rake, Sweat laughed softly and said, "Poor Billy Silver. He smelled the wrong horse!"

I remember wishing that those days could breeze on forever—the mornings over coffee and doughnuts at the truck outside the barn, the hours spent watching the red colt walk to the track and gallop once around, the days absorbing the rhythms of the life around the horse. I had been following racehorses since I was 12, back in the days of Native Dancer, and now I was an observer on an odyssey, a quest for the Triple Crown. It had been 25 years since Citation had won racing's Holy Grail. But for me the adventure really began in the early morning of March 14, when Laurin lifted Turcotte aboard Secretariat and said, "Let him roll, Ronnie."

The colt had filled out substantially since I had last seen him under tack, in the fall, and he looked like some medieval charger—his thick neck bowed and his chin drawn up beneath its mass, his huge shoulders shifting as he strode, his coat radiant and his eyes darting left and right. He was walking to the track for his final workout, a three-eighths-of-a-mile drill designed to light the fire in him for the seven-furlong Bay Shore Stakes three days later. Laurin, Tweedy and I went to the clubhouse fence near the finish line, where we watched and waited as Turcotte headed toward the pole and let Secretariat rip. Laurin clicked his stopwatch.

The colt was all by himself through the lane, and the sight and sound of him racing toward us is etched forever in memory: Turcotte was bent over him, his jacket blown up like a parachute, and the horse was reaching out with his forelegs in that distinctive way he had, raising them high and then, at the top of the lift, snapping them out straight and with tremendous force, the snapping hard as bone, the hooves striking the ground and folding it beneath him. Laurin clicked his watch as Secretariat raced under the wire. "Oh, my god!" he cried. "Thirty-three and three-fifths!" Horses rarely break 34 seconds in three-furlong moves.

Looking ashen, fearing the colt might have gone too fast, Laurin headed for the telephone under the clubhouse to call the upstairs clocker, Jules Watson: "Hello there, Jules. How fast did you get him?"

I watched Laurin's face grow longer as he listened, until he looked thunderstruck: *"Thirty-two and three fifths?"* A full second faster than Laurin's own clocking, it was the fastest three-furlong workout I had ever heard of. Tweedy smiled cheerily and said, "Well, that ought to open his pipes!"

Oh, it did that. Three days later, blocked by a wall of horses in the Bay Shore, Secretariat plunged through like a fullback, 220 yards from the wire, and bounded off to win the race by 4½ lengths. I could hear a man screaming behind me. I turned and saw Roger Laurin, Lucien's son, raising his arms in the air and shouting, "He's too much horse! They can't stop him. They can't even stop him with a wall of horses!"

I had ridden horses during my youth in Morton Grove, Ill., and I remember one summer I took a little black bullet of a thoroughbred filly out of the barn and walked her to the track that rimmed the polo field across Golf Road. I had been to the races a few times, had seen the jockeys ride, and I wanted to feel what it was like. So I hitched up my stirrups and galloped her around the east turn, standing straight up. Coming off the turn, I dropped into a crouch and clucked to her. She took off like a sprinter leaving the blocks—

swoooosh!—and the wind started whipping in my eyes. I could feel the tears streaming down my face, and then I looked down and saw her knees pumping like pistons. I didn't think she would make the second turn, the woods were looming ahead, big trees coming up, and so I leaned a little to the left, and she made the turn before she started pulling up. No car ever took me on a ride like that. And no roller coaster, either. Running loose, without rails, she gave me the wildest, most thrilling ride I had ever had.

But that was nothing like the ride Secretariat gave me in the 12 weeks from the Bay Shore through the Belmont Stakes. Three weeks after the Bay Shore, Turcotte sent the colt to the lead down the backstretch in the one-mile Gotham. It looked like they were going to get beat when Champagne Charlie drove to within a half length at the top of the stretch—I held my breath—but Turcotte sent Secretariat on, and the colt pulled away to win by three, tying the track record of 1:33⅗.

By then I had begun visiting Charles Hatton, a columnist for the *Daily Racing Form* who the previous summer had proclaimed Secretariat the finest physical specimen he had ever seen. At 67, Hatton had seen them all. After my morning work was over, I would trudge up to Hatton's private aerie at Belmont Park and tell him what I had learned. I was his backstretch eyes, he my personal guru. One morning Hatton told me that Secretariat had galloped a quarter mile past the finish line at the Gotham, and the clockers had timed him pulling up at 1:59⅗, three fifths of a second faster than Northern Dancer's Kentucky Derby record for 1¼ miles.

"This sucker breaks records pulling up," Hatton said. "He might be the best racehorse I ever saw. Better than Man o' War."

Those were giddy, heady days coming to the nine-furlong Wood Memorial, the colt's last major prep before the Kentucky Derby. On the day of the Wood, I drove directly to Aqueduct and spent the hour before the race in the receiving barn with Sweat, exercise rider Charlie Davis and Secretariat. When the voice over the loudspeaker asked the grooms to ready their horses, Sweat approached the colt with the bridle. Secretariat always took the bit easily, opening his mouth when Sweat moved to fit it in, but that afternoon it took Sweat a full five minutes to bridle him. Secretariat threw his nose in the air, backed up, shook his head. After a few minutes passed, I asked, "What's wrong with him, Eddie?"

Sweat brushed it off: "He's just edgy."

In fact, just that morning, Dr. Manuel Gilman, the track veterinarian, had lifted the colt's upper lip to check his identity tattoo and had discovered a painful abscess about the size of a quarter. Laurin decided to run Secretariat anyway—the colt needed the race—but he never told anyone else about the boil. Worse than the abscess, though, was the fact that Secretariat had had the feeblest workout of his career four days earlier when Turcotte, seeing a riderless horse on the track, had slowed the colt to protect him from a collision. Secretariat finished the mile that day in 1:42⅗, five seconds slower than Laurin wanted him to go. Thus he came to the Wood doubly compromised.

The race was a disaster. Turcotte held the colt back early, but when he tried to get Secretariat to pick up the bit and run, he got no response. I could see at the far turn that the horse was dead. He never made a race of it, struggling to finish third, beaten by four lengths by his own stablemate, Angle Light, and by Sham. Standing near the owner's box, I saw Laurin turn to Tweedy and yell, "Who won it?"

"You won it!" Tweedy told him.

"Angle Light won it," I said to him.

"Angle Light?" he howled back.

But of course! Laurin trained him, too, and so Laurin had just won the Wood, but with the wrong horse.

I was sick. All those hours at the barn, all those early mornings at the shed, all that time and energy for naught. And in the most important race of his career, Secretariat had come up as hollow as a gourd. The next two weeks were among the most agonizing of my life. As great a stallion as he was, Bold Ruler had been essentially a speed sire and had never produced a single winner of a Triple Crown race. I couldn't help but suspect that Secretariat was another Bold Ruler, who ran into walls beyond a mile. In the next two weeks Churchill Downs became a nest of rumors that Secretariat was unsound. Jimmy (the Greek) Snyder caused an uproar when he said the colt had a bum knee that was being treated with ice packs. I *knew* that wasn't true. I had been around Secretariat all spring, and the most ice I had seen near him was in a glass of tea.

All I could hope for, in those final days before the Derby, was that the colt had been suffering from a bellyache on the day of the Wood and had not been up to it. I remained ignorant of the abscess for weeks, and I had not yet divined the truth about Secretariat's training: He needed hard, blistering workouts before he ran, and that slow mile before the Wood had been inadequate. The night before the Derby, I made my selections for the newspaper, and the next day, two hours before post time, I climbed the stairs to the Churchill Downs jockeys' room to see Turcotte. He greeted me in an anteroom, looking surprisingly relaxed. Gilman had taken him aside a few days earlier and told him of the abscess. Turcotte saw that the boil had been treated and had disappeared. The news had made him euphoric, telling him all he needed to know about the Wood.

"You nervous?" he asked.

I shrugged. "I don't think you'll win," I said. "I picked My Gallant and Sham one-two, and you third."

"I'll tell you something," Turcotte said. "He'll beat these horses if he runs his race."

"What about the Wood?" I asked.

He shook me off. "I don't believe the Wood," he said. "I'm telling you. Something was wrong. But he's O.K. now. That's all I can tell you."

I shook his hand, wished him luck and left. Despite what Turcotte had said, I was resigned to the worst, and Secretariat looked hopelessly beaten as the field of 13 dashed past the finish line the first time. He was dead last. Transfixed, I could not take my eyes off him. In the first turn Turcotte swung him to the outside, and Secretariat began passing horses, and down the back side I watched the jockey move him boldly from eighth to seventh to sixth. Secretariat was fifth around the far turn and gaining fast on the outside. I began chanting, "Ride him, Ronnie! Ride him!" Sham was in front, turning for home, but then there was Secretariat, joining him at the top of the stretch. Laffit Pincay, on Sham, glanced over and saw Secretariat and went to the whip. Turcotte lashed Secretariat. The two raced head and head for 100 yards, until gradually Secretariat pulled away. He won by 2½ lengths. The crowd roared, and I glanced at the tote board: 1:59⅖! A new track and Derby record.

Throwing decorum to the wind, I vaulted from my seat and dashed madly through the press box, jubilantly throwing a fist in the air. Handicapper Steve Davidowitz came racing toward me from the other end. We clasped arms and spun a jig in front of the copy machine. "Unbelievable!" Davidowitz cried.

I bounded down a staircase, three steps at a time. Turcotte had dismounted and was crossing the racetrack when I reached him. "What a ride!" I yelled.

"What did I tell you, Mr. Bill?" he said.

I had just witnessed the greatest Kentucky Derby performance of all time. Secretariat's quarter-mile splits were unprecedented—:25⅕, :24, :23⅘, :23⅖ and :23. He ran each quarter faster than the preceding one. Not even the most veteran racetracker could recall a horse who had done this in a mile-and-a-quarter race. As quickly as his legions (I among them) had abandoned him following the Wood, so did they now proclaim Secretariat a superhorse.

We all followed him to Pimlico for the Preakness two weeks later, and he trained as if he couldn't get enough of it. He thrived on work and the racetrack routine. Most every afternoon, long after the crowds had dispersed, Sweat would graze the colt on a patch of grass outside the shed, then lead him back into his stall and while away the hours doing chores. One afternoon I was folded in a chair outside the colt's stall when Secretariat came to the door shaking his head and stretching his neck, curling his upper lip like a camel does. "What's botherin' you, Red?" Sweat asked. The groom stepped forward, plucked something off the colt's whiskers and blew it into the air. "Just a pigeon feather itchin' him," said Sweat. The feather floated into the palm of my hand. So it ended up in my wallet, along with the $2 pari-mutuel ticket that I had on Secretariat to win the Preakness.

In its own way Secretariat's performance in the 1¾₆-mile Preakness was even more brilliant than his race in the Derby. He dropped back to last out of the gate, but as the field dashed into the first turn, Turcotte nudged his right rein as subtly as a man adjusting his cuff, and the colt took off like a flushed deer. The turns at Pimlico are tight, and it had always been considered suicidal to take the first bend too fast, but Secretariat sprinted full-bore around it, and by the time he turned into the back side, he was racing to the lead. Here Turcotte hit the cruise control. Sham gave chase in vain, and Secretariat coasted home to win by 2½. The electric timer malfunctioned, and Pimlico eventually settled on 1:54⅖ as the official time, but two *Daily Racing Form* clockers caught Secretariat in 1:53⅖, a track record by three fifths of a second.

I can still see Clem Florio shaking his head in disbelief. He had seen thousands of Pimlico races and dozens of Preaknesses but never anything like this. "Horses don't *do* what he did here today," he kept saying. "They just don't *do* that and win."

Secretariat wasn't just winning. He was performing like an original, making it all up as he went along. And everything was moving so fast, so unexpectedly, that I was having trouble keeping a perspective on it. Not three months before, after less than a year of working as a turf writer, I had started driving to the racetrack to see this one horse. For weeks I was often the only visitor there, and on many afternoons it was just Sweat, the horse and me in the fine dust with the pregnant stable cat. And then came the Derby and the Preakness, and two weeks later the colt was on the cover of *Time, Sports Illustrated* and *Newsweek,* and he was a staple of the morning and evening news. Secretariat suddenly transcended horse racing and became a cultural phenomenon, a sort of undeclared national holiday from the tortures of Watergate and the Vietnam War.

I threw myself with a passion into that final week before the Belmont. Out to the barn every morning, home late at night, I became almost manic.

The night before the race I called Laurin at home, and we talked for a long while about the horse and the Belmont. I kept wondering, What is Secretariat going to do for an encore? Laurin said, "I think he's going to win by more than he has ever won in his life. I think he'll win by 10."

I slept at the *Newsday* offices that night, and at 2 A.M. I drove to Belmont Park to begin my vigil at the barn. I circled around to the back of the shed, lay down against a tree and fell asleep. I awoke to the crowing of a cock and watched as the stable workers showed up. At 6:07 Hoeffner strode into the shed, looked at Secretariat and called out to Sweat, "Get the big horse ready! Let's walk him about 15 minutes."

Sweat slipped into the stall, put the lead shank on Secretariat and handed it to Charlie Davis, who led the colt to the outdoor walking ring. In a small stable not 30 feet away, pony girl Robin Edelstein knocked a water bucket against the wall. Secretariat, normally a docile colt on a shank, rose up on his hind legs, pawing at the sky, and started walking in circles. Davis cowered below, as if beneath a thunderclap, snatching at the chain and begging the horse to come down. Secretariat floated back to earth. He danced around the ring as if on springs, his nostrils flared and snorting, his eyes rimmed in white.

Unaware of the scene she was causing, Edelstein rattled the bucket again, and Secretariat spun in a circle, bucked and leaped in the air, kicking and spraying cinders along the walls of the pony barn. In a panic Davis tugged at the shank, and the horse went up again, higher and higher, and Davis bent back, yelling "Come on down! Come on down!"

I stood in awe. I had never seen a horse so fit. The Derby and Preakness had wound him as tight as a watch, and he seemed about to burst out of his coat. I had no idea what to expect that day in the Belmont, with him going a mile and a half, but I sensed we would see more of him than we had ever seen before.

Secretariat ran flat into legend, started running right out of the gate and never stopped, ran poor Sham into defeat around the first turn and down the backstretch and sprinted clear, opening two lengths, four, then five. He dashed to the three-quarter pole in 1:09⅘, the fastest six-furlong clocking in Belmont history. I dropped my head and cursed Turcotte: *What is he thinking about? Has he lost his mind?* The colt raced into the far turn, opening seven lengths past the half-mile pole. The timer flashed his astonishing mile mark: 1:34⅕!

I was seeing it but not believing it. Secretariat was still sprinting. The four horses behind him disappeared. He opened 10. Then 12. Halfway around the turn he was 14 in front . . . 15 . . . 16 . . . 17. Belmont Park began to shake. The whole place was on its feet. Turning for home, Secretariat was 20 in front, having run the mile and a quarter in 1:59 flat, faster than his Derby time.

He came home alone. He opened his lead to 25 . . . 26 . . . 27 . . . 28. As rhythmic as a rocking horse, he never missed a beat. I remember seeing Turcotte look over to the timer, and I looked over, too. It was blinking 2:19, 2:20. The record was 2:26⅘. Turcotte scrubbed on the colt, opening 30 lengths, finally 31. The clock flashed crazily: 2:22 . . . 2:23. The place was one long, deafening roar. The colt seemed to dive for the finish, snipping it clean at 2:24.

I bolted up the press box stairs with exultant shouts and there yielded a part of myself to that horse forever.

I didn't see Lawrence Robinson that day last October. The next morning I returned to Claiborne to interview Seth Hancock. On my way through the farm's offices, I saw one of the employees crying at her desk. Treading lightly, I passed farm manager John Sosby's office. I stopped, and he called me in. He looked like a chaplain whose duty was to tell the news to the victim's family.

"Have you heard about Secretariat?" he asked quietly.

I felt the skin tighten on the back of my neck. "Heard what?" I asked. "Is he all right?"

"We might lose the horse," Sosby said. "He came down with laminitis last month. We thought we had it under control, but he took a bad turn this morning. He's a very sick horse. He may not make it.

"By the way, why are you here?"

I had thought I knew, but now I wasn't sure.

Down the hall, sitting at his desk, Hancock appeared tired, despairing and anxious, a man facing a decision he didn't want to make. What Sosby had told me was just beginning to sink in. "What's the prognosis?" I asked.

"Ten days to two weeks," Hancock said.

"Two weeks? Are you serious?" I blurted.

"You asked me the question," he said.

I sank back in my chair. "I'm not ready for this," I told him.

"How do you think I feel?" he said. "Ten thousand people come to this farm every year, and all they want to see is Secretariat. They don't give a hoot about the other studs. You want to know who Secretariat is in human terms? Just imagine the greatest athlete in the world. The greatest. Now make him six foot three, the perfect height. Make him real intelligent and kind. And on top of that, make him the best-lookin' guy ever to come down the pike. He was all those things as a horse. He isn't even a horse anymore. He's a legend. So how do you think I feel?"

Before I left I asked Hancock to call me in Lexington if he decided to put the horse down. We agreed to meet at his mother's house the next morning. "By the way, can I see him?" I asked.

"I'd rather you not," he said. I told Hancock I had been to Robinson's house the day before, and I had seen Secretariat from a distance, grazing. "That's fine," Hancock said. "Remember how you saw him, that way. He doesn't look good."

Secretariat was suffering the intense pain in the hooves that is common to laminitis. That morning Anderson had risen at dawn to check on the horse, and Secretariat had lifted his head and nickered very loudly. "It was like he was beggin' me for help," Anderson would later recall.

I left Claiborne stunned. That night I made a dozen phone calls to friends, telling them the news, and I sat up late, dreading the next day. I woke up early and went to breakfast and came back to the room. The message light was dark. It was Wednesday, Oct. 4. I drove out to Dell Hancock's place in Paris. "It doesn't look good," she said. We had talked for more than an hour when Seth, looking shaken and pale, walked through the front door. "I'm afraid to ask," I said.

"It's very bad," he said. "We're going to have to put him down today."

"When?"

He did not answer. I left the house, and an hour later I was back in my room in Lexington. I had just taken off my coat when I saw it, the red blinking light on my phone. I knew. I walked around the room. Out the door and down the hall. Back into the room. Out the door and down to the lobby. Back into the room. I called sometime after noon. "Claiborne Farm called," said the message operator.

I phoned Annette Covault, an old friend who is the mare booker at Claiborne, and she was crying when she read the message: "Secretariat was euthanized at 11:45 A.M. today to prevent further suffering from an incurable condition. . . ."

The last time I remember really crying was on St. Valentine's Day 1982, when my wife called to tell me that my father had died. At the moment she called, I was sitting in a purple room in Caesars Palace, in Las Vegas, waiting for an interview with the heavyweight champion, Larry Holmes. Now here I was, in a different hotel room in a different town, suddenly feeling like a very old and tired man of 48, leaning with my back against a wall and sobbing for a long time with my face in my hands.

Nona Garson

From the New Jersey *Star-Ledger,* May 1997

BY NANCY JAFFER

Nancy Jaffer, the award-winning reporter who specializes in equestrian sports, has covered five Olympics, seven World Championships, and 16 World Cup finals. She has written the equestrian column in The New Jersey *Star Ledger* for three decades.

Since this profile was written four years ago, Nona Garson accomplished one of her primary goals when she rode Rhythmical on the United States Equestrian Team's show jumping squad at the 2000 Olympics in Sydney, Australia.

The sport of show jumping turns a glamorous face to the world, with stops in Palm Beach County, Fla., during the winter, Europe and the Hamptons during the summer. There are champagne victory celebrations and chicly outfitted wealthy patrons, necessary to supply horses that cost six figures or more.

But when the competition is over and the TV cameras leave, the top riders can't just go home and relax. Horses take seven-day-a-week dedication and endless schooling that doesn't always pay off. Despite their size, they are fragile creatures. They also have minds of their own. The frustrations resulting from that combination are endless.

Success requires many early mornings and late nights, more of which are spent on the road than at home. Most purses in U.S. competitions run between $25,000 and $50,000, with the winner's share a small portion of that. Any real money is made from training and selling horses; subsistence comes from giving lessons. A lot of time is spent wondering how to make ends meet. For every equestrian at the top of the standings, there are scores at the bottom, hoping for the right horse and the big break that will boost them out of the local circuit into the big time.

Nona Garson of Tewksbury, N.J., once knew just the flip side of show jumping's dazzle, going from the dusty rings at one small New Jersey show to the dusty rings at another, performing only for friends, family and a few interested spectators.

Still, she was fascinated by it.

"I think jumping is the biggest thrill of all. It's the closest thing to flying," said the 38-year-old equestrian, as exuberant as if she had discovered it yesterday. "Nothing feels better than galloping down to a big jump and having the horse take flight. It's like being superhuman."

Before each event, riders go into the ring without their horses and scout the layout, which is always different. In grands prix, the highest form of competition, it's not uncommon to find the jump rails standing up to 5-feet, 3-inches, and obstacles stretching more than 6 feet wide. Course designers concentrate on the distance between the fences, requiring riders to figure out how to adjust their horses' strides so they meet each of the brightly colored obstacles perfectly.

Knocking down a pole means a 4-point penalty, and the horse with the least penalties wins, usually after a timed tie-breaker.

"Some days, you walk the course and it looks impossible," said Garson, now ranked sixth in the country. "You wonder, how could you get that high in the air, but you do it. It's just such a feeling. I've been dedicated to that feeling my whole life."

She and her late father, George Garson, who was divorced when Nona was a child, moved to Tewksbury from Westfield, N.J., more than 30 years ago. "I'm the only person I know in the sport who spent my whole life in one place," said Garson, flashing her trademark perky smile.

Her farm is called The Ridge, and it commands an impressive view of Round Valley Reservoir, green fields and plenty of trees. From her 200-year-old farmhouse, painted a Colonial shade of blue, Garson can see her stables and paddocks.

That was where she began riding when she was five, on a half-wild Shetland pony named Maple Sugar. "I proceeded to fall off that pony at least three times a day, every day that I had it. I was on the ground more than I was on the pony," said Garson. That just honed her determination, forming her rough-and-ready approach. It brought success on the Jersey circuit, even if it didn't give her a reputation for being a smooth stylist.

After lessons with instructors in the area, Garson improved and won dozens of state championships, though she didn't seem destined for anything more. "She was the local girl hero. But if anybody had ever said Nona Garson would be one of the top grand prix riders in the country, I would have been amazed," said Scott Milne, a trainer who was traveling the Jersey circuit when Garson was doing well there. "I never watched her and thought, 'This girl is such a talent,' though she did have guts. She made it to the top of the jumper ranks from out of nowhere."

"You have to be patient. You have to believe," she said. "You can't get hung up on what's gone wrong. Riding is an exercise in optimism."

Her breakthrough came in the final Pan American Games trials in 1995, over a rigorous course on which many experienced riders had failed and fallen. There couldn't have been a more difficult, or controversial, victory—people had a hard time believing she had won.

She showed them all by becoming a regular in the ribbons on the grand prix circuit. Last fall, Garson took a class at the National Horse Show in Madison Square Garden. That fulfilled an ambition she had held since she was a wide-eyed little girl in Mary Jane shoes and white ankle socks, traveling to Manhattan to see the venerable show for the first time.

One of her horses, the snowy-coated Derrek, whom she owns with Toni and Leon Andors, has been brought along by Garson since he was an un-schooled two-year-old. Another, Rhythmical, is a Russian-bred with enough ability to make him one of the world's best show jumpers. She has successfully solicited friends and neighbors, like Rhythmical's co-owners, the Kamine family, to buy her horses, a must for someone without an independent fortune.

These days, her business at home is run by Liz Perry, who has taken over the 30-horse operation, where Garson trains and gives lessons when she can. She never forgets her equestrian roots, however, unlike some riders who have no interest in the small shows where they developed their skills.

After her father died in 1990, Garson decided it was the moment to see how far she could go with show jumping. "It took me a long time to figure out how to do it," she said. "I always had to make a living. Some people have the luxury of not doing that. I took a big chance, because I had a good business at home. If my dad were alive, he would not have approved."

He wouldn't have been the only one.

"I've had 100 people tell me, 'You shouldn't do this. You don't have the money, you don't have the talent, you're not going to make it.' There are always doubters, but I don't worry about what other people think." She began training with George Morris, the best known of America's instructors in the sport, and co-chef d'equipe (team manager) for show jumping with the U.S. Equestrian Team.

"Nona's very talented," observed Morris, shortly after she started working with him. "She's been a local star, but she could do very well in the big time. She's got to go to the big time and learn to 'live' there."

It wasn't an easy move.

One of the worst moments on her Florida circuit grand prix debut involved getting thrown into a water jump and having to drag herself out, dripping wet, in front of spectators and the elite riders whose ranks she was trying to join. Others might have given up, but Garson had learned not to do that from her earliest moments with Maple Sugar and his successor, a feisty mare named Peppermint.

The weekend before she went to Sweden for this month's Volvo Show Jumping World Cup finals, Garson was at a small show in Moorestown (cq), N.J., coaching riders competing in children's and adult jumper classes over fences that were miniscule, compared to what she's been jumping.

"It's nice to come back and see all the people I grew up with," said Garson, "and I still enjoy teaching."

Although she was on the bronze medal team at the 1995 Pan American Games, where she finished 12th individually, the World Cup was her biggest test so far. Practically every great rider on earth was on hand to try their luck in an arena filled with fabulous flower arrangements and an electricity generated by thousands of eager screaming, stomping Swedes.

She managed to finish 25th of 42, with several better-known riders below her in the standings. Garson has no doubt she'll be back another year and do better, while continuing to pursue her goal of riding in next year's World Equestrian Games and the 2000 Olympics.

The rider has little time for anything but horses, though she does try to take a break occasionally. She took up tennis. "It's fun to do other things, but I don't forsee myself at Wimbledon," the trim, 5-foot-2 athlete said with a sly smile. Riders' personal lives inevitably suffer with the demands of their sport. Garson was wed briefly to another trainer, but that didn't work out. "At this level, show jumping is all-consuming," she explained. "It's definitely a situation where you're married to the job."

"I tell people who don't know about show business that, 'I'm like the girl swinging on the flying trapeze in the circus. We travel from town to town and everybody stays in hotels. It's a major commitment in your life.

"Some understand it and some don't. But I have a good time and I love all the people I'm with. And I believe the right man will find me."

Her enjoyment hasn't waned with the demands of her work, or with the knowledge that she has made the big time. "On the worst day, I think I have the best job in the world. To me, it's such a treat to be able to do this," she said.

That enthusiasm is catching. Two-time World Cup winner Ian Millar of Canada is among the great riders who have learned to accept and appreciate Garson. "I have a great respect for her competitive instincts, dedication and focus," he said. "She's an inspiration for people who want to realize a dream."

The star of Garson's string is the Russian-bred Rhythmical, whom she spotted in a class for young riders two years ago in Sweden. The Russians originally sold him as part of a group of horses to a Finn—for $10,000 U.S. and 150 used washing machines. Times were bad after the collapse of the USSR, and machinery was more valuable than money.

"This horse, I'm sure if he could talk, he'd have some tales," said Garson, and shook her head. Scars and tattooed identification numbers bear mute testimony to the 12-year-old's past. While Rhythmical now travels in luxury in an enclosed van, it wasn't so long ago that he was shipped on an open truck.

In Finland, he became a lowly lesson horse. "The first people who bought him couldn't train him," explained Garson. He's difficult-natured. Nobody wanted to ride him; he's too fresh."

Her affinity for such temperaments helped her get to the root of his personality, and work from there until animal and rider bonded.

"He's a lot of horse, more powerful than the average horse," she said. Even Garson didn't realize how special he was at first, however.

"I knew I had a really good competitive horse, big-hearted and really fast. I wasn't sure how much sheer scope he had. But I thought my determination and his physical ability could make up for that, and he's risen to the occasion. I've never not had enough horse. His scope is endless; just the opposite of what you see when you look at him."

Compact and trim, his chestnut coat glinting red in the sun, Rhythmical doesn't have a special aura until he gets to the bottom of a jump, where he explodes over it like a starburst. His attributes have convinced Garson she'd like to have another Russian horse, but this is probably not the moment to go looking for one. "It's a dangerous trip right now," she noted. "He comes from the south of Russia, and it's difficult to get there. You can only fly to a certain point. Then you have to take a train or a car." And after that, she pointed out, who knows what you'll encounter.

She doesn't ever want to part with Rhythmical. But another trainer has made a standing offer: He jokingly told her he'd be happy to buy the horse for 10 VCRs.

A Royal Rip-Off at Kingdom Hill

BY DICK FRANCIS

The thirty mystery novels by the ex-steeplechase jockey Dick Francis did more to promote racing over fences than anything this side of *National Velvet.* He also wrote a handful of short fiction. This one investigates the age-old search if not for a foolproof handicapping system then the extent to which horseplayers will go to circumvent the laws of probability.

Thursday afternoon Tricksy Wilcox scratched his armpit absentmindedly and decided Claypits wasn't worth backing in the 2:30. Tricksy Wilcox sprawled in his sagging armchair with a half-drunk can of beer within comforting reach and a huge color television bringing him the blow-by-blow from the opening race of the three-day meeting at Kingdom Hill. Only mugs, he reflected complacently, would be putting in a 9 to 5 stint in the sort of July heatwave that would have done justice to the Sahara. Sensible guys like himself sat around at home with the windows open and their shirts off, letting their beards grow while the sticky afternoon waned toward opening time.

In winter Tricksy was of the opinion that only mugs struggled to travel to work through snow and sleet, while sensible guys stayed warm in front of the TV, betting on the jumpers; and in spring there was rain, and in the autumn, fog. Tricksy at 34 had brought unemployment to a fine art and considered the idea of a full honest day's work to be a joke. It was Tricksy's wife who went out in all weathers to her job in the supermarket, Tricksy's wife who paid the rent of the council flat and left the exact money for the milkman. Eleven years of Tricksy had left her cheerful, unresentful and practical. She had waited without emotion through his two nine-month spells in prison and accepted that one day would find him back there. Her dad had been in and out all through her childhood. She felt at home with the minor criminal mind.

Tricksy watched Claypits win the 2:30 with insulting ease and drank down his dented self-esteem with the last of the beer. Nothing he bloody touched, he thought gloomily, was any bloody good these days. He was distinctly short of the readies and had once or twice had to cut down on necessities like drink and cigarettes. What he wanted, now, was a nice little wheeze, a nice little tickle, to con a lot of unsuspecting mugs into opening their wallets. The scarce ticket racket, now, that had done him proud for years, until the coppers nicked him with a stack of forged duplicates in his pocket at Wimbledon. And tourists these days were too flaky by half; you couldn't sell them subscriptions to nonexistent magazines, let alone London Bridge.

He could never afterwards work out exactly what gave him the Great Bandwagon Idea. One minute he was peacefully watching the 3 o'clock at Kingdom Hill, and the next he was flooded with a breathtaking, wild and unholy glee.

He laughed aloud. He slapped his thigh. He stood up and jigged about, unable to bear, sitting down, the audacity of his thoughts.

"O Moses," he said, gulping for air. "Money for old rope. Kingdom Hill, here I come."

Tricksy Wilcox was not the most intelligent of men.

Friday morning, Major Kevin Cawdor-Jones, manager of Kingdom Hill racecourse, took his briefcase to the routine meeting of the executive committee, most of whom detested each other. Owned and run by a small private company constantly engaged in boardroom wars, the racecourse suffered from the results of spiteful internecine decisions and never made the profit it could have done.

The appointment of Cawdor-Jones was typical of the mismanagement. Third on the list of possible candidates, and far less able than one or two, he had been chosen solely to sidestep the bitter deadlock between the pro-one line up and the pro-two. Kingdom Hill in consequence acquired a mediocre administrator; and the squabbling committee usually thwarted his more sensible suggestions.

As a soldier Cawdor-Jones had been impulsive, rashly courageous and easy-going, qualities which had ensured that he had not been given the essential promotion to colonel. As a man he was lazy and likable, and as a manager soft.

The Friday meeting habitually wasted little time in coming to blows.

"Massive step-up of security," repeated Bellamy positively. "Number one priority. Starting at once. Today."

Thin and sharp-featured, Bellamy glared aggressively round the table, and Roskin as usual with drawling voice opposed him.

"Security costs money, my dear Bellamy."

Roskin spoke patronizingly, knowing that nothing infuriated Bellamy more. Bellamy's face darkened with anger, and the security of the racecourse, like so much else, was left to the outcome of a personal quarrel.

Bellamy insisted, "We need bigger barriers, specialized extra locks on all internal doors, and double the number of police. Work must start at once."

"Racecrowds are not *hooligans,* my dear Bellamy."

Cawdor-Jones inwardly groaned. He found it tedious enough already, on non-race days, to make his tours of inspection, and he was inclined anyway not to stick punctiliously to those safeguards that already existed. Bigger barriers between enclosures would mean he could no longer climb over or through, but would have to walk the long way round. More locks meant more keys, more time-wasting, more nuisance. And all presumably for the sake of frustrating the very few scroungers who tried to cross from cheaper to more expensive enclosures without paying. He thought he would much prefer the status quo.

Tempers rose around him, and voices also. He waited resignedly for a gap.

"Er . . ." he said, clearing his throat.

The heated pro-Bellamy faction and the sneering pro-Roskin clique both turned toward him hopefully. Cawdor-Jones was their mutual safety valve; except, that was, when his solution was genuinely constructive. Then they both vetoed it because they wished they'd thought of it themselves.

"A lot of extra security would mean more work for our staff," he said diffidently. "We might have to take on an extra man or two to cope with it . . . and after the big initial outlay there would always be maintenance . . . and . . . er . . . well, what real harm can anyone do to a racecourse?"

This weak oil stilled the waters enough for both sides to begin their retreat with positions and opinions intact.

"You have a point about the staff," Bellamy conceded grudgingly, knowing that two extra men would cost a great deal more than locks, and the racecourse couldn't afford them. "But I still maintain that tighter security is essential and very much overdue."

Cawdor-Jones, in his easy-going way, privately disagreed. Nothing had ever happened to date. Why should anything ever happen in the future?

The discussion grumbled on for half an hour, and nothing at all was done.

Friday afternoon, having pinched a tenner from his wife's holiday fund in the best teapot, Tricksy Wilcox went to the races. His trip was a reconnoitering mission to spy out the land, and Tricksy, walking around with greedy eyes wide-open, couldn't stop himself from chuckling. It did occur to him once or twice that his light-hearted singlehanded approach was a waste: the big boys would have had it all planned to a second and would have set their sights high in their humorless way. But Tricksy was a loner who avoided gang life on the grounds that it was too much like hard work; bossed around all the time, and with no pension rights into the bargain.

He downed half-pints of beer at various bars and wagered smallish amounts on the Tote. He looked at the horses in the parade ring and identified the jockeys whose faces he knew from TV, and he attentively watched the races. At the end of the afternoon, with modest winnings keeping him solvent, he chuckled his way home.

Friday afternoon Mrs. Angelisa Ludville sold two one-pound Tote tickets to Tricksy Wilcox, and hundreds to other people whom she knew as little. Her mind was not on her job but on the worrying pile of unpaid bills on the bookshelf at home. Life had treated her unkindly since her 50th birthday, robbing her of her looks, because of worry, and her husband, because of a blonde. Deserted, divorced and childless, she could nevertheless have adapted contentedly to life alone had it not been for the drastic drop in comfort. Natural optimism and good humor were gradually draining away in the constant grinding struggle to make shortening ends meet.

Angelisa Ludville eyed longingly the money she took through her Tote window. Wads of the stuff passed through her hands each working day, and only a fraction of what the public wasted on gambling would, she felt, solve all her problems handsomely. But honesty was a lifetime habit; and besides, stealing from the Tote was impossible. The takings for each race were collected and checked immediately. Theft would be instantly revealed. Angelisa sighed and tried to resign herself to the imminent cutting off of her telephone.

Saturday morning, Tricksy Wilcox dressed himself carefully for the job in hand. His wife, had she not been stacking baked beans in the supermarket, would have advised against the fluorescent orange socks. Tricksy, seeing his image in the bedroom mirror only as far down as the knees, was confident that the dark suit, dim tie and bowler hat gave him the look of a proper race-going gent. He had even, without reluctance, cut two inches off his hair and removed a flourishing moustache. Complete with outsize binoculars case slung over his shoulder, he smirked at his transformation with approval and set out with a light step to catch the train to Kingdom Hill.

On the racecourse Major Kevin Cawdor-Jones made his race-day round of inspection with his usual lack of thoroughness. Slipshod holes in his management resulted also in the police contingent's arriving half an hour late and under strength; and not enough racecards had been ordered from the printers.

"Not to worry," said Cawdor-Jones, shrugging it off easily.

Mrs. Angelisa Ludville traveled to the course in the Tote's own coach, along with 50 colleagues. She looked out of the window at the passing suburbs and thought gloomily about the price of electricity. Saturday afternoon at 2:30 she was immersed in the routine of issuing tickets and taking money, concentrating on her work and feeling reasonably happy. She arranged before her the fresh batch of tickets, those for the 3 o'clock, the biggest race of the meeting. The extra-long queues would be forming soon outside, and speed and efficiency in serving the bettors was not only her job but, indeed, her pride.

At 2:55 Cawdor-Jones was in his office next to the weighing room trying to sort out a muddle over the day laborers' pay. At 2:57 the telephone at his elbow rang for about the 20th time in the past two hours, and he picked up the receiver with his mind still on the disputed hourly rates due to the stickers-back of kicked-up chunks of turf.

"Cawdor-Jones," he announced himself automatically.

A man with an Irish accent began speaking quietly.

"What?" said Cawdor-Jones. "Speak up, can't you. There's too much noise here. . . . I can't hear you."

The man with the Irish accent repeated his message in the same soft half-whisper.

"*What?*" said Cawdor-Jones. But his caller had rung off.

"Oh, my God," said Cawdor-Jones, and stretched a hand to the switch that connected him to the internal broadcasting system. He glanced urgently at the clock. Its hands clicked round to 2:59, and at that moment the 14 runners for the 3 o'clock race were being led into the starting stalls.

"Ladies and gentlemen," said Cawdor-Jones, his voice reverberating from every loud-speaker on the racecourse. "We have been warned that a bomb has been placed somewhere in the stands. Would you please all leave at once and go over to the center of the course while the police arrange a search."

The moment of general shock lasted less than a second. Then the huge race-crowd streamed like a river down from the steps, up from the tunnels, out of the doors, running, pelting, elbowing toward the safety of the open spaces on the far side of the track.

Bars emptied dramatically with half-full glasses overturned and smashed in the panic. The Tote queues melted instantaneously, and the ticket-sellers followed them helter-skelter. The stewards vacated their high box at a dignified downhill rush, and the racing press pell-melled for the exit without hanging about to alert their papers. City editors could wait half an hour. Bombs wouldn't.

The scrambling thousands deserted all the racecourse buildings within a space of two minutes. Only a very few stayed behind, and chief of those was Kevin Cawdor-Jones, who had never lacked for personal courage and now saw it as his duty as a soldier to remain at his post.

The under-strength of policemen collected bit by bit outside the weighing room, each man hiding his natural apprehension under a reassuring front. Probably another bloody hoax, they told one another. It was always a hoax. Or . . . nearly always. Their officer took charge of organizing the search and told the civilian Cawdor-Jones to remove himself to safety.

"No, no," said Cawdor-Jones. "While you look for the bomb, I'll make quite sure that everyone's out." He smiled a little anxiously and dived purposely into the weighing room.

All clear there, he thought, peering rapidly round the jockeys' washroom. All clear in the judges' box, the photofinish developing room, the kitchens, the boiler room, the Tote, the offices, the stores. He bustled from building to building, knowing all the back rooms, the nooks and crannies where some deaf member of the public might be sitting unawares.

He saw no people. He saw no bomb. He returned almost out of breath to the space outside the weighing room and awaited a report from the slower police.

Around the stands Tricksy Wilcox was putting the Great Bandwagon Idea into sloppy execution. Chuckling away internally over the memory of an Irish impersonation good enough for an entry to Actors Equity, he bustled speedily from bar to bar and in and out of doors, filling his large, empty binocular case with provender. It was amazing, he thought, giggling, how *careless* people were in a panic.

Twice he came face to face with the searching policemen.

"All clear in there, Officer," he said pompously, each time pointing back to where he had been. And each time the police gaze flickered unsuspectingly over the bowler hat, the dark suit, the dim tie. The police took him for one of the racecourse staff.

Only the orange socks stopped him getting clean away. One policeman, watching his receding back view, frowned uncertainly at the brilliant segments between trouser leg and shoe, and started slowly after him.

"Hey. . . ." he said.

Tricksy turned his head, saw the Law advancing, lost his nerve and then bolted. Tricksy was not the most intelligent of men.

Saturday afternoon precisely at 4 o'clock, Cawdor-Jones made another announcement.

"It appears the bomb warning was just another hoax. It is now safe for everyone to return to the stands."

The crowd streamed back in reverse and made for the bars. The barmaids returned to their posts and immediately raised hands and voices in a screeching chorus of affronted horror.

"Someone's pinched all the takings!"

"The cheek of it. He's taken our tips and all!"

In the various Tote buildings, the ticket sellers stood appalled. Most of the huge intake for the biggest race of the meeting had simply vanished.

Angelisa Ludville looked with utter disbelief at her own plundered cash box. White, shaking, she joined the clamor of voices. "The money's gone. . . ."

Cawdor-Jones received report after report with a face of anxious despair. He knew no doors had been locked after the stampede to the exits. He knew no security measures whatever had been taken. The racecourse wasn't equipped to deal with such a situation. The committee would undoubtedly blame him. Might even give him the sack.

At 4:30 he listened with astounded gratitude to news from the police that a man had been apprehended and was now helping to explain how his binoculars case came to be crammed to overflowing with used treasury notes, many of them bearing a fresh circular watermark resulting from the use of a wet beer glass as a paperweight.

Monday morning Tricksy Wilcox appeared gloomily before a magistrate and was remanded in custody for seven days. The Great Bandwagon Idea hadn't been so hot after all, and undoubtedly they would send him down for more than nine months this time.

Only one thought brightened his future. The police had tried all weekend to get information out of him, and he had kept his mouth tight shut. Where, they wanted to know, had he hidden the biggest part of the loot?

Tricksy said nothing.

There had only been room in the binoculars case for one tenth of the stolen money. Where had he put the bulk?

Tricksy wasn't telling.

He would get off more lightly, they said, if he surrendered the rest.

Tricksy didn't believe it. He grinned sardonically and shook his head. Tricksy knew from past experiences that he would have a much easier time inside as the owner of a large hidden cache. He'd be respected. Treated with proper awe. He'd have status. Nothing on earth could have persuaded him to spill the beans.

Monday morning Major Cawdor-Jones took his red face to an emergency meeting of his executive committee and agreed helplessly with Bellamy's sharply reiterated opinion that the racecourse security was a disgrace.

"I warned you," Bellamy repeated for the 10th self-righteous time. "I warned you all. We need more locks. There are some excellent slam-shut devices available for the cash boxes in the Tote. I'm told that all money can be secured in five seconds. I propose that these devices be installed immediately throughout the racecourse."

He glared belligerently round the table. Roskin kept his eyes down and merely pursed his mouth, and Kingdom Hill voted to bolt its doors now that the horse was gone.

Monday evening Angelisa Ludville poured a double gin, switched on the television and put her feet up. She sighed contentedly. Never, she thought, would she forget the shock of seeing her empty till. Never would she get over the fright it had given her. Never would she forget the rush of relief when she realized that everyone had been robbed, not just herself. Because she knew perfectly well that it was one of the five-pound windows whose take she had scooped up in the scramble to the door. It would have been plain stupid to have lifted the money from her own place. And besides . . . there was far more cash at the five-pound window than at hers.

Monday evening Kevin Cawdor-Jones sat in his bachelor flat thinking about the second search of Kingdom Hill. All day Sunday the police had repeated the nook-and-cranny inspection, only this time slowly, without fear, looking not for a bang but a hidden bank. Cawdor-Jones had given his willing assistance, but nothing at all had been found.

"Tricksy must have had a partner," said an officer morosely. "But we can't get a dickybird out of him."

Cawdor-Jones, still the manager of Kingdom Hill, smiled gently at the memory of the past two days. Cawdor-Jones, impulsive and rashly courageous, had made the most of the opportunity Tricksy Wilcox had provided. Cawdor-Jones, whose nerve could never be doubted, had driven away on Saturday evening with the jack pot from the Tote.

He leaned over the arm of his chair and fondly patted his bulging briefcase.

Breakneck Hill

BY ESTHER FORBES

Esther Forbes is best known to generations of young adults as the author of *Johnny Tremaine,* the Revolutionary War novel about Paul Revere's apprentice. The story that appears here reveals a perceptive and moving appreciation of all that it means to say goodbye to a beloved horse.

Down Holly Street the tide had set in for church. It was a proper, dilatory tide. Every silk hat glistened, every shoe was blacked, the flowers on the women's hats were as fresh as the daffodils against the house fronts. Few met face to face, now and then a faster walker would catch up with acquaintances and join them or, with a flash of raised hat, bow, and pass on down the stream.

Then the current met an obstacle. A man, young and graceful and very much preoccupied, walked through the churchgoers, faced in the opposite direction. His riding breeches and boots showed in spite of the loose overcoat worn to cover them. He bowed continually, like royalty from a landau, almost as mechanically, and answered the remarks that greeted him.

"Hello, Geth."

"Hello."

"Good morning, Mr. Gething. Not going to church this morning." This from a friend of his mother.

"Good morning. No, not this morning." He met a chum.

"Good riding day, eh?"

"Great."

"Well, Geth, don't break your neck."

"You bet not."

"I'll put a P.S. on the prayer for you," said the wag.

"Thanks a lot." The wag was always late—even to church on Easter morning. So Gething knew the tail of the deluge was reached and past. He had the street almost to himself. It was noticeable that the man had not once called an acquaintance by name or made the first remark. His answers had been as re-flex as his walking. Geth was thinking, and in the sombre eyes was the dumb look of a pain that would not be told—perhaps he considered it too slight.

He left Holly Street and turned into Holly Park. Here from the grass that bristled so freshly, so ferociously green, the tree trunks rose black and damp. Brown pools of water reflected a blue radiant sky through blossoming branches. Gething subsided on a bench well removed from the children and nursemaids. First he glanced at the corner of Holly Street and the Boulevard where a man from his father's racing stable would meet him with his horse. His face, his figure, his alert bearing, even his clothes promised a horseman. The way his stirrups had worn his boots would class him as a rider. He rode with his foot "through" as the hunter, steeplechaser, and polo player do—not on the ball of his foot in park fashion.

He pulled off his hat and ran his hand over his close-cropped head. Evidently he was still thinking. Across his face the look of pain ebbed and re-turned, then he grew impatient. His wristwatch showed him his horse was late and he was in a hurry to be started, for what must be done had best be done quickly. Done quickly and forgotten, then he could give his attention to the other horses. There was Happiness—an hysterical child, and Goblin, who needed training over water jumps, and Sans Souci, whose leg should be co-cained to locate the trouble—all of his father's stable of great thoroughbreds needed something except Cuddy, who waited only for the bullet. Gething's square brown hand went to his breeches pocket, settled on something that was cold as ice and drew it out—the revolver. The horse he had raced so many times at Piping Rock, Brookline, Saratoga had earned the right to die by this hand which had guided him. Cuddy's high-bred face came vividly before his eyes and the white star would be the mark. He thrust the revolver back in his pocket hastily, for a child had stopped to look at him, then slowly rose and fell to pacing the gravel walk. A jay screamed overhead, "Jay, jay, jay!"

"You fool," Geth called to him and then muttered to himself. "Fool, fool—oh, Geth—" From the boulevard a voice called him.

"Mr. Gething—if you please, sir—!" It was Willet the trainer.

"All right, Willet." The trainer was mounted holding a lean greyhound of a horse. Gething pulled down the stirrups.

"I meant to tell you to bring Cuddy for me to ride, last time, you know."

"Not that devil. I could never lead him in. Frenchman, here, is well be-haved in cities."

Gething swung up. He sat very relaxed upon a horse. There was a life-time of practice behind that graceful seat and manner with the reins. The horse started a low shuffling gait that would take them rapidly out of the city to the Gething country place and stables.

"You know," Geth broke silence, "Cuddy's got his—going to be shot."

"Not one of us, sir," said Willet, "but will sing Hallelujah! He kicked a hole in Muggins yesterday. None of the boys dare touch him, so he hasn't been groomed proper since your father said he was to go. It's more dangerous wipin' him off than to steeplechase the others." Geth agreed. "I know it isn't right to keep a brute like that."

"No, sir. When he was young and winning stakes it seemed different. I tell you what, we'll all pay a dollar a cake for soap made our 'er old Cuddy."

"There'll no be soap made out of old Cuddy," Gething interrupted him, "I'll ride him out—up to the top of Breakneck Hill and shoot him there. You'd better begin the trench by noon. When it's dug I'll take him to the top and—"

"But nobody's been on his back since your father said it was useless to try to make him over. Too old for steeplechasing and too much the racer for anything else, and too much the devil to keep for a suvnor."

"Well, I'll ride him once again."

"But, Mr. Geth, he's just been standing in his box or the paddock for four weeks now. We've been waiting for you to say when he was to be shot. He's in a sweet temper and d'yer know, I think, I do—"

"What do you think?" Willet blushed purple.

"I think Cuddy's got something in his head, some plan if he gets out. I think he wants to kill someone before he dies. Yes, sir, *kill* him. And you know if he gets the start of you there is no stopping the dirty devil."

"Yes, he does tear a bit," Geth admitted. "But I never was on a surer jumper. Lord! How the old horse can lift you!" Gething dropped into a dis-consolate silence, interrupted before long by Willet.

"Happiness will get Cuddy's box—she's in a stall. Cuddy was always mean to her—used to go out of his way to kick her—and she, sweet as a kitten."

"So you'll give her his box in revenge?"

"Revenge? Oh, no, sir. Just common sense." Any thought of a senti-mental revenge was distasteful to the trainer, but he was glad that good Happi-ness should get his box and disappointed about the soap. It would have lent relish to his somewhat perfunctory washings to say to himself, "Doubtless this here bit of soap is a piece of old Cuddy."

"How long will the trench take?"

"A good bit of time, sir. Cuddy isn't no kitten we're laying by. I'll put them gardeners on the job—with your permission—and they know how to shovel. You'll want an old saddle on him?"

"No, no, the one I've raced him in, number twelve, and his old bridle with the chain bit."

"Well, well," said Willet rubbing his veiny nose.

He considered the horse unworthy of any distinction, but in his desire to please Geth, took pains to prepare Cuddy for his death and burial. Gething was still at the big house although it was four o'clock and the men on Breakneck Hill were busy with their digging. Willet called them the sextons.

"And we, Joey," he addressed a stableboy, "we're the undertakers. Handsome corpse, what?" Cuddy stood in the centre of the barn floor fastened to be groomed. He was handsome, built on the cleanest lines of speed and strength, lean as an anatomical study, perfect for his type. The depth of chest made his legs, neck, and head look fragile. His face was unusually beautiful— the white-starred face which had been before Geth's eyes as he had sat in Holly Park. His pricked ears strained to hear, his eyes to see. The men working over him were beneath his notice.

"Look at him," complained Joey, "he pays no more attention to us than as if we weren't here." Cuddy usually kicked during grooming, but his present indifference was more insulting.

"Huh!" said Willet, "he knows them sextons went to Breakneck to dig the grave for him. Don't yer, Devil? Say, Joey, look at him listening like he was counting the number of spadefuls it takes to make a horse's grave. He's thinking, old Cuddy is, and scheming what he'd like to do. I wouldn't ride him from here to Breakneck, not for a thousand dollars." He began rapidly with the body brush on Cuddy's powerful haunch, then burst out:

"He thinks he'll be good and we'll think he's hit the sawdust trail, or perhaps he wants to look pretty in his coffin. Huh! Give me that curry. You wash off his face a bit." Cuddy turned his aristocratic face away from the wet cloth and blew tremulously. Joey tapped the blazing star on his forehead.

"Right there," he explained to Willet, "but anyhow he's begun to show his age." He pointed to the muzzle, which had the run-forward look of an old horse, and to the pits above the eyes. The grooming was finished but neither Gething came to the stable from the big house nor the trench diggers from Breakneck to say that their work was done.

"Say, Joey," suggested Willet, "I'll do up his mane in red and yellow worsteds, like he was going to be exhibited. Red and yellow look well on a bay. You get to the paddock and see Frenchman hasn't slipped his blanket while I fetch the worsteds from the office."

Cuddy, left alone, stopped his listening and began pulling at his halter. It held him firm. From the brown dusk of their box-stalls two lines of expectant horses' faces watched him. The pretty chestnut, Happiness, already had been transferred to his old box; her white striped face was barely visible. Farther down, on the same side, Goblin stood staring stupidly, and beyond were the heads of the three brothers, Sans Pareil, Sans Peur and the famous Sans Souci, who could clear seven feet of timber (and now was lame). Opposite stood Bohemia, cold blood in her veins as a certain thickness about the throat testified, and little Martini, the flat racer. On either side of him were Hotspur and Meteor and there were a dozen others as famous. Above each stall was hung the brass plate giving the name and pedigree and above that up to the roof the hay was piled sweet and dusty-smelling. The barn swallows twittered by an open window in the loft. In front of Cuddy the great double doors were open to the fields and pastures, the gray hills and the radiant sky. Cuddy reared abruptly, striking out with his front legs, crouched and sprang against his halter again, but it held him fast. Willet, on returning with his worsted, found him as he had left him, motionless as a bronze horse on a black marble clock.

Willet stood on a stool the better to work on the horse's neck. His practiced fingers twisted and knotted the mane and worsted, then cut the ends into hard tassels. The horse's withers were reached and the tassels bobbing rakishly gave a hilarious look to the condemned animal.

Four men, very sweaty, carrying spades entered.

"It's done," said the first, nodding, "and it's a big grave. Glad pet horses don't die oftener."

"This ain't a pet," snapped Willet. "He's just that much property and being of no more use is thrown away—just like an old tin can. No more sense in burying one than the other. If I had my way about it I'd—" But Geth entered. With his coat off he gave an impression of greater size; like Cuddy his lines were graceful enough to minimize his weight.

"Hole dug? Well, let's saddle up and start out." He did not go up to Cuddy to speak to him as he usually would have done, but as if trying to avoid him, he fell to patting Happiness's striped face. She was fretful in her new quarters. "Perhaps," thought Willet, "she knows it's old Cuddy, and *he's* gone out for good." All the horses seemed nervous and unhappy. It was as if they knew that one of their number was to be taken out to an inglorious death—not the fortune to die on the turf track as a steeplechaser might wish, but ignominiously, on a hilltop, after a soft canter through spring meadows.

Cuddy stood saddled and bridled and then Willet turned in last appeal to his master's son.

"Mr. Geth, I wouldn't ride him—not even if I rode as well as you, which I don't. That horse has grown worse and worse these last months. He wants to kill someone, that's what he wants." Geth shook his head.

"No use, Willet, trying to scare me. I know what I'm doing, eh Cuddy?" He went to the horse and rubbed the base of his ears. The satin head dropped forward on to the man's chest, a rare response from Cuddy. Gething led him out of the stable; Willet held his head as the man mounted. As he thrust his foot in the stirrup Cuddy lunged at Willet; his savage yellow teeth crushed into his shoulder. The rider pulled him off, striking him with his heavy hunting whip. The horse squealed, arched himself in the air and sidled down the driveway. He did not try to run or buck, but seemed intent on twisting himself into curves and figures. The two went past the big house with its gables and numberless chimneys and down to the end of the driveway.

There is a four foot masonry wall around the Gething countryplace ("farm" they call it). The horse saw it and began jerking at his bit and dancing, for ever since colthood walls had had but one meaning for him.

"Well, at it, old man," laughed Gething. At a signal Cuddy flew at it, rose into the air with magnificent strength and landed like thistledown.

"Cuddy," cried the man, "there never was a jumper like you. Breakneck will keep, we'll find some more walls first."

He crossed the road and entered a rough pasture. It was a day of such abounding life one could pity the worm the robin pulled. For on such a day everything seemed to have the right to live and be happy. The crows sauntered across the sky, carefree as hoboes. Underfoot the meadow turf oozed water, the shad-bush petals fell like confetti before the rough assault of horse and rider. Gething liked this day of wind and sunshine. In the city there had been the smell of oiled streets to show that spring had come, here was the smell of damp earth, pollen, and burnt brush. Suddenly he realized that Cuddy, too, was pleased and contented, for he was going quietly now; occasionally he threw up his head and blew "Heh, heh!" through his nostrils. Strange that Willet had thought Cuddy wanted to kill someone—all he really wanted was a bit of a canter.

A brook was reached. It was wide, marshy, edged with cowslips. It would take a long jump to clear it. Gething felt the back gather beneath him, the tense body flung into the air, the flight through space, then the landing well upon the firm bank.

"Bravo, Cuddy!" The horse plunged and whipped his head between his forelegs, trying to get the reins from the rider's hands. Gething let himself be jerked forward until his face almost rested on the veiny neck.

"Old tricks, Cuddy. I knew *that* one before you wore your first shoes." He still had easy control and began to really let him out. There was a succession of walls and fences and mad racing through fields when the horse plunged in his gait and frightened birds fluttered from the thicket and Gething hissed between his teeth as he always did when he felt a horse going strong beneath him.

Then they came to a hill that rose out of green meadows. It was covered with dingy pine trees except the top that was bared like a tonsure. A trail ran through the woods; a trail singularly morose and unattractive. The pines looked shabby and black in comparison to the sun on the spring meadows. This was Breakneck Hill. Perhaps Cuddy felt his rider stiffen in the saddle, for he refused passionately to take the path. He set his will against Gething's and fought, bucking and rearing. When a horse is capable of a six-foot jump into the air his great strength and agility made his bucking terrible. The bronco is a child in size and strength compared to Cuddy's race of superhorse. Twice Geth went loose in his flat saddle and once Cuddy almost threw himself. The chain bit had torn the edges of his mouth and blood colored his froth. Suddenly he acquiesced and quieted again; he took the sombre path. Geth thrust his right hand into his pocket; the revolver was still there. His hand left it and rested on the bobbing, tasseled mane.

"Old man," he addressed the horse, "I know you don't know where you're going and I know you don't remember much, but you must remember Saratoga and how we beat them all. And Cuddy, you'd understand—if you could—how it's all over now and why I want to do it for you myself."

The woods were cleared. It was good to leave their muffled dampness for the pure sunshine of the crest. On the very top of the hill clean-cut against the sky stood a great wind-misshaped pine. At the foot of this pine was a bank of fresh earth and Gething knew that beyond the bank was the trench. He bent in his saddle and pressed his forehead against the warm neck. Before his eyes was the past they had been together, the sweep of the turf course, the grandstand aflutter, grooms with blankets, jockeys and gentlemen in silk, owners' wives with cameras, then the race that always seemed so short—a rush of horses, the stretching over the jumps, and the purse or not, it did not matter.

He straightened up with a grim set to his jaw and gathered the loosened reins. Cuddy went into a canter and so approached the earth bank. Suddenly he refused to advance and again the two wills fought, but not so furiously. Cuddy was shaking with fear. The bank was a strange thing, a fearsome thing, and the trench beyond, ghastly. His neck stretched forward. "Heh, heh!" he blew through his nostrils.

"Six steps nearer, Cuddy." Geth struck him lightly with his spurs. The horse paused by the bank and began rocking slightly.

"Sist! be quiet," for they were on the spot Gething wished. The horse gathered himself, started to rear, then sprang into the air, cleared earth-mound and trench and bounded down the hill. The tremendous buck-jump he had so unexpectedly taken, combined with his frantic descent, gave Gething no chance to get control until the level was reached. Then, with the first pull on the bridle, he realized it was too late. For a while at least Cuddy was in command. Gething tried all his tricks with the reins; the horse dashed on like a furious gust of wind; he whirled through the valley, across a ploughed field, over a fence and into more pastures. Gething, never cooler, fought for the control. The froth blown back against his white shirt was rosy with blood. Cuddy was beyond realizing his bit. Then Gething relaxed a little and let him go. He could guide him to a certain extent. Stop him he could not.

The horse was now running flatly and rapidly. He made no attempt to throw his rider. What jumps were in his way he took precisely. Unlike the crazed runaway of the city streets Cuddy never took better care of himself. It seemed that he was running for some purpose and Gething thought of Willet's often repeated remark, "Look at 'im—old Cuddy, he's thinking." Two miles had been covered and the gait had become businesslike. Gething, guiding always to the left, was turning him in a huge circle. The horse reeked with sweat. "Now," thought Gething, "he's had enough," but at the first pressure on the bit Cuddy increased his speed. His breath caught in his throat. There was another mile and the wonderful run grew slower. The man felt the great horse trip and recover himself. He was tired out. Again the fight between master and horse began. Cuddy resisted weakly, then threw up his beautiful, white-starred face as if in entreaty.

"Oh, I'm—" muttered Gething and let the reins lie loose on his neck, "your own way, Cuddy. Your way is better than mine. Old friend, I'll not try to stop you again." For he knew if he tried he could now gain control. The early dusk of spring had begun to settle on the surface of the fields in a hazy radiance, a marvellous light that seemed to breathe out from the earth and stream through the sky. A mile to the east upon a hill was a farm house. The orange light from the sunset found every window, blinded them and left them blank oblongs of orange. The horse and rider passed closer to this farm. Two collies rushed forward, then stopped to bark and jump. The light enveloped them and gave each a golden halo.

Again Gething turned, still keeping toward the left. A hill began to rise before them and up it the horse sped, his breath whirring and rattling in his throat, but his strength still unspent. To the very top he made his way and paused dazed. "Oh, Cuddy," cried Gething, "this is Breakneck." For there was the wind-warped pine, the bank of earth, the trench. The horse came to a shivering standstill. The bank looked strange to him. He stood sobbing, his body rocking slightly, rocking gently, then with a sigh, came slowly down on to the turf. Gething was on his feet, his hand on the dripping neck.

"You always were a bad horse and I always loved you," he whispered, "and that was a great ride, and now—" He rose abruptly and turned away as he realized himself alone in the soft twilight. The horse was dead. Then he returned to the tense body, so strangely thin and wet, and removed saddle and bridle. With these hung on his arm he took the sombre path through the pines for home.

The Horse Whisperer

BY PAUL TRACHTMAN

lthough it may have taken a novel and a movie to popularize the term "horse whisperer," Buck Brannaman's skills at starting and re-training horses have long been well known to western riders and trainers. This article by Paul Trachtman that appeared in *Smithsonian* reveals Brannaman's thoughtful approach and its underlying sensible philosophy.

"The way a person sits on a horse is exactly the way a mountain lion would, climbing on its back with your legs reaching down over it," says Buck Brannaman, a lanky Wyoming cowboy, as he gets ready to mount a skittish colt for the first time. "So it's easy to understand why a horse wouldn't be that interested in a person crawling up on top of him like some would-be mountain lion and clamping down his feet!" It's the way Buck sees the world, from the horse's point of view.

He's been working with the colt for more than an hour, getting it used to a lead rope, a halter, then a saddle, and letting it know he won't hurt it. "He hasn't been worked with before," Buck says, lifting himself on the stirrup, leaning over the saddle, letting the horse adjust to his weight, then getting back down. "He's scared. And he should be scared. That's how he survives on the range. What you're dealing with is thousands of years of self-preservation that you're asking the horse to just ignore, and allow you to be there." Now he gets a foot in the stirrup again and swings up into the saddle. The colt flinches a little, its muscles quivering. Buck rubs its mane, and the colt settles down, chewing things over and deciding the cowboy's not a predator after all.

"He's pretty flinchy, but in time he won't be," Buck says. "He's not mean. But whether they're scared and bucking you off, or spoiled and bucking you off, gravity works about the same either way." He laughs, knowingly. "So you need to get them comfortable, to where they don't mind you being around them."

Buck flaps his feet lightly in the stirrups, and the horse starts forward. Before you know it, horse and human look as comfortable with each other as two partners dancing a waltz. What is going on here is ordinarily accomplished by "breaking" a horse, using methods more suited to the rodeo than the ballroom. But Buck is no ordinary horseman. He is demonstrating his way of turning frightened horses into friends, a way that has more to do with respect and trust than mastery or manhandling.

This particular demonstration is taking place at the National Western Stock Show, Rodeo and Horse Show in Denver, Colorado, an event regarded as the Super Bowl of stock shows. Although Buck has been giving clinics in horsemanship for more than 15 years in every part of the United States and abroad, this is his first brush with stock show celebrity. He's more than ready for it. He had to fly in from California for the event, straight from a set for the Robert Redford movie, *The Horse Whisperer,* opening this month in theaters around the country. For the film, Buck taught Redford to handle horses with the Brannaman touch.

The name "horse whisperer" appears to be an ancient one from the British Isles, given to people whose rapport with horses seemed almost mystical. For Buck, it's just a romantic metaphor for what he does every day. In fact, Redford's movie and the best-selling novel from which it is adapted were largely inspired by the real character of Buck Brannaman. But he isn't putting much stock in all the celebrity. "When the dust dies down and this movie's in the bargain bin at Kmart," he laughs, "I'll still have my day job that I had before all this started."

That "day job" takes Buck on the road nine months of the year, March through November, driving a two-ton Freightliner truck and hauling a 24-foot horse trailer with five or six of his own horses in it, to clinics where, for two or three days at a time, he helps people with starting colts, horsemanship, ranch roping, cow working. This year he's scheduled for 45 clinics and demonstrations in 16 states, from Limerick, Maine, to Bakersfield, California. Along the way, he tries to fit in a couple of clinics in Sheridan, Wyoming, where he runs a small ranch with his wife, Mary, and their three girls.

For Buck, his day job is as much a passion as a profession. He is carrying on a tradition of horsemanship that he learned from Ray Hunt, now a 67-year-old cowboy who preaches a gospel of "thinking harmony with horses." That tradition was handed down from Hunt's own guru, a living legend in the horse world named Tom Dorrance. Now in his 80s, Dorrance is still giving clinics and teaching what he calls "true unity," or the willing communication between horse and human. When Ray once asked where *he'd* learned this, Tom said, "Ray, I learned it from the horse."

Buck still recalls the day that, as a young ranch hand, he first saw Ray Hunt "work magic" with horses at a clinic in Bozeman, Montana. "I watched the entire day and left amazed and confused and a little ashamed," he says. "Everything I couldn't do on a horse, he could do." From that day on, he was a Ray Hunt disciple. At that same clinic, he also met Tom Dorrance. "Tom Dorrance," he says now, "has compiled so much information in his mind in the past 80 years that he has to get the credit for this revolution of new methods of working with horses." According to one admirer of all three men, they represent a direct lineage: "Tom Dorrance is Yoda, Ray Hunt is Obi-Wan Kenobi and Buck Brannaman is Luke Skywalker!"

Buck would dismiss this as another romantic metaphor, but there's a lot to it. George Lucas has said that *Star Wars* was about redemption. What Buck's mentors have handed down is also something akin to a spiritual quest, a way to rid oneself of one's own devils in learning to become one with the horse. "So often people start horses with a sort of caveman mentality," Buck says. "For some people, working with the horse is just a way of stroking their own egos. Sometimes they have a lot of emotional baggage. Sometimes they lack awareness of their surroundings. That's why horses have so many problems with humans."

The first time I talked to Buck, I asked if there was anything I could read to help me understand what he does. He didn't mention his own book about starting horses, but a slim volume about communication and consciousness called *A Kinship With All Life*. That book describes all animals as spiritual and mental beings who can read our hidden intentions and thoughts. At Buck's clinics, there's not much talk about this aspect of horsemanship. The word "spiritual" isn't part of his cowboy vocabulary. "People might get hung up on some cosmic image of it all," he says. "And it's really not that, it's something perfectly natural, something that the horse has to offer us, that some of us have to offer the horse. I think it's there for anybody who wants it."

Those who come to his clinics, whether they are starting colts or improving their riding skills, aren't given much of a chance to think cosmic thoughts: there's more than enough work to do as Buck points out that their timing is off, their balance isn't right, their awareness isn't sharp enough to catch what the horse is trying to tell them through its expression, its body language, its "feel"—or that they just don't know what to look for. Buck shows them why a troubled horse gets troubled, and what to do about it. There is plenty of practical advice, and plain horse sense.

After roping a colt around the neck, he lets it run around the pen at the end of his lasso. "Think of the rope as elastic," he says. "If it pulls, I keep the tension but let it slide through my hand a little, so it doesn't jerk the horse. I'm asking the horse to yield to the pressure of the rope, letting him find a way to come off that pressure. Any time the rope jerks, a horse will pull back, but it's the human that teaches it to pull back." As the colt realizes that the rope is not going to hurt him, his eye darts toward Buck. Instantly Buck releases the tension on the rope, and the colt stops and turns in to face him, as if asking, what's going on? It's the beginning of a friendship rather than a fight.

This is far from the old cowboy way, which Teddy Roosevelt, a rancher before becoming President, described in his 1896 book on ranch life. After roping a horse, he said, a broncobuster holds the rope against his hip, "at the same time leaning so far back, with the legs straight in front, that the heels dig deep into the ground when the strain comes, and the horse, running out with the slack of the rope, is brought up standing, or even turned head over heels by the shock."

Buck makes what he does look so ordinary that it's hard to see why this way of working with horses is still so uncommon. If this is "horse whispering," where's the mystery? In search of answers, I drive up into the northern reaches of the Cowboy State, across the wind-punished, frostbitten Wyoming landscape of red clay, scrub pine, sagebrush and open grassland spotted with herds of stoic livestock, scattered windmills, old battlefields, and remote ranch houses cowering beneath huge cottonwoods. I'm heading for Buck's ranch on the outskirts of Sheridan, a city where the local high school teams are called the Broncs and Lady Broncs, in a state whose license plate is stamped with a bucking horse and rider. An outdoor thermometer nailed to the door of a café has zero degrees in the middle of the scale, with the temperature markings going as far below zero as above. There's nothing gentle about the landscape, or the weather or the history of this place where Buck Brannaman makes his home. But I forget all that, warming up in the kitchen of the ranch. Buck is getting ready to head for a big barnlike arena he's just built, to start some young colts he hasn't worked with before. His wife, Mary, is dressing their 3-year-old daughter, Reata, named for a Spanish-style braided rawhide rope used by the old vaqueros of California. Reata is clutching a toy compact, and Mary patiently tells her, "You have to leave that here. You can't take this to the barn. Cowgirls don't wear makeup in the barn."

Watching Buck work with these horses from the ground up over the next few days is, in fact, a lot like learning a new language, one in which the flick of an ear, a sidelong glance, a licking of lips or a shift of weight may be all the horse offers, while the human responds with a slight change in posture, a step back or to the side, a lifted hand, or sometimes something as intangible as a change of expression. "There's no secret to this," he says. "I just know what we need to do in order for both of us to speak the same language and dance the same dance."

He's working in a round corral, with no corners where a colt could get into trouble, and working mostly from the saddle of a gelding named Abe, who seems to go where Buck wants without his asking. Buck goes through the same basic steps in starting all the colts, adjusting things to fit each different personality. First he ropes a colt, and works with the colt on the end of the lasso rope, helping it to free up its hindquarters and frontquarters so that its feet aren't stuck with fear. Next, he wants to desensitize the colt to things that might frighten it, bothering it with a flag, tossing a saddle blanket over its back, slapping its sides with the coils of his rope, until it isn't so bothered anymore. Then he fastens a halter over its head and works with the colt on the end of the halter rope: more practice to free up its front and hindquarters, and teaching it to back up and to follow his lead. When he senses a change, even a slight effort to do what he asks, he puts slack in the rope and rubs the colt's face or neck reassuringly.

After this, he saddles the colt and drives it off around the pen until it is comfortable with the saddle, and then draws its attention in toward him as he steps back and stands still at the middle of the pen. As the horse turns away from the fence to face him—a wonderful moment called hooking on—something important has been accomplished: "I've got the horse to focus on me mentally," Buck says, "without being physically pulled. I want him to feel he'd rather be with me than anywhere else." Before very long the colt is following him around the pen without any rope. "It should never be a fight," he says. "If it's a fight, you've lost ground."

After several days on the ranch, it's easy to see why Buck calls himself "the horse's friend" and how fluent he is in its native language. But I suspect there's more to what he does than meets the eye. I don't get a chance to ask him about this just yet. He's too busy getting his gear together, loading two horses into a trailer and heading off with a friend to try to catch a steer that's been running wild in the foothills behind a neighboring ranch since it escaped the roundup last fall.

Buck and his partner disappear over a frozen ridge, silhouetted against the morning sun. When they return that afternoon, they've got a roped steer and a story that gets better with each telling. Buck is leading the steer with a rope around its neck, and his partner trails with a rope on its hind leg. The steer has been "on the fight" all the way down. Finally, it digs in and won't go another step.

Buck spends a good deal of the next couple of hours trying to get the steer more interested in moving than in staying put, leaning back in his saddle to put a little tension on the rope, flicking the rope so it bothers the steer, getting his partner to bother the animal from the rear, waving a tarpaulin flag at it, talking to it and just waiting. All he gets in return are a few steps or a few yards at a time, or a sudden lunge as the steer tries to hook Brannaman's horse with its horns. Just as you'd think he'd have lost all patience, Buck leans over in the saddle, looks the steer in the eye and says, "Come on, honey!" It's almost dark when they finally collect some lengths of metal fencing and build a small pen around the steer, right where it is, figuring they'll load it into a trailer tomorrow.

Later Buck tells the story of the chase, how they heard the steer sneaking through the brush at the bottom of a deep, narrow draw. When the steer emerged out the other end of the draw, Buck roped it. Then he let it run until it slowed down and suddenly turned back and ran right under his horse, a sorrel gelding named Biff. But Biff was quick enough, and the steer didn't have much in the way of horns, so the horse wasn't hurt. The real danger was chasing the steer through a prairie dog town. "There was a hole about every four feet," Buck says, "but Biff was raised in country where they had lots of badger and gopher holes, so I just kind of closed my eyes and left it up to him."

Biff was almost an outlaw when Buck bought him and started to work with him, a horse who'd outfought his owners and never been broken. "He'd paw you or kick you or strike you anyway he could. He was very dangerous to be around for a couple of years," Buck says. "And he's no prettier now than when I got him, but on the inside he's very attractive. He's made it, and he's my friend."

On my last day at the ranch, I corner Buck and ask, What is it he sees in a horse that others don't? Is it the "spiritual part of the horse," as Tom Dorrance calls it? He doesn't answer right away. Instead, he tells me about his own life, growing up in Whitehall, Montana. "I was always kind of scared of my dad," he says. "He was pretty mean to us boys. I remember we'd come home from school for lunch, and my mom would drop me off at school again on the way to work. She was a waitress in a town about 50 miles away, and my dad had a shoe repair and saddle shop in town. I remember from about 8 or 9 years old, I would beg her not to go to work every day, 'cause I was terrified of being at home alone with my dad for the four or five hours after school, before she'd get home. I feel terrible for her now, 'cause every day I made her cry.

"She died of diabetes when I was 11. My dad really loved my mother, and he just didn't want to live anymore. He told us he wanted to be with her, and he started drinking. He moved us to Ennis, Montana. We ended up on a little ranch where my dad was putting up hay for a fellow, and he really started getting rough on us boys. He would drink and rant at us and keep us up all night and make us listen to him, and then send us to school on a half hour's sleep. Some nights he'd knock the hell out of you and some nights he'd just holler at you all night long, and you'd about rather get beat up and go to bed and get some sleep than listen to him all night.

"I remember one night, he got to chasing us around the house. There was sort of a little island in the middle of the house, so you could kind of work in a circle when he was real drunk, and stay ahead of him. I was in the lead and my older brother Smokie was right behind me, and just as my brother came around a corner in the kitchen he jerked a drawer open and grabbed a knife. And I told him real quietly, 'Put it back!' And he did. If my dad saw it, Smokie would've had to use it. It was one of those moments that define a person's life.

"The fellow who really saved us was a deputy sheriff of Madison County, Johnny France. A teacher of ours tipped him off, and he was the only one of the law enforcement people who had the guts to take us out of there. He arranged for a place for us to live, with the people who had raised him, in the same kind of a deal."

When I talk to Johnny France later, he recalls that the couple, Forrest and Betsy Shirley in Norris, Montana, had taken him in from a broken home and encouraged him to finish high school. After graduation, he'd told them he didn't know how he could repay them, and Betsy had said, "Some day, when you run across a similar situation, if you do for another child what we did for you, we'd consider that payment."

Buck still remembers how comfortable he felt with Betsy Shirley that first night. "It was the first time in a long while I knew I was going to get to sleep." But Forrest was out of town and due back the next day, and Buck was worried: maybe he didn't like kids! "I happened to be standing in the yard when he showed up," Buck recalls, "and he got out of the truck, walked over to me and said, 'You must be Buck,' and I just kind of nodded my head, and he said, 'Well, I'm Forrest,' and he handed me a brand-new pair of leather gloves, real nice deerskin gloves for work, and he said, 'Get in.' And we got in the ranch truck, which always had fencing material in it, and he never said a word. We went out for hours that day, and just fixed fence, stretched wire, put in posts. He didn't say anything to me, and I was so happy that he didn't. I never realized at that age how wise he was, but I'm sure Forrest had put quite a bit of thought into that. I think he figured, just get him busy doing something and let him alone. We spent quite a few days together before he said much to me at all. And finally, about the time I was thinking, 'I wish he'd talk to me a little bit,' he did just that. At that point, that's where his influence really began with me. He was a good old cowboy."

While in high school, Buck learned to ride colts with Forrest at the ranch, tried his hand as a saddle bronc rider at local rodeos and took jobs starting colts for neighboring ranches to make some money. "I got tough horses to ride," he says. "What else are you going to give a 14-year-old kid you don't know anything about? If I wrecked the horse, they'd just send it to the sale ring. It wasn't pretty, but I could get it done after a fashion."

After high school, Buck went to work for the Madison River Cattle Company near Three Forks, Montana. He also got serious about trick roping, a skill his father had forced upon him from the age of 3, and eventually set a world's record for jumping through the smallest "butterfly" loop, with a perimeter of just over nine feet.

When he first asked for a job at Madison River, Buck was sent into Bozeman to see the manager of the ranch, who was at a Ray Hunt clinic. "I'd heard about this Ray Hunt in high school," Buck laughs, "but I was a cocky teenager and said I don't need any of that! It's just a bunch of BS!" But when he got to the clinic, he was so amazed by what he saw that he forgot to ask for the job that day. When he did get hired, the manager began sending Buck and other hands to more of Hunt's clinics, each time with a trailer load of young broncs, and Hunt would start the horses and try to educate the cowboys.

Buck had a lot to learn. "In those days when I'd start a horse," he recalls, "I was so afraid I couldn't get him saddled that I'd tie up a hind foot, tie him to the fence, and if that didn't work, I'd tie up a front foot along with it. Well, eventually I got the saddle on. But Ray made a horse feel comfortable about being worked with and saddled!"

The young cowboy was a convert. For Buck, as much as the horses, Ray Hunt was offering a different way of life. "The ranch boss saw what a passion I had for becoming a good hand," Buck says, "so he gave me the nod, and sent me to clinics to ride with Ray over the next five years."

Ray Hunt's approach with horses was remarkably like Forrest Shirley's with Buck in their first few days together. Where Forrest hadn't said much until Buck was really wishing he would, Ray Hunt didn't try to make a horse do anything; he "set it up for the horse," explains Buck, and made it easy for the horse to find out what he wanted. "Ray was teaching us to let the horse figure it out," Buck says, "to let it be the horse's idea." This meant communicating with the horse, not overpowering it.

"Tom and Ray both speak of feel, timing and balance, and *that one other thing,*" Buck says. There's a Zenlike indirectness in their teachings, leaving the essence of training up to the horse.

Ray Hunt and his wife, Carolyn, soon became like family to Buck. He was learning about more than horses. Like a Zen master, Hunt offers up his wisdom in epigrams that people remember for a lifetime. One Buck will never forget is: "You're not working on the horse, you're working on yourself." His foster mother, Betsy, remembers Buck's temper as a boy, recalling times he was grounded because he beat the cow when something went wrong as he milked it. And Buck remembers the day he realized that Ray Hunt knew of his temper. It was a turning point in his life. "I so wanted him to appreciate me and I thought I'd fooled him, but he knew," Buck recalls, "and I made a commitment to work on my temper, every day of my life if that's what it took."

It was a turning point with the horses, too. "The horse is so intimidated by someone who's angry," Buck explains. "Some horses are so sensitive that if they find out you have this warlike part of your psyche, you might never get anything accomplished."

As he made Ray Hunt's methods his own, Buck's relationship with horses became more than a meeting of minds, it became an affair of the heart. And like all such affairs, it had its painful moments. One of these left an indelible impression. He had moved to a ranch near Bozeman, enrolled in college and worked on the ranch after classes. In addition to Buck, who rode other people's colts, the owner had hired trainers for his own horses, and the trainers had their own ideas. Their way was to force a halter on a colt in a stall, lead it around with its mare until the pair got close to a fence, then tie the colt to the fence and lead the mare away. "And these babies," Buck recalls, "having never worn a halter before, would pull back and thrash around and slam their head into the fence and throw themselves upside down. It was horrible."

"I came back from classes one afternoon," he recalls, "and there was a weanling filly they'd tied up to the fence. They were beating her, to make her get up. She didn't understand how to give to the pressure of the rope, so she'd thrash around and get up and throw herself back down again. They were taking the snap on the end of the rope and hitting her with it, in the head. These guys had been making fun of me because of my Ray Hunt stuff, even after I bailed them out a few times. So I just stood back and stayed out of it at first. One fellow went into the barn and got a bucket of water, and he poured water down the filly's ears. And of course that drove her insane. She jumped up right away, for a moment, and as soon as she felt the halter rope come tight she threw herself again, and squealed. If you've ever heard the sound a young horse makes just before it dies, that's what she sounded like.

"But they thought," Buck continues, "they'd done so well there with the water because they did get her up, that the next thing you know this fellow was dragging the hose out of the stall barn. Evidently he was going to run more water down her ears: at that point, I took over. I walked up and un-snapped this filly from the fence and snapped in a lead shank. It didn't take me but just a few seconds to get her up, and within five minutes I had her leading all over with no conflict whatsoever. I handed the lead rope to my boss, and he didn't so much as look ashamed. So I walked to the house and packed my bags and I was gone, in search of someone who I wanted to be around."

Not long afterward, Buck rented an arena and started giving his first clinics. He was in his third year of college, majoring in accounting, when his adviser, after hearing local people talk about what he was doing with horses, called Buck into his office. "I was at the top of my class," Buck laughs, "but he told me the best thing I could do was to dump my book bag into the garbage can and pursue my horse career! And I did just that."

The idea of starting horses gently isn't new. Teddy Roosevelt actually bucked convention and adopted the practice on his own ranch, and Will James, a popular author of the 1920s and '30s, described the rare cowboy who used a gentle touch, and "started" horses instead of breaking them. What is new is the idea of the horse as an intelligent individual who has more to teach us than we imagine. This is an idea handed down from Tom Dorrance to Ray Hunt and Buck Brannaman, and to the thousands of students who have been to their clinics.

There is a growing interest in more humane ways of working with horses. The field is producing a bumper crop of instructors, clinics, magazines, videos and books, including a controversial best-seller by another horse trainer, Monty Roberts. With the huge success of Nicholas Evans' novel, *The Horse Whisperer,* and the arrival of Redford's movie version, the field is expanding like a prairie fire. Some of what's offered is gentler than the old ways, but still far from what Buck and his teachers have in mind.

When Buck agreed to work on the *Horse Whisperer* movie with Redford, he had mixed feelings about the publicity it would produce. "There's a horse whisperer behind every bush these days," he laughs. As for himself, he adds, "I don't think of myself as a horse whisperer. I never heard of a horse whisperer until Nick Evans wrote about it. If you want to give me a label, just call me a cowboy and leave it at that."

At the same time, he's seen so much abuse of horses that he thinks the movie offers a real moment of hope. "Most people don't want to be mean to horses or abuse them," he says. "Sometimes it happens as a result of ignorance. In my entire life of working my tail off, I could never reach as many people with this message as this movie will, with its vast exposure. There's a possibility for it to change horsemanship in a positive way, on a huge scale."

When Nicholas Evans was planning his novel, he heard about Buck Brannaman and showed up at one of his clinics. "I realized how sincere he was," Buck says, "and I gave him quite a bit of my time over those few days. Then he went on his way. Next thing I know, he's sold about a bazillion books." When Redford decided to make the movie, both directing it and starring as Tom Booker, a Montana cowboy who heals a fear-crazed horse along with the mother and daughter who bring it to him, Buck was a natural choice as the film's technical adviser. But what happened on the set was more than technical.

"In the beginning," Buck says, "I was a bridge between what was real and what was a movie. I think they believed that it's really just fiction, just a story that they were trying to create, through illusion or the magic of motion pictures. But there's nothing phony or made up about the horsemanship in this book. As the filming progressed through the summer, something changed. Everyone began to realize they were making a story about real life, a story that involved these matters of the heart. Even people that were grips and lighting technicians and electricians really started to take hold of what it was all about. They would see me work with some of the horses, and then see Bob Redford working with my horses, and see the human and the horse relate to each other, and they really started to understand. I was real pleased at how he could take on the role. And he didn't have me covering for him doing all the action, making him look like a horseman. He did it himself."

In the arena at the National Western Stock Show in Denver, Buck is under pressure. He's had to fly in from working on the movie, and has to fly out right after his demonstration. He's got three hours to saddle and ride a colt that's never been ridden: if he gets it done there's another horse waiting. After two hours the first horse does anything Buck asks, as if they are reading each other's minds. He starts working with the second one, a dun filly that comes in bucking, its muscles rippling with fear, its feet scarcely finding the ground. As before, Buck tries to show the horse there's nothing to fear, helping her to free up her hindquarters, soften her neck, move her feet. "That's what made her buck," he says, "too afraid, too upset to move her feet." But time's short; Buck tells the crowd he's going to get on her before she's really ready, and do the rest from the saddle. She kicks up her heels when he gets the saddle on, and bucks around the corral after he cinches it up.

He gets her quiet again and climbs on, and the crowd gets to see a rare sight: Buck Brannaman riding a bucking horse. He's a good enough bronc rider to stay on, but there's a difference between this ride and the ones at the stock show rodeo the night before. Here the filly just seems to change her mind, and stops bucking. "Some people might be pretty punishing when the horse bucks," he says. "But I didn't want her to have any trouble. If you no-ticed, when she was bucking I was trying to pet her. There's no hard feelings."

After the demonstration, I ask Buck if he's ever met a horse he didn't like. "Not me. No," he says. "I've run across some people I don't like, but not a horse. The people I don't like are the ones who are mean to their horses, or to other people. I'm the horse's friend, so if you're mean to a horse, you're mean to my friend."

A Vote for Ta Wee

BY RED SMITH

Winner of the 1976 Pulitzer Prize for distinguished commentary, Red Smith (1905–1982) brought elegance, wit and a keen understanding of human nature to the sports pages of whichever newspaper his columns graced. Choosing only one column to reprint here was difficult, but this one, "A Vote For Ta Wee," got my vote.

1970

Betty Friedan, stay as sweet as you are, don't take any wooden nickels, and may 1971 be the year you'll run all chauvinist male pigs back to the dishpan where they belong. And, dear, if you're uncertain where to hit first with your troops from Women's Lib, you might consider the offices of the Thoroughbred Racing Association, the Triangle Publications, *Turf and Sport Digest,* and *Newsweek.*

These are the strongholds of the misogynists who perpetrated the grossest injustice of 1970 upon a member of the deadlier sex. They denied little Ta Wee the title of Horse of the Year, a distinction she deserved as richly as they deserve a dainty shoe in the blouse of the breeches.

There were wide differences of opinion among the electorate who voted in the annual polls to designate racing champions in 1970. The TRA poll picked out Personality as the boss hoss. Staff members of Triangle Publications—the *Daily Racing Form* and the *Morning Telegraph*—chose Fort Marcy. So did *Turf and Sport Digest.* Pete Axthelm, sports editor of *Newsweek,* went for Personality.

Pooh. The perspicacious Mike Casale, the perceptive Dave Alexander of the *Thoroughbred Record, The New York Times*'s discerning James Pilkington Roach, and the pertinacious Red Smith say Ta Wee.

Let us compare credentials.

61

Fort Marcy was beyond question the best grass horse of the year. He had no peer on this continent, and he polished off a picked field from abroad in the Washington, D.C. International at Laurel. This was his third straight victory in a $100,000 stakes, following scores in the United Nations and the Man O'War.

He has more than a million dollars in the bank, less than his owner, Paul Mellon, but more than his trainer, the gifted Elliott Burch.

However, Fort Marcy was not a standout on dirt, and that is the surface for all but a few major races in the United States. In the view of Pete Axthelm and others who plumbed for Personality, that disqualified Fort Marcy.

Personality ran on skinned tracks and his eight victories included scores in the Preakness, the Wood Memorial, the Jersey Derby, the Jim Dandy, and the Woodward.

Bred by the late Hirsch Jacobs, he is a versatile son of the brilliant Hail to Reason and Affectionately, the Jacobs family's pet mare. Hirsch Jacobs considered Personality the finest horse he ever bred but did not live to see the colt succeed. John Jacobs, Hirsch's son, trained the horse and his stablemate, High Echelon. When Personality caught the sniffles a few days before the Belmont Stakes, John Jacobs sent High Echelon out to win that mile-and-a-half climax of the Triple Crown series.

Hirsch Jacobs was America's leading trainer over many years, but he never had a winner of the Kentucky Derby, the Preakness, or the Belmont, which make up the Triple Crown. John Jacobs won two of the three, and had two different three-year-olds fit enough to collaborate on the job.

That made him trainer of the year in this book, but Personality was only the best three-year-old. Neither he nor any other colt could carry Ta Wee's shoes.

Five times a winner and twice second in seven starts, the lady was unmatched for consistency. However, it was neither the number of races won nor the times she registered on the clock that puts her in a class by herself. She is simply the greatest weight-carrying filly of our time and one of the two best on this continent in any time.

The legendary Pan Zareta, whose owners ran her to death for $39,000 in purses half a century ago, is the only name in American racing history fit to be bracketed with Ta Wee's. Pan Zareta won a race in Juarez, Mexico, carrying 146 pounds.

In the Correction Handicap, which was Ta Wee's first start of 1970, she won under 131 pounds. Never again did they let her go to the post with only the kitchen stove on her back. They kept piling on the furniture until Tartan

Stable entered her against colts in the Fall Highweight Handicap at Belmont. Tommy Trotter gave her 140 pounds, something the New York racing secretary had never in his life done to a girl. She won, so when she rejoined the ladies for the Interborough Handicap, he gave her 142. She won.

In more than three hundred years of New York racing, no filly or mare had ever lugged such a load on the flat. In a sense the voters were right. She isn't Horse of the Year. She's the Horse of Three Centuries.

Concerning the Imperial Spanish Riding School in Vienna

From *Florian*

BY FELIX SALTEN

Felix Salten, the creator of the children's classic *Bambi,* recognized the grace of other four-legged creatures too. This chapter from his novel *Florian* captures classical dressage and the surrounding splendor that is still to be seen at Vienna's Spanish Riding School.

The Imperial Spanish Riding School in Vienna existed for over two hundred years for the sole purpose of breeding and training their beautiful Leppizan horses and in developing that type of riding known as "Haute Ecole." Whether one believes that Haute Ecole is the acme of fine horsemanship, or whether one is of the school of thought that it is so artificial as to be completely useless, does not change the fact that the interpretation of the will of the rider by the horse (and his desire to comply instantly with that will) approaches the uncanny. The "High School" rider and his mount were as near one as it is possible for man and beast to be. They did not perform for glory or gain as does the Arabian on his war mare, the polo player, or the jockey; horse and man devoted their entire lives to perfecting what they considered a fine art for the sheer love of that art.

The Spanish School disappeared with the death of Franz Joseph at the beginning of World War I. It was revived for a short time, but I fear it has succumbed again. A few of the horses, or their descendants, are still to be seen doing the simplest of the Haute Ecole movements in circuses and vaudeville acts, but when the trainers who learned from the great Ritmeisters *are gone it is questionable whether there will be any to take their places.*

"To the degree that an Asil—highborn horse—possesses thy heart will she respond to thee. She will humble thy enemies and honor thy friends. Willingly she will carry thee upon her back, but she will consent to no humiliation. She is at once aware whether she carrieth a friend or an enemy of God. The mare that lives by Divine orders as a mute and obedient companion of man, has an insight into the mind of her master whom she may even prefer to her own kind."—Mnahi.

DRINKERS OF THE WIND by Carl Raswan

A brief "Good morning" from the Emperor was accompanied by a circular movement of his hand. The moment he sat down, a door in the opposite wall was thrown wide, and four horsemen rode into the arena. In a straight line they swept toward the Court Box and stopped at an appropriate distance. Simultaneously they doffed their two-cornered hats and swung them until their arms were horizontal. Then they wheeled and to the strains of the *Gypsy Baron* began their quadrille.

The circle and capers cut by the four horses were precisely alike, and gave the effect of music in the flowing rhythm of their execution. The regularity of the horses' strides, and the horsemanship of the four riders aroused the spectators to a gay pitch, no one could have said why; it was sheer rapture evoked by the beautiful, blooded animals and their artistry.

The quadrille was over, the horsemen had made their exit. The wooden door remained wide open.

Next seven mounted stallions entered and filed in front of the Court Box. Seven bicornes were removed from seven heads, swung to a horizontal position, and replaced.

Florian stood in the center. To his right stood three older stallions, thoroughly trained, and to his left three equally tested ones. He resembled a fiery youth among men. In a row of white steeds he stood out as the only *pure* white one. His snowy skin, unmarred by a single speck, called up memories of cloudless sunny days, of Nature's gracious gifts. His liquid dark eyes, from whose depths his very soul shone forth, sparkled with inner fire and energy and health. Ennsbauer sat in the saddle like a carved image. With his brown frock-coat, his chiseled, reddish brown features and his fixed mien, he seemed to have been poured in metal.

The Emperor had just remarked, "Ennsbauer uses no stirrups or spurs," when the sextet began to play.

The horses walked alongside the grayish-white wainscoting. Their tails were braided with gold, with gold also their waving manes. Pair by pair they were led through the steps of the High School; approached from the far side toward the middle, and went into their syncopated, cadenced stride.

The Emperor had no eyes for any but Florian. Him he watched, deeply engrossed. His connoisseur's eye tested the animal, tested the rider, and could find no flaw that might belie the unstinted praise he had heard showered on them. His right hand played with his mustache, slowly, not with the impatient flick that spelled disappointment over something.

Ennsbauer felt the Emperor's glance like a physical touch. He stiffened. He could hope for no advancement. Nor did he need fear a fall. Now—in the saddle, under him this unexcelled stallion whose breathing he could feel between his legs and whose readiness and willingness to obey he could sense like some organic outpouring—now doubt and pessimism vanished. The calm-collected, resolute animal gave him calmness, collectedness, and resolution.

At last he rode for the applause of the Emperor, of Franz Joseph himself, and by Imperial accolade for enduring fame. Now it was his turn. . . .

Away from the wall he guided Florian, into the center of the ring. An invisible sign, and Florian, as if waiting for it, fell into the Spanish step.

Gracefully and solemnly, he lifted his legs as though one with the rhythm of the music. He gave the impression of carrying his rider collectedly and slowly by his own free will and for his own enjoyment. Jealous of space, he placed one hoof directly in front of the other.

The old Archduke Rainer could not contain himself: "Never have I see a horse *piaffe* like that!"

Ennsbauer wanted to lead Florian out of the Spanish walk, to grant him a moment's respite before the next tour. But Florian insisted on prolonging it and Ennsbauer submitted.

Florian strode as those horses strode who, centuries ago, triumphantly and conscious of their triumphant occasion, bore Caesars and conquerors into vanquished cities or in homecoming processions. The rigid curved neck, such as the ancient sculptors modeled; the heavy short body that seemed to rock on the springs of his legs, the interplay of muscle and joint, together constituted a stately performance, one that amazed the more as it gradually compelled the recognition of its rising out of the will to perfect performance. Every single movement of Florian's revealed nobility, grace, significance and distinction all in one; and in each of his poses he was the ideal model for a sculptor, the composite of all the equestrian statues of history.

The music continued and Florian, chin pressed against chest, deliberately bowed his head to the left, to the right.

"Do you remember," Elizabeth whispered to her husband, "what our boy once said about Florian? He sings—only one does not hear it."

Ennsbauer also was thinking of the words of little Leopold von Neustift as he led Florian from the Spanish step directly into the *volte.* The delight with which Florian took the change, the effortless ease with which he glided into the short, sharply cadenced gallop, encouraged Ennsbauer to try the most precise and exacting form of the *volte,* the *redoppe,* and to follow that with the *pirouette.*

As though he intended to stamp a circle into the tanbark of the floor, Florian pivoted with his hindlegs fixed to the same place, giving the breathtaking impression of a horse in full gallop that could not bolt loose from the spot, nailed to the ground by a sorcerer or by inner compulsion.

And when, right afterward, with but a short gallop around, Florian rose into the *pesade,* his two forelegs high in the air and hindlegs bent low, and accomplished this difficult feat of balance twice, three times, as if it were child's play, he needed no more spurring on. Ennsbauer simply let him be, as he began to *courbette,* stiffly erect. His forelegs did not beat the air, now, but hung limply side by side, folded at the knee. Thus he carried his rider, hopped forward five times without stretching his hindlegs. In the eyes of the spectators Florian's execution of the *courbette* did not impress by its bravura, or by the conquest of body heaviness by careful dressure and rehearsal, but rather as an exuberant means of getting rid of a superabundance of controlled gigantic energy.

Another short canter around the ring was shortened by Florian's own impatience when he voluntarily fell into the Spanish step. He enjoyed the music, rocked with its rhythm. These men and women and their rank were as nothing to him. Still, the presence of onlookers fired him from the very outset. He wanted to please, he had a sharp longing for applause, for admiration; his ambition, goaded on by the music, threw him into a state of intoxication; youth and fettle raced through his veins like a stream overflowing on a steep grade. Nothing was difficult any longer. With his rider and with all these human beings around him, he celebrated a feast. He did not feel the ground under his feet, the light burden on his back. Gliding, dancing with the melody, he could have flown had the gay strains asked for it.

On Florian's back as he hopped on his hindlegs once, twice, Ennsbauer sat stunned, amazed.

Following two successive *croupades,* a tremendous feat, Florian went into the Spanish step still again. Tense and at the same time visibly exuberant, proud and amused, his joyously shining eyes made light of his exertions. From the *ballotade* he thrust himself into the *capriole,* rose high in the air from the standing position, forelegs and hindlegs horizontal. He soared above ground, his head high in jubilation. Conquering!

Frenetic applause burst out all over the hall, like many fans opening and shutting, like the rustle of stiff paper being torn.

Surrounded by the six other stallions Florian stepped before the Court Box, and while the riders swung their hats in unison, he bowed his proud head just once, conscious, it seemed, of the fact that the ovation was for him and giving gracious thanks in return.

Sleeping Sickness

BY BEN K. GREEN

Ben K. "Doc" Green was a Texas veterinarian whose collections of stories, including *Horse Tradin'* and *Wild Cow Tales,* chronicled life in the American West as it was really lived (no Hollywood glamour there). For realistic hands-on views of horse doctoring on the range, Doc Green had no peer, as this reminiscence shows.

Charlie Baker, the sheriff of Pecos County, rushed into my office about nine o'clock one hot August morning and said, "Doc, there's four or five horses over at the Sheriff's posse barn fallin' around, and I know they've got the blind staggers. I've seen some of it when I farmed back East and they're got it if I ever saw it, and I'm afraid that the rest of the horses over there are goin' to start staggerin' soon. Ben K. is already weavin' a little when he walks. (Ben K. was a horse I had given him.) You know everybody that's got a horse over there thinks as much of them as they do of their families and you got to do somethin' fast."

"Charlie, it ain't likely that there is any blind staggers in this old desert country because it's generally caused by horses bein' fed moldy corn or some other feed that's in the process of sourin' after it's been wet."

"Well, I'll swear it looks just like blind staggers."

As I stepped into my car, I said, "I'll follow you to the posse barn."

News had spread fast and there were several of the fellows who had horses in the posse barn already there when I drove up. They were leading and holding four horses out in the corral in front of the barn that were having a hard time being still or walking straight. At a glance I knew that we had a fresh outbreak of sleeping sickness, and I explained to everybody that it might be easier to cure and stop the spread of it than blind staggers because there were serum injections for the treatment of sleeping sickness and vaccines to stop it from spreading.

Encephalomyelitis is a disease of horses that is spread by blood-sucking insects that transmit the disease from one horse to another; this explains why it is a late-summer and fall disease, for it is then that the transporting hosts are most prevalent. It is commonly referred to among horsemen as "sleeping sickness."

When a horse has been bitten by an insect carrying the virus, he will slowly develop the virus in his blood stream; it takes about five or six days. When the disease becomes apparent, the first symptoms are nervousness and a difficulty with vision, and a gentle horse will have trouble recognizing the person who has been handling him.

After this first stage, the horse becomes unsteady on his feet and wobbles and staggers and stands with his head lowered toward the ground, and as he becomes worse, he will find a fence or tree or some other solid object to push against with his breast or shoulder to steady himself. This is getting into the last stages.

The next step in the disease is that the horse falls to the ground and is unable to regain his equilibrium. After this happens, no matter how much treatment and care a horse may get, should he recover he will never be the same because the damage to his central nervous system will leave him more or less stupid and without good coordination, even though he may appear to be normal.

There had been a few cases of sleeping sickness in the area in the late summer every year. This had been a rainy summer, so to speak, for a desert region and flies and mosquitoes were plentiful. A good many of my regular clients had me vaccinate their horses for sleeping sickness early enough to prevent the disease. However, these horses would amount to a very small percentage of the horse population in the Trans-Pecos, Edwards Plateau, and Davis Mountains Region. These areas had gotten to be my over-all territory.

In late August I was called for a few cases of sleeping sickness that were widely scattered over my practicing territory. By the first week in September there was a full-scale epidemic of sleeping sickness raging among the horse population. I was ordering vaccine for the inoculations and anti-serum for the treatment in such high amounts that the laboratories were beginning to short my orders but were sending all they could, which in many instances wasn't enough. I began phoning drugstores and other practitioners in regions where there had not been an outbreak and buying up all the available stock I could find while the laboratories hurried in their efforts to produce fresh supplies.

The harder and the faster I worked, it seemed the more the epidemic got out of hand. There were thousands of stock horses, brood mares, yearlings, two's, and so forth that weren't being vaccinated and were a constant source of new infestation to the gentle horses that were in the working remuda on the various ranches. It seemed that horses being kept on feed around ranch headquarters or in town so that they would be available for immediate and everyday use were getting sick in greater numbers than range horses. This was true because of the additional population of flies and mosquitoes around barns, corrals, watering places, and the like.

The vaccination was a 1-cc. live-virus injection administered between the layers of the skin (interdermal). Because of the slow absorption of this skin shot it took at least nine days to begin to furnish some immunity, and it was necessary to vaccinate the horse with a second shot seven days after the first one. Within three weeks I had vaccinated about three thousand horses and had about two hundred and fifty active cases of sleeping sickness under treatment.

The usual treatment for a horse already stricken with the disease was to inject into the jugular vein 250-cc.'s of anti-serum. In addition to this I always gave some heart stimulant, the purpose of which was to keep the horse on his feet. Often when an owner would describe a horse's condition to me over the phone and I knew that it would be a few hours before I could possibly get to him, I would instruct that a quart of strong black coffee to be given by mouth every two hours until I got there. This was another way to keep a horse awake and on his feet. Many of those good telephone operators who served the ranch country of the Far Southwest mercifully would sometimes be guilty of listening in and asking somebody that couldn't get in touch with me how sick their horse was and several learned to tell them to drench their horses with a quart of strong black coffee until they could reach me.

This was a big ranch country and I was driving unbelievable distances, making very few stops other than to get gas and supplies. These were the war years and the local ration officer caught up with me about noon one day and told me there was a man from Washington, D.C., in his office who came to check my gas mileage and would ride along with me for a few days in my practice. I had had very little sleep, ate when I could get to it, and was drawn down pretty hard and mean, so I said, "Brush the brain-washed civil service idiot out on the curb and I'll suck him up directly."

I whipped by the courthouse and this very nice precise gentleman of about thirty-five was standing on the curb in front of the courthouse when I stopped. As I got out of the car, he asked, "Are you Dr. Green?"

I told him, "Yeah," and he introduced himself by saying that he was the civil service idiot who I was supposed to suck up. He had been on an extension line when Mr. Johnson, the chairman of our local board, was talking to me.

I had started to Marathon sixty miles south on a graded road. As we pulled out of town he took out a pencil and pad and went to figurin' and explainin' to me at the suggested word rate that at the speed of 45 mph in a tenhour day with time out for meals and stops, it was hardly possible for one driver to drive one car more than three hundred miles. The record showed that I was consistently getting over five hundred miles of gas-ration stamps a day, figured at the rate of fifteen miles per gallon.

At the time he was makin' me this speech, I was driving at 85 mph. I hadn't driven less than eighteen to twenty-four hours a day in over two weeks and wasn't payin' a hell of a lot of attention to what he was sayin'. However, I had looked him over pretty good as was my habit with livestock, women, and civil service employees.

He had the ruddy complexion of a freshly peeled banana and his eyes were sort of marble-like of an indeterminate color, and when you glanced at him through those thick horn-rim glasses, you could almost see a column of figures crossing the stare he wore. His nose and chin and the rest of his face were narrow and sharp and you could have jabbed both his eyes out with a hairpin without spreadin' it. His hairline hovered down close to his eyebrows, and the back of his head ran down his neck. After lookin' at him carefully, I would say that he had a very typical kind of a government head, and he had adorned it with a small crown, narrow-brimmed brown hat that you could barely get thumb-hold on.

We drove up to the Hess Ranch and the foreman by the name of Hill waved me to come on down to the barn. I got out and started talking with him and walked into the corral where the sick horses were and also those that he had to vaccinate. He glanced over the fence and saw my passenger sittin' in the car with the door open and asked, "What's that?"

I told him who this passenger was and why he was along and that he was a native of Maryland. Hill walked back to the car with me, and on the way he said he wanted to take a closer look at this gov'ment man.

I introduced Mr. Hill to Mr. Stratsford. Hill stuck his long, strong callused hand out, and as he shook hands, you could tell he was tryin' to break every bone in that pencil-muscled hand as he said, "Hello, 'Fed.' I'm glad the gov'ment has begun to pay old Doc some mind."

We circled by Alpine from Marathon and out to some ranches and back down the public highway between Alpine and Fort Stockton to the

Hoovey Draw country. By now it was dark and I was still going from ranch to ranch treating horses that were already stricken with sleeping sickness. Along about five o'clock in the afternoon I noticed that he had put his little scratch pad and pen in his pocket.

We came out on the Balmorhea-Fort Stockton highway and turned toward town, a distance of about thirty miles. When I let him out about eleven o'clock that night at the Springhurst Hotel, I had crisscrossed and driven about three hundred miles since I picked him up. He had insisted that I not make any calls without him so I told him to eat something, get some rest, and I would pick him up just as soon as I had to make a call.

I had my living quarters in the back of my office, so I went in and started to go to bed when the phone rang. It was another case at Imperial, which was forty miles north of town, and I told them I would be right out. The telephone operators voluntarily kept tickets on my incoming calls and promised people who were phoning me that they would give me the message when they found me or when I called in.

I pulled up in front of the hotel and told Benny Walker, the night porter, to get my man for me. He had barely had time to take a bath, so he put on his clothes and came back down lookin' rather shocked, worn, and surprised that I would answer another call so soon.

The morning before he had taken a reading of my speedometer and had forgotten to look at it again when we got in that night. As we started off he looked at the speedometer and you could see some surprise come over his Maryland-bred, Washington-trained countenance.

I had some twenty-five or thirty horses to treat and vaccinate at Imperial between then and daylight. The telephone operator from Fort Stockton caught me at the country café in Imperial and so I made some more calls north and west to Grand Falls and Monahans. Then we whipped back by Crane and McCamey and were back in Fort Stockton about three o'clock that afternoon. This was another three hundred plus miles, which made a total of more than six hundred miles in about twenty-four hours which was the distance between the places where I worked.

Between nine and ten o'clock that night I had a call from Jim Nance, the sheriff at Sanderson, about a horse of his that was at Charlie Gregory's ranch ten miles west of Sanderson. I went by the hotel and picked up the "Fed" and we started sixty miles south to Sanderson. Jim's horse was sick but was in the early stages and I almost knew that the one treatment would be all that he would need, but by flashlight and lantern we vaccinated Charlie's best brood mares and saddle horses.

In the meantime, Frank Warren had put in a call from the Circle Dot Ranch in the Big Canyon that had been relayed to me by Jim Vance, so we went from Sanderson to the Circle Dot. Frank didn't have his horses ready and told me when I could catch the time that I could come, call him in a day or so, since he didn't actually have a sick horse and this was just a vaccination call.

I went from the Circle Dot to Sheffield, about another seventy miles, and vaccinated horses there early the next morning and then we ate a bite of breakfast at one of the country cafés. I had had calls catch up with me to go to Iraan, where I vaccinated a bunch of horses and treated for Mr. Lee a horse that was already in secondary stages, which meant that I would have to double-check and stop by there every chance I got the next few days and nights.

Val Gobert went with us around Iraan to show us where all the different horses were that people had ready for me to vaccinate and he opened gates and entertained Mr. Fed for two or three hours. By now I had calls back to Sanderson.

We drove in under the long driveway at McKnight's Garage at Sanderson. It was a big old garage with a lot of loafers' benches just under the shade of the driveway and a big café at the end of the building. We got out of the car, so it could be serviced while we went in to eat. There were several loafers on the old car seats that were set out for that purpose. They all got up to shake hands and ask about people over the country. I had a pretty good audience, so I turned to my passenger and said, "Boys, I want you to meet Uncle Sam."

They all shook hands kind of polite as they looked him over, and as Monte Cordor shook hands with him, he said, "Doc's kind of a smart aleck. What's your real name?"

He put the Maryland brogue to it and told him the name was Stratsford. Between the length of the name and his foreign accent, another cowboy spoke up and said, "Monte, don't you wished you hadn't asked?"

I explained to him his mission in the Far Southwest and the reason he was with me, and as we turned to walk into the café, somebody said in a loud voice, "Why don't you let him drive some. We need to get our money's worth out of that kind of gov'ment help."

They served good Western grub and it was about middle of the afternoon, and Uncle Sam's appetite improved to the point where he ate as much as I did.

On the way back to Fort Stockton we went by Frank Hinde's and I introduced Frank to Uncle Sam. Frank took an aerial view of him from his six feet eight inches, and he wore a high-crown broad-brimmed hat that made him look even taller. He shook hands with him and was so polite and nice that you could tell he didn't really mean it. It was gettin' real late in the afternoon, so Uncle Sam stayed in the car.

As Frank and I walked to the corral, Frank said, "What's the matter with that damn feller's head?"

I said, "I haven't diagnosed it yet."

"Well, it looks like he should cover it up with a bigger hat so he wouldn't look so bad."

That was a good enough opening for me to cut an old friend, so I said, "That explains why you wear such a damn big hat."

As we were driving into town that night, Uncle Sam began to break down. He had seen more country, more horses, and more rough roads and a different breed of people than he had ever imagined existed. He had seen us vaccinate wild horses in chutes or rope and choke them down and vaccinate them in a matter of a split second before they could get off the ground, and all in all he was impressed beyond words with his experiences and my professional talent combined with my cowboy and ranch background.

As we drove down the road between stops, I had explained to him some of the finer points that made it possible to work with a horse affected by sleeping sickness, even one that was staggering, and told him that you might slap a horse on the side where you were standing or raise your voice some and holler in his ear but never push against him because he would think that he had found something to lean against and you couldn't possibly hold him up and he would very likely fall on you. As I walked with a horse trying to put a needle in his jugular vein, I would put my free hand on the other side of his neck and pull toward me, which would cause him to stagger away from me, making it safer to give him an injection.

Whether Uncle Sam knew it or not, he was seein' cowboy'n' and horse handlin' at its best by lifetime experts.

As we got nearer town, he said that if he wrote his report and tried to explain the distances between calls and the vast amount of country I was covering, and describe the friendly, informality of the people, from his experience, Washington would send out another "brain-washed civil service idiot" to see if his report was true. He readily confessed that he never would have believed any part of what he had seen if it had just been told to him or written up in a report. For ten miles he was almost a human being and actually showed some kind of admiration for me, my clients, and the great Far Southwest.

I let Mr. Civil Service Expert out at the hotel and told him I would call him when I had to leave town again. It was about four o'clock in the afternoon and I lay down to take a nap and slept until almost dark. This was the first time in over a week I had been on a bed. I would catch a nap here and yonder in my car while I would be waiting for an owner to get his horses in the corral or during some other short delay.

My phone rang a little after dark and I had several calls stacked up in a matter of a few minutes. I loaded the refrigerated vaccine boxes in the back of my car and picked up other fresh supplies.

I pulled up in front of the hotel and told Benny to get my man. He said, "Doc, what have you done done to that feller! He took a bath and took a plane, an' he acted plum fitified about gettin' a taxi to take 'im to the airport and get away from hea'. He looked like he needed some res'."

Every horse owner had vaccinated every active case and the neighbors who had pet horses and using horses had all vaccinated too, but it seemed that there would be no end to the epidemic; and now after three weeks, the disease was still spreading and I hadn't turned down a call and had lost very few cases. Any horse being treated for a disease that is accompanied by high fever and severe dehydration might get over the disease but die from the exhaustion and malnutrition that had occurred during the time of the most severe part of the sickness. Almost any sick animal with a raging fever will have the presence of mind or enough instinct to drink, but few if any will eat feed. All the cases that I had that were not beyond the secondary stage and hadn't gotten down, I fed by means of stomach tube and pump. I carried hundred-pound sacks of oatmeal and gallon jugs of molasses in the back of my car and as soon as a horse showed response to treatment, I would mix up in a tub a gruel of oatmeal, syrup, and sufficient water to make the mixture thin enough to go through a stomach pump. With the nursing and care of the owners, we rarely lost a horse that was still standing when I got to him for the first time.

Dick Arnold, a transplanted Vermonter who had come to the Far Southwest as a very young man and had aged out in the business, was still looked on by many of his neighbors as misplaced rather than transplanted. Dick had lots of horses and I was always doing some practice for him. He called early in the morning to tell me that he had three sick hosses and for me to come pa'pared to treat and vaccinate all his hosses.

Tires were very scarce, and although I had three permits from the ration board in my pocket to buy tires, there were no tires available; I had borrowed the spare tire from three different people's cars. I owned one tire that was on the ground, hopin' every day that some of the filling stations in town would be lucky enough to get a shipment of what we called war tires, which were mostly synthetic rubber.

Dick's ranch was between fifty and sixty miles south and I got to within about a mile of the ranch house when I blew out a tire. It was a country road with very little traffic, and after I blared my horn and hollered a few times, Dick drove up the road in a new Packard to see about me.

We loaded in his car all the medicine and vaccine that I would need to treat his hosses, and I decided that I would worry about the tire when I got through with the stock. During this period everybody tried to help those of us who needed to travel in order to be of service to the community, and I knew that Dick would have his men help me repair that tire one way or another.

He did have three very sick horses that we treated first and then vaccinated one hundred and four head. It was noon and Dick had a good housekeeper and cook who called from the back porch that dinner was ready. By now I had noticed that both of Dick's pickup trucks had brand-new tires on them, and as we went into the screen porch, layin' over in one corner were two more new tires, but I could see at a glance that they were truck tires and wouldn't fit my car. The thought ran through my mind that Dick had some better source of gettin' tires, black market or otherwise, than I did.

We got in place, as was the custom of the country, and went by the kitchen stove and helped ourselves to the barbecue, beans, and potatoes that were in Dutch ovens on the top of the stove. After I had eaten a big dinner in a hurry, I stepped up from the table, reached for my hat, and said, "Dick, I've got to go."

He said, "Don't hurry me. I'll get my hat."

While he was comin' off the porch, I stepped in that big new Packard about two hundred feet away, started the motor, and slammed the door as I waved at Dick, I hollered to him, "Bring my car to town after you get new tires on it."

I looked back in the mirror and saw him stompin' the ground and whippin' himself with his hat: I had thought about askin' him for a pickup, for he would have gladly loaned me one, but then he wouldn't have been worried about gettin' me new tires for my car. Since he always owed me a good deal more than a set of tires would cost, I knew that he would make the necessary arrangements, fair or foul, to get that new Packard back as soon as possible.

On the third morning at about daylight he drove up in front of the office in my car, which had four new tires on the ground and a spare in the turtle. We both had a big laugh and went up to the hotel and had breakfast together and traded automobile keys and drove on.

My day's work started by heading east to the Baker-White Ranch Company, where Pete TenyCke was foreman. He didn't have a sick horse, but he had a bunch of good horses that he wanted vaccinated.

Next I had a lot of work to do at the Elrod Ranch at Sheffield and went on across the Pecos River to Vic Montgomery's, where I vaccinated his horses and treated a sick stud, but not for sleeping sickness: he had a heart condition. I went on to Ozona and treated several horses in town in people's backlots.

By now it was night and I was way past due up north of Ozona around Rankin and Crane. I drove into Crane that night and gave some further treatment to horses that I had treated a few days before. I went on into Midland, where there was a Chrysler garage that had an all-night service department.

Midland was one hundred and ten miles north of Fort Stockton and sort of the north edge of my territory. I got over there rather often and the night crew always serviced my car while I went across the block to the Scarborough Hotel and got some sleep; because I was away from home the chances were good that I wouldn't be bothered. The next morning I would start out in a car that had been well serviced while I slept.

I was never a very good businessman and always a poor bookkeeper and this Chrysler car was sort of a dirty sand color, so I used the outside of the cab for bookkeeping purposes. When I made a call, either before I left or the next time I stopped I would take my pencil and write the amount of the call somewhere on the outside of the car and put an initial of some kind on it so I would know whose it was and then draw a circle around it. This was all the bookkeeping system I needed since I rarely sent out bills. When a rancher would see me in town and say that he had sold something, such as lambs, wool, or cattle, and wanted to pay me, we would walk out to my car and I would look around on it for his bill. During the time we were doing this, we would be discussin' what all we did to the livestock the time that I made his call.

I cared very little about a car; it was just a means of transportation. And although I had one serviced, I never had one washed. This particular night after I had gone, the service crew were talkin' about all the business I gave them and the fact that I never got a wash job, and to show their appreciation for me coming by, after they got through greasin' and packin' the wheels, they just gave me a great big wash job, free—and I lost my books!

People who have never lived horseback and are not familiar with the big pastures in rough country would not understand the feeling that is developed among all members of a ranch family for certain individual horses. During this epidemic I rarely, if ever, heard discussed the value in dollars of a horse that was sick. The conversation about an older horse would concern the "good he had done" in helping establish a ranch or in helping raise the kids. In talking about one of the younger horses that were hard from constant use, the stories would be about the bad spots he had carried his rider through in working stock and how much endurance he had in rough country.

One night I was treating a horse that was sick and staggering bad but had not been down on the ground. As I walked and staggered with him, trying to get a needle in his jugular vein, the old cowboy leadin' him and holdin' his head and talkin' to him said, "Doc, I've dropped my rope into lots of wars on this old friend and we always won 'em, and we sure need to save him if we can." This meant that he caught lots of fightin' cattle and horses and brought them in and this horse was worth saving.

It was a common thing for a rider to leave the headquarters early in the morning and if in the late afternoon, he hadn't gotten back, when word got out, the first conversation would be about the horse he was ridin'. If his wife or somebody spoke up and said he was on a certain old horse that was known to be trustworthy, there would be a feeling of reassurance that he just had had some trouble but would be in after a while.

In the event a rider was past due to come in and someone remarked that he was ridin' a "green" horse (an inexperienced animal) or a horse that had a lot of endurance and was used for hard rides but was known not to be dependable in a tight, then whoever was around and whoever could be called easily would start lookin' for the rider, who might be crippled or killed. Horses that had no affection for people and were undependable would rarely come back to a headquarters and would usually be found grazin' or at a water hole.

When I was doctor'n' a horse, the story would come up about what he had done and who he had saved and they'd say, "Save him if you can!" Nobody in the ranch country ever insulted a good horse by talking about what it would cost to replace him and the telephone operators whose help was indispensable in this particular epidemic were mostly all girls and women with ranch background or were married to a cowboy and the general thought in treating horses was never about money but instead was to save the horse for the good he had done or for what he meant to somebody.

One night I was way below Sanderson on the Rio Grande River treating some horses and the ranch wife came to the corral and said, "We just talked to the telephone operators and they have gotten together and figured out that you haven't been to bed in about nine days. They told me to tell you that so far as they know, your calls are sort of caught up, and I should put you to bed."

This kind of concern was very touching, but I had more work lined up than they knew about, so I thanked the good woman and kept on doctorin' horses. When I left the ranch and pulled out into the highway, I noticed several hot biscuits stuffed with venison steak layin' in the seat of my car. During these several weeks, the ranchwomen in the country kept me fed by havin' food ready at the most ungodly hours or by puttin' it in the car so I could eat on the way.

By the end of the fifth week the epidemic slowed up and by then I had vaccinated (two injections) over four thousand horses and had treated three hundred and seventy-five active cases and had driven over thirteen thousand miles. Outside of the cavalry, there have never been this many horses vaccinated or treated during the same length of time and over as wide a territory. This siege could not have been brought under control without the help of everyone who was interested in the horses of the great Southwest. The highly mechanized, direct-dialing telephone systems now in existence could have never performed the service to the ranch people and to me that those switchboard operators had, voluntarily and without any thought of gain or reward. Filling-station operators, café waitresses, druggists, and some few others all helped by taking and relaying messages.

Tallyho and Tribulation

BY STEPHEN BUDIANSKY

H e who would ride a horse must learn to fall," goes a Spanish proverb. Stephen Budiansky, the eminent scientist and author, examines this proposition in the context of foxhunting and cross-country riding. His conclusions will be well received by anyone of us who ever executed an involuntary dismount.

For other of the author's observations on the species, try *The Nature of Horses: Exploring Equine Evolution, Intelligence and Behavior.*

When I dream about horses, as I sometimes do, I often dream about my own horse, a large and touchy palomino, on the one day in ten years of fox hunting when everything went right. On that October day the red-tailed hawks whistled overhead, the soft early sunlight angled through the mist rising from the woods, the autumn smells of sumac and fallen leaves and damp earth filled the air, and my horse was the palomino Pegasus. He soared over every fence as if he had wings. He never pulled at the bit or crowded the horses in front of him or embarrassed me by running wildly past the master as all the field looked on. He didn't fidget and paw and buck at a halt and force me to walk him nervously around in a circle. He didn't stop suddenly at a jump and send me soaring over the fence as if I had wings. He stood neatly to the side when the huntsman with his red coat and the hounds with their heedlessness came dashing toward us on a narrow path in the woods, not blundering into their way at the last second owing to that perverse quirk of human and equine psychology that all too often leads us somehow to signal, and horses somehow to heed, the one thing we are trying with all our conscious might to tell them not to do. He was, in short, the perfect horse on the perfect day. And then he threw a shoe, and I took him home. I have not taken a survey among fox hunters, but I think one (almost) perfect day in ten years is well above the mean.

There are few sports in which image and reality are as far apart as they are in fox hunting. The literature of fox hunting is all noisy insiders' bluster; the public spectacle is all anachronism and pomp; the politics (here in America less so, but ineluctably in animal-loving and class-resentful Britain) is all about privilege and cruelty. The reality is none of these things. Fox hunting is essentially an inner struggle against dashed hopes. It is an elemental experience for horse and human being alike. For the coddled horse it is a day of behaving like the herd animal that a horse fundamentally is—a day of milling about with a few dozen other horses and then (what horses do best) stampeding. For the coddled human being, used to controlling at least some things in his modern life, it is a raw exposure to all the powers of fate and misadventure that used to constitute human existence, and for which we were not always the worse.

I don't mean danger, necessarily, though there is some of that. What I really mean is things not going right. Things never go right in fox hunting. I could write an epic of dashed hopes on the subject of horseshoes alone. And as for getting over fences, one lifetime would scarcely be enough to record all the heartbreak that fences represent.

To outsiders, fox hunting probably seems incomprehensible, or at least very odd. There are 168 organized fox hunts in the United States, nearly all supported by their dues-paying members, many of which hire a professional huntsman to take care of, train, and hunt the hounds two or three days a week during the season, which runs from fall to early spring. Its elitist image notwithstanding, even in eighteenth-century England hunting was quirkily egalitarian: farmers and dukes rode side by side, and the Prince Regent could tell a tall but not actually implausible tale of having gotten into a scuffle on the hunt field with a Brighton butcher who had "rode slap over my favorite bitch, Ruby." In some ways American hunting in the early twentieth century, when it became officially organized with associations and "recognized" hunts, was more English than the English, a way for nouveau riche northern plutocrats and faded-glory southern gentry to burnish their self-styled aristocratic images. But that has all been more or less swept aside, not so much by American democracy as by the American middle-class enthusiasm that is the chief characteristic of most participatory sports these days. The people who were in it for the social cachet have long since found easier ways to make a social statement. In most hunts well over half the members are women, mirroring the general demographics of equestrian enthusiasm. And hunting is no more expensive than golf or skiing or sailing—other pursuits once exclusively for the idle rich.

About half the foxhound packs in North America hunt coyotes, which are rapidly taking over the habitat of the red fox in the United States and Canada. In American hunting it is far and away the exception for hounds actually to catch and kill a fox (there are U.S. fox hunts that have hunted for thirty years without making a kill), and foxhounds almost never catch a coyote (coyotes are faster than hounds, and woe betide any hound that does manage to catch up with a coyote). Serious hunters talk about the pleasures of watching hounds work a line of scent and of hearing them speak, and they are not talking through their hats. I thought that one woman who rides with my local hunt, a nurse who arranges her shifts in the pediatric intensive-care unit around her hunting schedule, was putting me on when a hound a quarter mile away would speak and she would name him, but I soon discovered that she did in fact know every one of fifty or so hounds both by looks and by sound. But most hunters, and I don't claim to be an exception, are attracted by the excitement of being able to gallop over big fields and jump big fences out in the real world. Fox hunting is an experience unlike anything available at the Merrymount School of Equitation, where riding around a ring in a horse show is as exciting as it gets.

In the ring, with a raked stone-dust footing and nicely painted standards holding a crossrail that obligingly drops to the ground if your horse's foot so much as brushes against it, you might, after years of lessons, jump a three-foot-high fence. In hunting there are four-foot jumps made of the most unforgivingly solid materials in the most awkward of spots: uphill, downhill, into the woods and out, some with extra rails on top to keep the cows in, some with a two-foot drop down a bank on the landing side. The fences that one jumps in the hunting field these days are usually modified for the purpose of jumping, but even so no two are alike in how they need to be ridden or in the ways they can cause trouble.

In the old days fox hunters just followed the hounds wherever they led, and when the horses came to a stone wall or a post-and-rail fence, they jumped at any likely spot. Then came wire fences, which only the borderline suicidal try to jump—horses have a hard time seeing a wire from a distance or judging its position in space, and so the likeliest outcome is that the horse stops short when he reaches the fence. The worst outcome is that he goes ahead and jumps, and misjudges it and catches a foreleg. When a thousand-pound animal trips in midair, a soft landing is not generally possible.

With the coming of wire, fox hunters sought farmers' permission to build short panels of wooden fencing into the fence lines, the most common pattern being the "coop"—two sloping wooden panels that straddle the wire in the shape of an inverted V, rather like an old-fashioned chicken coop. Coops are solid and have a clearly visible ground line, which horses need to judge the location and depth of an obstacle properly. With only one jumpable spot per fence line, rides can't always follow the hounds in a straight line, but at least the jumps offer a way of getting across a fence at *some* point. Head out onto a back road near Woodstock, Vermont, or in parts of Dutchess County, New York, or drive out of Washington, D.C., for about an hour in a westerly or northwesterly direction and start prowling around what's left of the countryside, and you'll see coops punctuating the fence lines of fields that used to be full of cows and sometimes still are (though at least where I live, outside Washington, they're as likely these days to be full of 6,000-square-foot houses built in the Tudor Norman Brick Colonial Tara architectural style).

Before paragliding, bungee jumping, snowboarding, and sky surfing there was fox hunting. The appeal in all cases is much the same. A retired Air Force pilot whom I used to see out hunting many Sundays, a kind and sympathetic man well into his seventies who took pity on a struggling beginner and would always let me ride right along with him and never said a word even when I was much too close behind him ("Do you want to get into my pocket, sir?" is what a furious fox hunter in a Trollope novel says in a similar circumstance), one day turned to me after we had galloped over three huge coops and said, "You know, it's just like flying a fighter plane." When everything goes right, it is blissful.

When things go wrong, you fall off. There are many ways to do that. The easiest is when your horse decides not to jump the fence he has been galloping toward and slams on the brakes at the last instant; in accordance with Newton's First Law of Motion, horse stops but rider does not. I have more than once done a 360-degree airborne flip and landed on my feet during this maneuver—something that a relatively unathletic six-foot, 185-pound man is unlikely ever to manage in everyday life. I have been dumped right into a coop this way, but one time I actually cleared the fence, almost landing on my feet on the other side and still holding the reins, and I stood there imagining the ignoble scene that was to follow (climb back over the coop, struggle back into the saddle, have another go at the fence with the same result, repeat until I slink away in shame or am carried off on a stretcher). My horse took a look at me standing there, decided that the fence mustn't be so bad after all, and leaped over to join me.

The other ways to fall off include simply losing one's balance on the far side of a jump, especially if the horses in the lead have made a sharp turn after landing and one's own horse, pulled ahead by the supermagnet of the herd instinct, takes an even sharper turn to follow. There is also a phenomenon almost identical to what the Air Force calls "pilot-induced oscillation" (the fighter-plane analogy again). This occurs when the person at the controls pushes the stick down too much and then reacts to the plane's sudden plunge by pulling the stick too far back up, causing the plane to nose up too far, and so on and on. With horse and rider it unfolds like this: Approaching a jump too quickly, the rider checks his horse by pulling back on the reins. The horse then hesitates or stops just before the jump, causing the rider to lose his balance and flop forward, suddenly loosening the reins, at which the horse goes ahead and jumps from a standstill, causing the rider to lose his balance and fall backward, jerking the horse in the mouth, which causes him to buck or react in some other uncontrollable manner upon landing. Falling off is sometimes dangerous, occasionally fatal, and always humiliating. In all my years of taking riding lessons I was so determined never to fall off that I never did; even the times I should have, my instructor would look over to see the spectacle of a man half out of the saddle defying the force of gravity by clutching his horse's mane with grim determination.

Then I started hunting, and fell off every other time I went riding. It never really worried me until last year, when the huntsman of one of the local hunts, schooling a horse he had ridden a hundred times, jumped a three-foot-high row of rails that he had jumped hundreds of times (one that I have jumped probably a dozen times), and his horse went one way, and he the other. He ended up rocketing headfirst into a tree and breaking two vertebrae in his neck; he's now paralyzed from the chest down.

As with all such sports, the whiff of danger is no doubt an element of the appeal, but that's more danger than I had bargained for. Still, along with the thrill comes an almost Zen dimension to jumping—or at least so I tell myself, for that is probably the only way to cope with day after day of frustration. Jumping over a fence on horseback is an almost utterly counterintuitive process. Getting it right is a trick of the mind as much as a physical skill, a process of learning at times to do the exact opposite of what the self-preservation instinct demands. In the perfect jump the rider feels as if he is the one soaring through space in a parabolic arc; the horse is just something below swiveling on gimbals, leaving the rider's balance unaffected. To achieve that result the rider must maintain his balance with supple knees and ankles—he must be, in effect, independent of the motion of his horse. Yet he can achieve that only by being fully aware of and at one with the horse's motion—and, indeed, the horse's anticipation. Riders in the ring are sometimes taught to deal with this contradiction by what has always struck me as a bastardized compromise: you sit firmly in the saddle, with your balance in the center of the horse; you keep your horse under an almost rigid control with your hands and your body weight; and then, at the last second, just as the horse pushes off the ground, you shift your balance forward into the airborne jump. The show-jumping ideal is to be able to choose the exact distance from a jump where you want to take off and "place" your horse at that precise spot. Riders who do this for a living on the Grand Prix show-jumping circuit can even make it look artistic and natural—some of them, anyway.

The show-ring style has always been strongly influenced by the close-order drill of the cavalry manual, with its emphasis on absolute control, synchronized movement, and a flashy, prancing gait with a tightly arched neck—an ideal of power that goes back to the ancient Greeks. In the hunting field, on uneven ground, with a herd of horses galloping off ahead, the Zen approach is a more prudent choice. It is, as well, the hunting ideal; as early as the seventeenth century practitioners of "scientific equitation" were expressing dismay about how English squires let their horses gallop during the hunt "as they would without a rider." Rather than sitting firmly in the saddle and trying to place your horse precisely where you want him every step of the way, you keep your weight off his back and your hands soft most of the time and let him do the driving. Achieving such a state of naturalness requires not so much that the rider become one with his horse as that both horse and rider become one with the very act of galloping and jumping. The paradoxical necessity when a horse is coming in to a jump too fast or awkwardly is to give him more rein, so that he will relax and be able to figure out the approach for himself.

The difference between a good jump and a bad jump is like the difference between playing in tune and playing out of tune—even a little bit off is awful. But in hunting there is the compensation, the wonderful compensation, of practicality: jumping over fences has the genuine purpose of getting from here to there. After years of brooding darkly over my imperfect days in the saddle (that is, all of them) I in realism adopted the binary system for rating my jumps. Forget the Olympic ten-point form scale; mine was one or zero—either I made it to the other side and was still in the saddle or I did not. (The time I got over and then immediately fell into a pond I secretly scored as a two.)

Living on a farm, and having seen a good measure of what nature routinely dishes out, I have never taken seriously the claims of cruelty leveled against fox hunting by animal-rights activists. In ten years of fox hunting I have seen far more foxes killed on the road by cars than killed by hounds. And foxes, themselves predators, are almost insouciant about being chivied around the woods, often doubling back to lay a confusing trail. I have even seen a hunted fox stopping to hunt mice when he had put a few minutes between himself and the hounds. For the most part American fox hunting has escaped the wrath of animal lovers, because of its emphasis on the chase over the kill, and because fox hunters are in many rural areas a major force for the preservation of open space and wildlife habitat.

I worry more about the change of affected quaintness: fox hunting when you hardly ever kill a fox, and when you haul your horse in a trailer behind a Ford pickup truck to the spot where you can ride, and when you jump panels that have been built into lines of wire fence expressly for the purpose of giving fox hunters a place to jump, is, as charged, contrived and anachronistic. But there is anachronism and anachronism: there is the kind in which you dress up as somebody's idea of a Renaissance character and go around saying "forsooth" for the tourists, and there is the kind in which you find a real bit of woods and field and submit yourself, if only for a few hours, to the full force of untamed pre-twentieth-century nature. Falling off and breaking your neck is a melodramatic way to make the point. But there are far worse ways to spend an autumn morning than leading your horse across three miles of fields and woods after he's thrown a shoe. You'd feel like a fool setting out to do that on purpose (uh, just taking my horse for a walk), but you never cease being grateful for such mornings. When scent or hounds or foxes fail to cooperate, there are days when nothing happens, and you stand around for three hours scarcely going anywhere, but there are worse ways, too, to spend a morning than to be sitting on horseback on a hillside while the rest of the world is listening to traffic reports on the radio.

And there is nothing contrived about the work of the hounds in following a scent and the reality of wind and weather and the huntsman's knowledge of every copse and path and the fact that one's day is in the lap of fortune. Hunts that spend most of their time puttering through the back yards of those 6,000-square-foot tract mansions are starting to seem like trail rides with dogs, but when the hounds can do their work, they force us to think like dogs and to think like foxes; they turn us from passive spectators and consumers of nature into participants. There are hunters who can hear a hound's cry and read a whole tale from it, hunters who while the chase is on live through the eyes—or the noses—of the hounds. Thoreau wrote of taking "rank hold on life" and living more as the animals do, of spending days fishing and hunting in order to approach nature with an honesty that philosophers and poets "who approach her with expectation" lack.

In this age of spectators I am not even sure that anyone would understand if fox hunters uttered the truth about what they do and why they do it. The friends of nature say they want wild, untouched nature, but what most people are really after is tame, pretty nature, and those who glower darkly out on a wood through the eyes of hounds and foxes are strangely out of keeping with the spirit of a time whose representative naturegoers are those nice extroverts in the L. L. Bean catalogue, with their ripstop-nylon parkas and their fresh faces aglow in wholesome recreation.

I realized recently that the breezy sportsmen's reports that pass for the literature of fox hunting are a fraud that hunters perpetrate on one another, a way to pretend that what they do is ordinary, routine, something like golf or woodworking, a pursuit for enthusiasts that is reducible to conventional narrative. A true narrative of the internal experience of a fox hunt would bear no resemblance to external appearance. The formal rituals of hunting—the black and red coats, the polished boots, the saddle-soaped tack, the well-brushed horses that immediately get muddy and disheveled—are there to keep the disguise propped in place. But then it slips, and the truth is out. I will never forget the horror and wonder and delight I felt the day the truth came to one huntsman, a man of decades of experience, a man whose living room is filled with silver trophies and plaques he has won for steeplechase racing, a man who knows hunting and hounds and every fence in the woods. I will never forget the words he shouted as he tumbled from his horse, a sudden burst of fury and truth: "Just one day! Just one day!" He, too, wondered why there can't be just one day when nothing goes wrong.

Why Is It that Girls Love Horses?

BY MAXINE KUMIN

P oet, novelist and author of children's books, Maxine Kumin won the
Pulitzer Prize for her 1972 collection, *Up Country: Poems of New
England*. This recollection/essay that first appeared in *MS Magazine*
offers as accurate an explanation of the bond between girls and horses
as has ever appeared in print.

For the last 21 days—ever since the mare's milk bag filled and gradually grew brick-hard—I have slept with the intercom open, relaying every
snort, yawn, cough, and chew into my waiting ear from 10 P.M. until dawn.
Nightly I have laid out my clothes on the floor next to the bed, like a fireper-
son. I have leaped up nine times in three weeks, yanked on jeans, socks, boots,
and hurled my half-conscious body downhill, across the road, over the snow-
banks, into the barn. False alarms, all of them. Just yesterday nature outwitted
me. The foal slipped silently into the world in his own time.

The annual foals are the best present of my middle age.

The best present of my childhood, a British storybook called *Silver
Snaffles,* by Primrose Cumming, arrived on my tenth birthday. In this fantasy
tale, a little girl walks through the dark corner of a draft-pony's stall into a sun-
lit world where articulate ponies with good English country-squire manners
and highly individual personalities give lessons to eager youngsters. The story
culminates in a joyous hunt staged by the foxes themselves, who are also great
conversationalists. Jenny, launched as a rider, learns that she is to be given a
pony of her own. Now she must relinquish her right to the magic password
and to the dark corner of Tattle's stall, through which she has melted every
evening into a better world. I thought it the saddest ending in the history of
literature.

By this age I had already begun to ride—an hour a week, one dollar an hour—on one of those patient livery horses who for most of their lives carry on their backs the timid and inept, the brash and graceless. Bob Ross of Ross-Del Riding Academy in Philadelphia, taught me how to post by riding so closely alongside old Charlie that he could keep one hand under my elbow and guide my risings and fallings in the saddle. Through Carpenter's Woods into Fairmont Park along Wissahickon Creek we rode decorously side by side. It was a safe excursion.

A year or two later, when I could wield a manure fork and manage a full-size wheelbarrow, I traded extra hours in the saddle for muckings-out, groomings, and the cleaning of worn school tack. It didn't especially matter to me whether I rode or not; I was happy just to be in the presence of horses. I wanted to inhale them, and I wanted them to take me in. Even though I had graduated to more challenging horses, I was happy just to perch on the top bar of Charlie's stall and admire him. I liked to watch the wrinkles on his muzzle crease as he chewed. Days that I wasn't allowed to walk two miles to the rental stable, I skulked abovestairs and reread *Silver Snaffles.*

Eventually, I wore this book out with ritual rereadings; somehow it disappeared from my life. When, 40-odd years later, I assumed my duties at the Library of Congress, it occurred to me that *Silver Snaffles* was undoubtedly housed in that enormous repository of knowledge. The day I found it in dusty stacks, I sat down on the marble floor and turned the familiar pages in disbelief. The book was real, after all! Then I carried it up to the Poetry Room that overlooks the Capitol and the Mall and read the story all over again, savoring the parts I had remembered verbatim, and wept.

I think I was crying for my lost childhood, but I'm still not sure. The cathartic effect of the book was not assuaged for me by Jenny's acquiring a pony of her own. Nothing would compensate for that loss of innocence, of the ability to speak the password and walk into a kingdom of virtue and honor. The deprivation that I felt when the female hero was denied continued access to Paradise was the loss of an intensity, a closeness for which I have no adequate words. This bonding, I believe, lies at the heart of horse fever.

For example, when my second daughter and her best friend were nine and 10 years old, they acted out elaborate scenarios involving plastic horses that were stabled in shoe boxes on bedding made of shredded newsprint. The horses had names, genders, and disparate personalities. "It had to do with thinking and feeling like a horse," she now says. "We could twitch our skin to shake off flies; we sucked water when we drank; and of course we pranced around a lot. It was better than ballet class."

This daughter is here for a visit during the last few weeks of her maternity leave. After the baby is fed and asleep in his carriage, she comes down to the barn while I muck stalls. She hauls the water buckets, rakes up loose hay, grooms the riding mares. Yes, she is still connected.

Such bonding is profoundly physical. We learn our horses' body language and they learn to respond to a body language we use—body pressures and positions called aids—to ask for changes in gait and direction. I still remember how astonished I was to discover, riding bareback under instruction, that my horse would move continually at a trot in a small circle without any recourse on my part to reins so long as I kept my body pivoted in that direction and asked him to do so with the pressure of my calf on that same side. There are a variety of body signals the rider gives the horse that ask it to come forward onto the bit, to use its hind legs, to halt squarely, back up, move off at a trot or canter, and so on. None of these responses is achieved by magic; all require patient repetition and forbearance. One day there is a little breakthrough. Then, another and another.

At the risk of sounding sexist—some wonderful trainers and handlers are male—I believe that women work best with horses in certain situations. I have seen a pigtailed 10-year-old girl quiet a raving, 17-hand thoroughbred who had glimpsed out of the corner of his eye the vet's approach and was plunging around his stall in a full-scale tantrum. The youngster simply walked in, caught a piece of her friend's mane as he whirled past her, took a firm pinch hold on his neck skin, and slipped a halter over his nose before three male stable attendants with whips and twitches could agree on who was to undo the door latch.

Women's empathy, subtlety, ability to read the nuance of difference that leads to change; our gift of timing; our socializing as nurturers—all contribute to our considerable successes, for example, in the large thoroughbred and standard-bred breeding farm operations; in the show ring; as exercise riders, grooms, and jockeys in the racing world; and as instructors at levels ranging from the local day-camp riding program to professional training establishments.

Granted, other elements enter into the young woman's passion for horses, and developing a sexuality may be one of these. But the stereotyped concept that girl children long to sit astride the muscular power and rhythmic motion of a horse out of deep sexual urges, and that, in time, they redirect this prepubescent desire toward its natural object of fulfillment, the adolescent boy, has always seemed to me too facile to be trusted. In the American West, where the cow pony represents not only the freedom to explore a space, but also the means to develop such working skills as cutting and roping and such recreational skills as rodeo riding or barrel-racing, males are still in the majority. Eastern pony clubs and 4-H horse groups have been for the most part the purview of mothers, perhaps as an alternate to such opportunities as Little League, which has belonged for the most part to competitive fathers.

I further mistrust the Freudian concept because it does not adequately explain the substantial number of adult females who, despite their comfortable adaptation to sex roles involving marriage and child-rearing, continue to lease, own, care for, ride, and raise horses.

I do not blink at the fact that a horse often comes into a young girl's life at a time when she feels a need to take control in some measure of what is essentially an uncontrollable environment. The key factor is that an animal's responses can be counted on. When all else shifts, changes, and disappoints, the horse can remain her one constant. Her best friend may turn against her; fickle boys forget their admiration; siblings bicker with her; parents exact a too ardent fealty. Her favorite teacher may suddenly grow aloof. The violence of the real world, the threat of nuclear war, the poverty and deprivation she is at least peripherally and probably acute aware of, all intensify her sense of adequacy to deal with these inequities. By comparison, the horse is predictable, manageable, kindly.

I asked Julia, my favorite 12-year-old working visitor, why she loves riding horseback. "It gives you a sense of freedom," she said. "You're sort of out of touch because you're higher up than everybody else." And then she added: "Taking care of horses makes you feel good because you're making somebody else feel good. It's sort of a comforting feeling when you get done with the evening barn chores because you've put the horses away and you know you've made them feel cozy and secure."

The bond with horses, no matter its origin, is enjoyed ultimately for its own worth. I like to think that my own obsession serves a greater good. Living with horses reminds me daily of my place in nature. Tending them, training, riding or driving them links me with my tribal past. My mother, who was born before the automobile and electric lights and lived to her eighty-fourth year in a nuclear age, remembered with piercing clarity the names and dispositions of all the horses of her childhood in rural Virginia—the driving team, the plow horse, the hackney pony, the delivery wagon mules. In a way, then, I am keeping the faith, taking my rightful place in the continuum.

"The horse," Gervase Markham wrote in 1614, "will take such delight in his keeper's company, that he shall never approach him but the horse will with a kind of cheerful or inward neighing show the joy he takes to behold him, and where this mutual love is knit and combined, there the beast must needs prosper and the rider reap reputation and profit."

Cheerful or inward neighing is what I would cross-stitch on a sampler, if I were assigned to work one, as my mother was. Hers read, in the astonishing even stitches of a 12-year-old: *He maketh me to lie down in green pastures.* An appropriate piety, under the circumstances.

Mustard-Pot, Matchmaker

BY GILBERT FRANKAU

I was in the initial stage of adolescent horse-craziness when I came across "Mustard-Pot, Matchmaker" in an anthology on a relative's bookshelf. Although I read the story dozens of times, it never lost its appeal. As I more recently discovered, the story comes from a collection entitled *Men, Maids—and Mustard Pot*. The volume is, alas, out of print, but look for it in libraries and second-hand book stores.

§1

My dear Victor, why not admit that you funked the place—and let it go at that?" Naomi Braunston flicked the lash of her heavy hunting-whip scientifi-cally at a twig in the leafless hedgerows, recoiled the thong round her hand, and trotted off—rising squarely as a man from her man's saddle—into the gathering twilight.

For a moment her companion thought to follow. Then, changing his mind, he walked his tired roan on up the hill. A flush deep as the mud-flecked scarlet of his hunting-coat mantled his wind-tanned cheeks. Under the auburn of the cropped mustache, his fine teeth bit hard on the lower lip. His eyes, steel-blue beneath the black brim of the high silk hat, were the eyes of a shamed school-boy.

And perhaps it *was* school-boyish for a man of thirty-eight with Vic-tor's service record to take such a remark seriously. But when you happen to have been born in the very center of that particular England which folk call the Shires; when, from the hour you first straddled a Shetland pony no bigger than the stable mastiff to the day you came back twice wounded and four times decorated from the conquered Rhine, everything you thought worth living for (and fighting for, and, if necessary, dying for) has been comprised in the three syllables of the word "fox-hunting"; when you're "damned if you know what to do with yourself" from the time of the "stinking violets" to the time when the "dahlias are dead"; when the only music you love is the high note of hounds breaking covert on a breast-high scent, and all the pictures you care to see are the pictures a man may espy from the back of a mettlestone horse as he follows the speeding pack; when, all about you, for forty hard-riding miles on either side, neither man, woman, nor child worries if you be lord or steeplechase jock, poet or profiteer, so long as you go straight at your fences and don't gallop more than absolutely necessary over Farmer Thompson's wheat; and when—in addition to all these things—you happen to be Lieutenant-Colonel Sir Victor Plowright Lomondham, Baronet, Royal Horse Artillery (retired), of Lomondham Hall, Leicestershire, and Charles Street, Mayfair, with thirty thousand pounds a year inherited income, a moderate conceit of yourself, and an immoderate desire to share hearth and home with your neighbor's daughter Naomi—then, quite conceivably, you allow that kind of remark, especially from her, to rankle.

Besides—and this was the worst of it—the remark happened to be true. Victor Lomondham—as he now admitted to his private soul—*had* funked not only the particular place of which Naomi spoke, a double-oxer with a nastyish ditch on the take-off side and a still nastier one on the landing, but half a hundred other leaps during the last half-dozen weeks. Ever since the opening meet of the season—to be perfectly frank with himself—he had been "going like a pair of boots." Something, some Peculiar Thing, seemed to have got him by the pit of the stomach. To-night, riding at a snail-pace toward the lights of his home, Lomondham knew, for the first time, that the name of that Peculiar Thing must be "Fear."

And at that he thought, grimly: "Afraid! Me. Good God, this won't do—this won't do at all." It seemed, you see, almost incredible that, after five years of warfare—years during which, inwardly, he had so often scoffed at others getting the wind up—Fear should have singled *him* out, in the hunting-field of all places, for its victim. "I *am* afraid," he thought. "I'm scared stiff of my own gee-gees."

The roan, as though in confirmation of his master's newly acquired self-knowledge, stumbled—sending the rider's heart into his mouth. Lomondham damned the beast, damned himself for his injustice (no horse stumbles on purpose), and so came past the lodge-gates of Lomondham Hall, round the drive, and into the great quadrangle of his stables. As he dismounted, a boy ran to take the horse, and Walters, the stud-groom—a burly, clean-shaven worthy who had been in the Lomondhams' service all his life—approached with touched cap and a deferentially cheerful, "How did it go after the change, Sir Victor?"

"Pretty fair, thanks, Walters." Lomondham stamped his booted feet on the gravel, and the pair of them followed the tired nag under the stable archway—for the habits of the Regular Army are not lightly discarded, nor was the master of Lomondham Hall one of those who leave the care of their horses to underlings, however trustworthy those underlings may appear.

§2

Hunting over for the day, his hour in stables had always been Lomondham's supreme and particular joy. But this evening—and weariness, even after the hardest galloped run, was rare with him—he felt weary, almost too weary to make his usual round. Yet the physical fatigue in him seemed paltry compared with the mental unease.

Breaking one of his own stable-rules, he lit himself a cigarette, and began to pace—the silent stud-groom at his elbow—disconsolately down the red-brick-floored, electric-lit corridors, opening each door as he came to it, entering here, merely peering in there, while the rugged occupants of the odorous stalls stamped and whinnied to his known approach.

Two dozen first-class hunters there were at Lomondham Hall—as fine a string as the poorest hunting-man ever dreamed of in his poverty; and master and stud-groom visited two and twenty of them, from Quicksilver, the chestnut pony with the white stockings, who had leaped Little Overdine Brook clean from poached bank to poached bank on the day when Farmer Thompson's cart-horses and tackle-chains had worked till dusk dragging bogged thoroughbreds from the mire, past the two gray Arabs, Selim and Ali, whose tails stuck up like gigantic ostrich-feathers, and whose actions were smooth as a cat's canter over turf, to the slim seventeen-hand Nigger Princess, with her ears bent wickedly backward, the whites of her eyeballs gleaming, and her hind hoofs itching to lash out at the visitors.

It was on Nigger Princess—quiet as a lamb once mounted, but a devil unleashed in stables—that Victor, just before "change of horses," had funked the "place" of which Naomi spoke; and he stood watching the mare for a long while, wondering whether she, too, realized her master's cowardice.

"About to-morrow, Sir Victor?" interrupted Walters, anxious for his tea.

"Selim and Ali's turn, ain't it? I sha'n't need the car—"

Lomondham stopped, chewing his mustache. To-morrow, thank the Lord! would be an easy day—the meet practically at his own gates, the country known to a post, Selim and Ali rides for a baby.

"Very good, Sir Victor." Walters, his duties almost over for the day, made a slight movement toward the last two loose-boxes, from one of which came the hiss and scrape of the stable-boy cleaning the roan. But his master halted him with a sharp, "Walters! Did you have Mustard-Pot shod this morning?"

"Yes, Sir Victor."

"Good. I'll have a look at him."

Master, a vague idea simmering at the back of his mind, and man, concealing his annoyance, made their way to the end loose-box of all, clicked on the light, opened the high grilled door, and passed in.

The first peculiarity which struck the observer's eye about Mustard-Pot was his color; the next his size. Stripped of his rugs, the enormous horse, standing prehistoric in the glare of the naked light-bulb above his manger, showed as near butter-yellow as a steed can be and live. In build, he might have been model to some equine sculptor of the gigantically symbolic. Judging from the slope of his huge shoulders, from the set of his lean pasterns, from the muscled swell of his gaskins, and the sinuous perfection of his hocks, any man might have said to himself—as Lomondham had said when he bought him, preternaturally cheap, at a little-frequented show: "Here is the leaper of the world."

And as a fact, in cold blood, over schooling-fences or the bar, Mustard-Pot could have held his own, and more than his own, with a kangaroo. As a show-jumper he had no equal; as a hack, his paces and his temper were no less perfect than his appearance was bizarre. It was only in the hunting-field—and possibly on the steeplechase course, though Victor, who at that period of his life hated racing, had never tried the experiment—that Mustard-Pot became entirely unmanageable. Whether, according to stable-legend, the animal had circus-blood in him and could only perform in a ring; whether he suffered from that obscure human complaint known as crowd-panic; or whether, in the words of Tom Sampey, the Little Overdine horse-breaker whom he had brought back white and shaking like a leaf after a three-mile bolt up and down the stiffest country in the Vale of Screever, "The trouble with him is that he's got a nose like a hound and follows scent on his own"—appeared to Mustard-Pot's owner, as he ground one spurred heel pensively into the clean peat-moss litter, the most unprofitable of speculations. Remained, a solid certainty, only the fact that if—instead of Selim—he rode the yellow horse on the morrow, nobody, not even Naomi, could accuse him of funking.

"I think I'll give the Arabs a day off," he said tersely. "We'll make it Mustard-Pot first, Quicksilver second"; and leaving the stud-groom to astonished speculations and the re-rugging of the horse, strode off.

§3

The dwelling-house of Lomondham Hall, a vast brownstone pile, tall of chimney-stack and mullioned of window, backed by the great oaks and green rides of Lomondham Wood, and fronted, mile upon mile, by the terracing down-sweep of Lomondham Vale, is separated from the stables by a good three hundred yards of gravel drive and shrubbery—distance enough, if a man take it slowly, for him to change his mind more than once. But Victor, having given his order to the stud-groom, did not turn back.

He came—a tall, powerful figure, the last person in the world one would have suspected of nerves—between the tall opal lights on either side of the open front door, up the steps, and into the big square-galleried hall. There he handed his hat, his gloves, and his hunting-whip to his waiting valet; sank into his big chair by the blazing fire; permitted himself to be served with tea and muffins from massive Georgian silver; patted the rough-haired terrier with a firm, capable hand; and thereafter went up the balustered staircase to his own particular bath-room as coolly as any other millionaire aristocrat without a care in the world save his own enjoyment.

Yet, inwardly, Sir Victor Plowright Lomondham, of Lomondham Hall, knew himself all one shivering apprehension. Dressing for dinner, in the beamed Tudor bedroom, he remembered the biblical phrase, "His bowels turned to water"; and found it amazingly applicable to the morrow. Dining, alone with his gloomy pictured ancestors, the men-servants manœuvering like trained shadows behind his back, it seemed to him that the rich foods were tasteless, that the rich wine soured in his mouth. In the smoking-room—his dinner over, a whisky and soda at his elbow, and a cigar between his teeth—he fell to wondering why, for the past month, he had never invited a guest.

Then he grew introspective; and in this mood of introspection, a mood never before experienced, he thought, suddenly, "I'm lonely, the most damnably lonely fellow in the world."

From which—and this, perhaps, furnishes the Freudian diagnosis that a psychoanalyst, had Sir Victor ever dreamed of consulting one, would have made of his mental condition—the baronet's thoughts switched, longingly, to Naomi.

Vividly and acutely he visualized her—the long lithe limbs, breeched knees gripping saddle, booted feet thrust home in the stirrup-irons; the broad shoulders and the deep bosom which the riding-coat hid without concealing; the hands capable as his own; the fine little head, beclustered with darkling tresses; the eyes, big and jet-black under jet-black brows; and the red ripe fullness of those lips which had said to him: "You funked the place—let it go at that."

Followed, hot on the heels of this sudden vision, a rage of self-questioning. Even admitting that he had got the wind up in the hunting-field, what the devil difference did that make to his marrying Naomi? Hadn't hundreds, thousands of other men been forced—sooner or later—to give up riding in the first flight? Didn't a man's nerve, naturally, break down when he reached a certain age? Weren't there cases of steeplechase jockeys, fellows cool as cucumbers in the sugar-my-neighbor leap-and-gallop between the flags of a marked and prepared course, who didn't dare—simply didn't dare—ride straight to hounds across a couple of miles of cut-and-laid and ridge and furrow? Didn't a chap's nerve come back, come back quite miraculously, if only he took a really good toss over timber? And, finally—finally, wouldn't Naomi, the very moment she saw him on Mustard-Pot, realize that her taunt had been unjust, and apologize for it?

That imagined apology, you see, was the real crux of the whole business. Lomondham had been on the verge, on the very verge of proposing. But a man, a man of his temperament and outlook, couldn't very well propose to a girl who—who had the whip-hand of him. In matrimony as in life, you see, the master of Lomondham Hall must be top dog; capable of controlling his woman as if controlling his staff and his gee-gees. "I'll ride the brute," he muttered. "I'll ride the brute if I break my neck."

Many a fox-hunter, by the way, has broken his neck for far less reason!

§4

Lomondham, according to custom, left the smoking-room at half-past ten to the tick, dismissed his valet at ten forty-five, got into bed at five minutes to eleven—and never slept a wink till four. Alternately, through the long restless hours, Naomi, Nigger Princess, and Mustard-Pot haunted him; and when at last he did sleep, the yellow horse gallopaded through his dreams—dreams in which he heard himself praying, voicelessly, to the heedless gods of the chase, for a frost severe enough to stop hunting for ever and ever, amen. Morning, however, brought neither frost nor storm, but a grayly perfect winter's day, almost warm and with hardly a breath of wind.

Morning, too, brought its mental reaction, so that it seemed to Naomi's lover, sitting down spurred and scarlet-clad to his ample breakfast, as though the night had never been. His mood of the moment was sheer recklessness—that particular kind of recklessness which is so often mistaken for true courage. He thought, a little bombastically, "I'll show that saffron quadruped, I'll show Naomi Braunston, who is master."

And this mood of swaggering recklessness—a mood as foreign to the real poised Lomondham as the introspection of the night before—endured all through breakfast-time, all through his post-breakfast cigar and his half-hour with his newspaper in the bow-windowed library, right up to the very moment when—at ten thirty to the second—Mustard-Pot's big hoofs halted on the gravel drive. Then, abruptly, nerves once more had their way with him.

Neither his hands, as—his gleaming silk hat well down on his head— he took his buckskin gloves and his short-handled, long-thonged whip from his man; nor his white-breeched, top-booted legs—as he stood on the broad steps looking down at the saddled horse—actually trembled: yet to prevent them from trembling took every ounce of his self-control. He wanted to say to Walters, whose curiosity had not been able to resist the temptation of allotting himself to the post of second horseman for the day, and who was even now wondering whether he should ask permission or simply go back to the stables and bring Quicksilver on, "I've changed my mind." He wanted to tell the stable-boy at the horse's head, "Take that brute away; and bring Selim round as quickly as ever you can."

Instead, he went silently down the broad stone steps; gentled the steady yellow muzzle; cast a quick eye over girthing and bridling; let out a link of the burnished curb-chain; thrust his foot into the iron; swung himself to saddle with a terse, "You needn't hold his head as if he were going to eat you, lad," to the stable-boy; gave Walters his orders about Quicksilver—and set off down the drive as though the curious domestic heads peering from the various windows did not exist.

All the same, when Mustard-Pot—apparently the gentlest creature ever foaled—stepped out daintily between the lodge-gates, Mustard-Pot's rider felt acutely self-conscious. With his terror—for now that he was actually astride that vast butter-colored back, only terror describes his emotion—mingled a peculiar pride. For the first time in his life he wanted, not merely to do things for the pleasure of doing them, but so that others, and more particularly Naomi, should be witness of his accomplishment.

Nor were spectators lacking to gratify the want! Already, a mile from Lomondham Ruffs, immaculate limousines occupied by immaculate sportsmen, fat farmers in grunting Fords, slim farmers' wives in smart traps, grooms with two horses and grooms with one, men in red frock-coats and men in black cut-aways, bowler-hatted girls astride and top-hatted women on side-saddles, boys on ponies and graybeards on cobs, folk on foot and folk on push-bikes, came crowding along the road and along the grass at roadside.

But soon Lomondham's thoughts were all for his horse. The great horse, already conscious of the chase, had pricked his ears. His neck arched to the reins. He tossed at his bit. His clipped skin twitched and twitched. His gentle walk became an amble; his amble a hand-canter. Checked, he began to dance among the crowd. The crowd scattered. The foot-folk drew to hedge-side. A hunting-mother shepherding two flapper daughters cursed "that ass of a Lomondham, who ought to know better than to bring that ass of a horse into the hunting-field."

Lomondham—his terror momentarily in abeyance—managed to simmer the dancer down just as Naomi on a big gray, accompanied by her father on a fat dun, trotted slowly out of the bridle-path from Little Lomondham on to the high-road.

She greeted him easily: "Good morning, Victor. So Tom Sampey managed to break Mustard-Pot for you, did he? I'm so glad. He *is* a topper."

Her father said: "Hallo, Lomondham. Going to give us all a lead, what?"

The master of Lomondham Hall looked at the big black-eyed, black-mustached landowner, at his tall, black-eyed, black-tressed daughter; and answering, "Yes, it's a good thing we've broken him to hounds at last," wondered what the devil *would* happen when hounds actually appeared.

Then Mustard-Pot began dancing again, and he had no time to think, no opportunity to observe that quick flash of apprehensive understanding in Naomi's eyes.

§5

Half an hour later, from the western edge of Lomondham Ruffs—a twenty-acre patch of gorse through which the green rides cut straight as cricket-pitches—three hundred horsemen and horsewomen listened to the shrill music of hounds in covert, listened for the twang of the silver horn and the loud "Gone away" which signals a fox departed. But the three-hundred-and-first horseman listened not at all.

Mustard-Pot, at first sight of the pack jig-jogging up the road, had been mad enough; now, hearing them, he seemed to have gone utterly crazy. The gentle hack had disappeared; in its place was a snorting, plunging, rearing, buck-jumping, pig-jumping saffron maniac whose one idea seemed to be to fling his rider out of the saddle and join the hounds on his own. Lomondham, wrenching at the near reins as a man wrenches at the tiller of a racing-yacht, had just managed to draw away from the rest of the field; and was still managing—though every leap of the crazed animal sapped a little more of his strength—to hold him from bolting into the gorse.

Curiously enough, the rider's terror had disappeared. Clinging—thigh, knee, and calf—to the smooth ox-hide; cursing—as only hunting-men can curse—at the back of Mustard-Pot's heedless ears; giving him every inch of rein he dared, yet aware that the inch too much would mean disaster; swaying to him as he spun like a top; leaning back to him as he buck-jumped, and forward, feet scarcely touching the irons, as he reared—he thought only: "Why don't the fox break? Why the devil don't he break?"

Love, pride, self-consciousness—all these, as well as terror, had momentarily taken wing from Lomondham's mind. Momentarily he was just a horseman; fighting for mastery; feeling—with each pitched second—that mastery at ebb from his hands and body; feeling the demon under him grow stronger and always stronger to his own weakness; knowing instinctively that his one chance, his one and only chance of ultimate victory lay in letting Mustard-Pot have his head and gallop till the power went out of his jaw-bones.

The fight went on, till Mustard-Pot, head between fore legs, hind heels over head, gave one final frenetical buck—and abruptly, from beyond the Ruffs, came the twang-twang of the huntsman's horn, the roared "Gone away—gone away" of a galloping whipper-in. Then, looking about him in the second of time the end of that buck allowed, Lomondham saw the rest of the field preparing to follow—an orderly stampede of horsemen and horsewomen, thrusters pushing to the front, second-flighters hanging back, wise ones rounding the gorse and weak ones making for road or bridle-paths—and gave the yellow gelding his head.

It wasn't a case of cutting down the field. Mustard-Pot, once loosed, went past the swiftest of them like a torpedo-boat past fishing-smacks; and as he went—the green turf thudding under him, the black turf flying from his flying heels—panic, the sheer panic of Things Uncontrollable, entered once again into his rider. For, instinctively, Lomondham knew that the fox would make due east for Saxenham; and instinctively—a map of the country beyond the Ruffs flashing through his mind—he tried to steer Mustard-Pot to the right, away from the most dangerous line in all the Vale.

But Mustard-Pot's long-checked curb might have been a watering-bridle. Straight for the Ruffs he made—his speed increasing with every gigantic bound; straight across them he went—his rider, feet back, body forward in the saddle—seeing rabbit-holes and bramble slide under and swirl past them as ground slides under and swirls past the mounting plane.

And now, as they flew for the far edge of the Ruffs, all hope went from Lomondham. At that pace not even Manifesto could have hoped to come safe across the one stone wall in the Vale, and up the big bank beyond the wall, and down the bank into Tupper's Lane. There was nothing—nothing in all the world to do save to sit down, and to sit still, and to pray that the fall would throw one clear. As for hounds, fox, whippers-in, or huntsmen—Lomondham had clean forgotten the lot of them.

Mustard-Pot, however, had not forgotten. Mustard-Pot's keen ears heard, away beyond the stone wall his eager eyes had just perceived, the eager music of the pack; and Lomondham, still praying, felt his mad pace check to the take-off; saw the jagged top of the wall racing at him; felt the saddle rise between his thigh-bones, as the horse up-ended for the leap; glimpsed the jagged wall-top flash below; knew one danger safely over-past; was conscious of the man-tall bank ahead, of Mustard-Pot hurling himself to top of it, of Mustard-Pot poised for the down-spring, of the green lane below and a gray thoroughbred checking in the lane, of his own back touching Mustard-Pot's croup as they alighted, and of the twelve-foot bullfinch—impenetrable as barbed wire—a bare six inches from his nose.

How horse and rider went through that bullfinch, Naomi, mud-splashed to the eyes, never knew. *She* merely saw Victor's scarlet whip-arm fling up to shield his face, and the yellow horse charge head down at the interlaced thorns, buck his way into them, and disappear to a crashing of wood and a thudding squelch of steel plates among rotten leaves and stagnant water.

As for Lomondham, he could see nothing. He was aware only of a million cats trying to scratch the skin from his face, the clothes from his body, and of a million claws trying to drag him backward over the cantle. Then—his hat snapped from its cord, his left spur wrenched off its strap, one red coat-tail left in the hedge and the other torn to tatters—he was through and in sight of the pack.

The pack, scoring to cry and so close on each other's sterns that they looked like one hound, were three good fields ahead; the huntsman and a whipper-in, alone in their glory, one.

At sight of them, a little of his nerve came back to Lomondham. The going—uphill across the switchback of deep furrows and high ridges which had been plowland in Cromwell's day—slowed Mustard-Pot's stride; and glancing over his right shoulder, the rider could see half a dozen horsemen pelting to be level with him. He thought, vaguely: "By gad, that was a short cut with a vengeance. We're giving 'em all a lead." Then he thought of Naomi's gray, checking in the lane—and shivered in his saddle at the realization that he might have jumped clean on top of her.

Followed realization of the fence ahead—a double post-and-rails with a thorn-filled ditch on the landing side. Mustard-Pot gathered speed again, hurling himself across the ridge and furrow. The wind of their going whipped through Lomondham's hair. Fifty yards from the timber he took a pull at his reins. But the yellow horse raced on unheeding, balanced himself in mid-career, and, clearing the obstacle with feet to spare, saw the two scarlet coats ahead.

No holding the lunatic yet! Still uphill, still over ridge and furrow, he tore like a steed possessed. The two scarlet coats were coming back. Back and back! Lomondham tried to steer round them. But the yellow horse held straight on and shot between the galloping pair, missing them by a hair's-breadth, scattering his clods in their faces. Lomondham heard the huntsman's outraged blasphemy die away down wind as Mustard-Pot took the next post-and-rails in his stride.

And now—now neither hill nor fence nor furrow checked them. For eight hundred yards the ground under hoof was flat as a race-course. Across that flat ground, hounds and quarry had gone like a flame—gone like a flame over the brow of the rise—gone like a flame for the heart of the Vale. And now desperately—desperately, as though his red nostrils told him the way they had traveled—desperately as a prairie-fire leaps the crackling grasses—Mustard-Pot went after them. No foam flecked his useless bit. No sweat darkled on his strid-ing muscles. He was still fresh—fresh and fearless and strong as the storm. But his rider was still afraid—afraid of the ground to come.

And now, suddenly, they were over the brow of the rise; and now, sud-denly, Lomondham saw the Vale below—bad lands dropping terrace-wise through patches of leafless coppice to a gray road and a brown, smoke-plumed village. Beyond these, broad as a river, gleamed the Saxenham Canal. "Steady, you fool! For God's sake, steady!" roared Lomondham, his shoulders back, his knees iron on the saddle-flaps, his hands iron on Mustard-Pot's curb.

But Mustard-Pot heeded not a whit. Mustard-Pot saw only the hounds—the towling-rowling hounds that poured like a cascade of black, white and tan down the slope of the Vale.

Ensued fantastic seconds—seconds of slip and slide and scramble, of plunge and stumble and miraculous recovery—seconds when it seemed to the horseman as though no power on earth could keep him from pitching yards over that enormous down-stretched yellow neck—seconds when the head, neck, and shoulders reared up like a giraffe's before his eyes as Mustard-Pot glissaded fifty sheer yards on his tail—seconds when the loose iron-stone of the hillside rained like shrapnel from their hoof-strokes—seconds when the tree-roots tip-tilted them at every bound—seconds when it seemed as though they left solid earth and flew, flew for dear life down the whistling void.

Down Mustard-Pot went, and down, scrambling over good land, scrambling over bad, scrambling over stone-heaps, scrambling through ditches, scrambling over fences, scrambling among tree-trunks, scrambling his rider's heart in his mouth as a servant-girl scrambles eggs in a pan.

Yet, even so, hounds gained on horse. Hounds made the Saxenham Road and flashed left along the grass at roadside five hundred yards clear ahead of the pair plunging like a scarlet and yellow plummet down Saxenham Hill. Hounds saw their fox streak dark across the gray road and swing away from the brown, smoke-plumed village just as Mustard-Pot—sweating at last—crashed through the young larch plantation at hill-foot and paused for the hundredth part of an instant, his ears cocking to their joyous music.

Lomondham, his face white as his hunting-stock, the sweat blinding his blue eyes, was too blown to take advantage of that instant's pausing; and before he could shorten rein, Mustard-Pot had leaped out of the plantation—into the road—over the road—up the bank and through the hedge on to ridge and furrow again.

One minute later, Saxenham Village, turning out to a man, cheered one hatless horseman over the "squire-trap" into Farmer Thompson's paddock. Two minutes later, Saxenham Village turning out to a boy, called: "Yes, sir. Yes, m'lady. That way, sir. That way m'lady," to the scattered field who came pounded and pounding, after him. Three minutes later, Saxenham Village, dashing, every mother's son and daughter of it, through the churchyard and up the slope behind, saw the dog-fox lolloping red across the chocolate loam that hid Farmer Thompson's winter wheat, and howled to Naomi Braunston as she galloped by: "You keep to the left, missie. He's making for the canal."

Taking the far hedge of the paddock, Lomondham—a little of the breath back in his body and a few of his wits back in his mind—wondered how much longer the horse under him could keep on bolting. He even began to wonder whether the horse were actually bolting. Mustard-Pot, for all that he refused to answer the reins, seemed to know his business. Foam-flecked, he still went straight as a railway-train. Nothing stopped him—neither the stile they cleared to a rap of steel horse-shoes on sodden plank—nor the double-oxer with the ditch beyond—nor the five-foot cut-and-laid on to the new-sown corn. And, "God help Thompson's wheat today," thought Lomondham, as they hared across it close behind the crazy hounds. Then he, too, heard voices howling: "You keep to the left, sir. He's making for the canal."

Before the meaning of those voices penetrated to the hatless horseman on the foam-flecked horse, Mustard-Pot was on turf again, barely a hundred yards behind the pack. But the pack, once off plowland, had the heels of him. They ran nearly mute now, their sterns straight as ramrods, their hackles up, fury in their eyes, and fire in their blood. For their fox was in view. Their fox sank as he ran—ran gasping for the water they could smell when their blood-frantic eyes lost him.

Lomondham, mute as the pack, watched the beaten fox across the tow-path; saw him tumble over the canal-bank; watched hound after hound tumble over after him; remembered the ten-foot drop to the twenty-foot water—and realized in one thrilling spout of superhuman exaltation that all fear had departed from him.

For at last, at good last, the hot dashing courage of Mustard-Pot was into Mustard-Pot's rider. For at last, at splendid last, Sir Victor Plowright Lomondham of Lomondham Hall rode straight again—rode straight and whooping for the kill. "Holla! Holla! Holla! little bitches," he whooped—the reins loose on his horse's neck, the huntsman behind him and the canal before.

And at that whoop, indomitably, incredibly, Mustard-Pot cracked on the last ounce of his astounding speed. No need to touch him with whip or spur! The very ground rocked under his drumming hoofs, as, bound on gigantic bound, he hurtled at the hazard.

The mud of the tow-path was fifty yards ahead—twenty—ten. Below it—still rippling to the passage of the pack—gleamed the brown and the desperate water. Beyond—up the bank—toiled the last eager hound. "Yooi, yooi, yooi to him, Winsome," whooped Lomondham.

Then he was aware of Mustard-Pot gathering himself as though to clear the moon, of the tow-path dropping away, of brown water scurrying under, of brown water leaping up, of a bombshell splash that flung white fountains high and high above his drowning eyes, and of a Force, a Force enormous and earthquake-like under his thighs, driving him up and up through the desperate waters. Then the fountains subsided; and Lomondham knew himself still in the saddle, knew his horse swimming like a swordfish to be in at the death.

Dripping steed under dripping rider scrambled out of Saxenham Canal and up the far bank of it just in time to see what came in after years to be known as "Mustard-Pot's fox" rolled over in the open.

§6

Mustard-Pot's fox had been torn and eaten a good ten minutes, but belated riders on blown horses were still clattering across the canal-bridge, when Lomondham—his reins over his bridle-arm, the water oozing over the tops of his boots—glanced up at a girl on a gray and remarked, meaningly: "I'm going to toddle home, Naomi. It looks to me as though Silver Glory's had about enough. You'd better come, too."

He swung to saddle with a squelch; and the yellow horse, after one regretful glance at the blooded pack, stepped daintily away—Naomi Braunston on a perfectly fit mare following them as obediently as a cavewoman her mate.

Item: Though Silver Glory, who usually grazes with him, seems confident that Lomondham saw something fall from Naomi's hand just at the very moment she confessed: "Victor, you—you mustn't ride like that again. It frightens me"; Mustard-Pot, from whom I had this first of many tales one summer afternoon as he grazed leisurely among the fragrant grasses of Lomondham Park, assures me that when, on their homeward way, the woman his master eventually married dropped her heavy hunting-whip, neither she nor Victor noticed the symbolism of a proceeding which shocked Silver Glory to the depths of her gray-mare-ish soul.

Horses and Horsemen

Born in 1915 in Alberta, Canada, Andy Russell has written about his life as a bronc-buster, rancher and professional guide in such books as *Grizzly Country* and *Trails of a Wilderness Wanderer*. Like most others for whom horses have been working partners, he sees no need to sentimentalize man's relationship with the critters, but that's not to say the reader won't come away without a fond view of what horses mean to the author.

When I was a youngster growing up on the east slope of the Rockies where Drywood Creek cuts down through the hills to join Yarrow Creek and Waterton River before making its contribution to the Saskatchewan, almost everything we did was done by our ability to work with horses. We rode horses to work stock and drove horses in harness to put up hay and haul supplies. Horses were a part of living on the frontier, besides being a means of having fun and a mark of prestige.

Probably no other living thing has had such an impact on our lives as the horse. Likely no other animal has exerted such an influence on the cultural and social development of man. Certainly the opening of the western frontiers of America was made possible by horses that were ridden and packed under saddle and those that worked in harness.

The equine influence reaches far back, to where the first captive horse was likely found in a bog by hunters somewhere in Europe or Asia. Or perhaps it was picked up as an orphan colt to be taken back to the camp alive, raised around the door of the cave and kept as a beast of burden. Maybe early man, tired of wearing down his callused feet on hard trails, watched, as I have done with a sudden lifting of the heart, a wild horse herd thunder by with tails and manes flying in the wind. Covetous of the speed and freedom promised by association with this grass eater, he may have woven a rope from rough strands of grass, or perhaps fashioned one from strips of green hide, and having tied a noose on one end, he hung it on a limb over a trail leading to water and hid to wait.

Who knows what things he caught before a horse put its head in the loop. That first one was likely a mare, for the mares are always in the lead, with the herd stallion bringing up the rear. One can picture that primitive man staring in wonder as his captive pawed the air, squealing and fighting to free itself of the rope. Maybe the horse choked itself into submission, or perhaps the man was crafty enough to use another rope to tie up its feet and bring it under his control. However it was done, it is quite within the realm of reason to suppose he likely collected a fair assortment of horse tracks on various parts of his anat-omy in the process. Before he finally straddled his captive's back, thus becoming the envy of every male who came to look, he probably had even more scars to prove the price he was paying for progress.

But suddenly he found that the size of his territory had broadened. Now he could easily journey to distant corners of the country—places he may have never seen before—and cause utter consternation in a strange village, maybe steal a woman, and far outdistance his pursuers on the way back to his own fire pit. Before this such raiding had been a risky business and very hard work besides. Now his movements were freed of much exertion; he could ride a long way and arrive still fresh enough to fight well. He was, for the first time in the history of mankind, independent of the limitations of his own two feet. He had become a personage of note in the eyes of his fellows—a very rich individual.

Then one warm night in spring, when the leaves were whispering among the trees on a soft breeze and the night birds sang, the musky, penetrating scent of the tethered mare carried on the wind to the questing nose of a stallion. And the strong magnetism of procreation drew him in close under cover of the velvety darkness, his muscles quivering at the smell of her. Unable to drive her away, he covered her where she stood, before her erstwhile captor could rouse himself from his sleeping skins and investigate the cause of the commotion. In due course what had been a one-horse sub-chief became a two-horse chief. The man's fortune had doubled within a few moons. He was now more than just a tamer of wild horses—he was a sort of hairy tycoon. His world had shrunk and grown infinitely bigger for the same reason. The location of his calluses had shifted a bit, from his feet to his rump. He was now a horseman.

Horsemen are a very special breed, for the acquisition and use of horses have always added a certain portion of healthy arrogance and pride to the character of man. Horses have also contributed greatly to the development of man's intelligence, for with horses to help him gather a living, his way of life became much easier. No longer did he find it necessary to work himself to the bone in pursuit of game to keep the stew pot full. His hunting was made much simpler, for the animals he preyed on took longer to realize the danger of his approach when hearing the feet of what had always been a harmless four-footed one coming through the forest. Upon jumping a herd of bison or wild oxen, the hunter could now charge in close with ease and lance a fat animal of his choice. If he missed the first try, he could stay with the fleeing animals for a second try or even a third. Perhaps the man's great surge of savage joy upon making a kill infected the wild heart of his mount, which made her something more than just a half-tamed beast—a part of his life.

The horses used in the settlement of the American west were more than just beasts of burden. They were an absolute necessity, without which the frontiersman would have been afoot and the opening of the west likely delayed by a half century at least. Worked in the harness puling stage coaches, carriages, and various types of freight wagons, the horse was a chief means of power for wheeled conveyances. And innumerable times the early trappers, traders, and cowboys found themselves in a tight spot, where their lives depended on the speed of their mounts. Many are the stories passed down through the years of wild rides through the roughest kind of country, when the penalty for a slow horse was the loss of a man's scalp, the price he paid for losing the race. Under such circumstances a man could easily become an enthusiast for fast horses.

Charlie Russell, the famous raconteur and western artist, told the story of the cowboy, who, for reasons best known to himself, was on the move to far pastures with a posse of grim riders in pursuit. He had outdistanced his pursuers and was enjoying the view of the near side of a getaway when his mount threw a shoe and went lame. This put him in a desperate situation, for a lame horse is not much better than being afoot, and under the circumstances he could feel the tightening of the noose on his neck.

Resting his horse, he was standing with the bridle reins looped over his arm on the rim of a valley, rolling a smoke, when he spotted salvation coming down a steep draw across the valley, heading for water. It was a bunch of wild horses, and among them was a magnificent sorrel gelding, deep of barrel, clean of limb, and in top condition. The draw they were following came out on a flat bar by the river just a bit below a point of a cutbank jutting out toward the water. By some careful and quick maneuvering, the cowboy rode his jaded horse into a bit of cover downwind from the mouth of the draw as close as he dared get.

With his cinch tight and his loop ready, the man waited for the horses to come down the trail onto the gravel bar. An old mare in the lead of the bunch trotted out to the edge of the water, and after a long look around put her head down to drink. The rest of the bunch lined up on each side of her, filling up. At this moment the cowboy made his play. Using every last ounce of his horse's strength and speed, he jumped in close, and in the momentary confusion as the wild ones wheeled and milled against the cutbank, the gelding reared high against another horse, and the cowboy's loop sailed out as straight and true as the strike of a snake to close around its neck.

For a moment or two the big gelding struck at the rope, squealing and fighting; but then he came up short facing the rider, his neck arched, fire in his eyes and ominous snorts rolling in his nostrils.

"When I heard them rollers in his nose, and seen the way his ears was cocked," the man remarked later, "I knew this bronc had seen a man before. When I seen all the brands he was wearin', I knew it for sure. He looked like a map of Montana and Wyoming with all the marks on him. It was a sure bet all the people that had owned him wanted to get rid of him for some good reason. So I begin to get fixed for some high ridin'!"

Untying the hair McCarthy rope off his hackamore, the cowboy threw a loop around the big sorrel's front feet. Right away the horse quieted down, and allowed the hackamore and bridle to be slipped over his head. Then came the saddle, and as it was cinched down the horse stood with his back humped up and his near ear drooping—a sure giveaway that he was getting set for a fight.

About this time the cowboy spotted movement on the hills above, and a moment later a bunch of mounted Indians came pouring down the slope as fast as their ponies could run. What they had in mind was not good, for they were all painted up and rigged for war. It was time to be moving.

The cowboy reached down and untied his hobble rope. Then in almost the same motion he grabbed the cheek strap of his bridle and hauled the sorrel's head around toward him, booted the near stirrup, and stepped up in the saddle. What happened next was the reason for all the brands. With a bawl like a wounded grizzly bear, that big horse put his head between his front legs and left the ground in a great stiff-legged jump. He came down in a jolting explosion of dust and went corkscrewing out along the flat by the river in a string of wild spine-snapping jumps.

A rider less inspired might have been thrown, but guns were going off somewhere behind and bullets were whispering by wide of their mark.

"I wasn't too worried about them savages," the man opined years later. "The way I was moving around they sure as hell didn't stand much chance of hitting me with a rifle slug. That big horse was sure doin' his best to break me in two and kick me out of the saddle at the same time. I lost a stirrup, my sixshooter and my hat. I pulled about everything that would come loose off him and my saddle from his ears back to his tail. But with all that shootin' and ki-yiin' in my ears, you couldn't have chopped me out of that saddle with an ax!"

Maybe a bullet kicked some dirt in his face. Maybe the horse realized his rider was going to stay. Suddenly he picked up his head and began to run. He could run even better than he could buck and in a couple of jumps the scenery was going by that cowboy in a blur. The singing of the wind was music in the man's ears, as the horse tore a hole through it like a spooked antelope heading for far horizons. The Indians pulled up their mounts and watched him go with envy, knowing they had no chance to stay in rifle range.

Without his hat and his gun, the rider felt half naked and a bit helpless in the face of the elements and the people who might be looking for him. But the sorrel carried him far to safety. To his dying day that cowboy claimed he owed his life to that big free-roaming outlaw horse.

Because range work did not allow much time for preliminary conditioning of a horse to accustom him to a rider, breaking methods were cruder and rougher than they are today. Most horses ran free on the range till five years old before being coralled, halter-broke, and then ridden by the bronc-buster of the ranch crew. Once started in their training for working cattle and becoming accustomed to rein, the broncs were turned over to the working crew for additional education through everyday use in working the stock. There were times when such horses were broke to ride before they were trained to lead on halter.

My friend and neighbor, John Wellman, tells of getting a job with a crew trailing a bunch of loose horses from eastern Washington into Montana when he was a youth in his teens. In those days nobody had as yet seen a motorcycle, and the young man of the day projected his image by claiming his prowess as a horseman. In this ride John had lots of opportunities.

The two hundred-odd horses they were trailing were mostly raw range broncs that had never had a rope over their heads. There were a few of them broke to ride, but not enough to keep the crew mounted for such a trip. So they broke horses to ride as they went. They were moving the bunch forty to fifty miles a day, and for the first few days it took some hard riding to keep the horses together in the rough breaks and steep valley country. John, being the ambitious kid of the crew, got plenty of chances to start building a reputation. As a matter of fact, he claimed that the whole crew from the foreman down were so solicitous and helpful he figured they were going to end up killing him. Every time his mount began to look leg weary, which was two or three times a day, they would throw a loop around a loose horse's front feet and throw him. Then they would help John transfer his saddle to the fresh bronc by poking the cinch under its belly with a stick as it lay on the ground. When the cinch had been tightened up and John was in the saddle, they let the bronc get back on its feet.

This first ride was not as rough as might be thought, for seeing the bunch running ahead and being confused, the bronc usually just lit out at a run to catch up. So John would find himself on a fresh horse running in the middle of the bunch. By the time his new mount began to take notice of what it was carrying on its back, it was beginning to tire a bit and answer the pull of the hackamore shank. When the horse began to show signs of lagging, his fellow riders would rope out a fresh one for him. The next time these horses were ridden, it was by the best riders of the crew, for after a rest and a chance to think things over, such horses would generally buck hard. So the trail drive went, and by the time they reached Montana most of the string were well on their way to being good saddle stock. John opined that they probably had more horses broke to ride that knew nothing about leading on halter than any other outfit in the country. In addition, the kid of the outfit had found out that a bronc rider's reputation is made by where he has been sitting and not very much by what he might have said.

All Horse Players Die Broke

BY DAMON RUNYON

I got the horse right here . . ." begins the musical comedy *"Guys and Dolls,"* which was based on newspaper columnist Damon Runyon's tales of Broadway's colorful denizens. Not to include one of these tales would have been criminal. I started to re-read this one while on a New York City bus; the driver would have been well within his rights to have summoned medical assistance to carry away his maniacally laughing passenger.

It is during the last race meeting at Saratoga, and one evening I am standing out under the elms in front of the Grand Union Hotel thinking what a beautiful world it is, to be sure, for what do I do in the afternoon at the track but grab myself a piece of a 10–to–1 shot.

I am thinking what a beautiful moon it is, indeed, that is shining down over the park where Mr. Dick Canfield once deals them higher than a cat's back, and how pure and balmy the air is, and also what nice-looking Judys are wandering around and about, although it is only the night before that I am standing in the same spot wondering where I can borrow a Betsy with which to shoot myself smack-dab through the pimple.

In fact, I go around to see a character I know by the name of Solly something, who owns a Betsy, but it seems he has only one cartridge to his name for this Betsy and he is thinking some of either using the cartridge to shoot his own self smack-dab through the pimple, or of going out to the race-course and shooting an old catfish by the name of Pair of Jacks that plays him false in the fifth race, and therefore Solly is not in a mood to lend his Betsy to anybody else.

So we try to figure out a way we can make one cartridge do for two pimples, and in the meantime Solly outs with a bottle of applejack, and after a couple of belts at this bottle we decide that the sensible thing to do is to take the Betsy out and peddle it for whatever we can, and maybe get a taw for the next day.

Well, it happens that we run into an Italian party from Passaic, N.J., by the name of Giuseppe Palladino, who is called Joe for short, and this Joe is in the money very good at the moment, and he is glad to lend us a pound note on the Betsy, because Joe is such a character as never knows when he may need an extra Betsy, and anyway it is the first time in his experience around the racetracks that anybody ever offers him collateral for a loan.

So there Solly and I are with a deuce apiece after we spend the odd dollar for breakfast the next day, and I run my deuce up to a total of twenty-two slugs on the 10-to-1 shot in the last heat of the day, and everything is certainly all right with me in every respect.

Well, while I am standing there under the elms, who comes along but a raggedy old Dutchman by the name of Unser Fritz, who is maybe seventy-five years old, come next grass, and who is following the giddyaps since the battle of Gettysburg, as near as anybody can figure out. In fact, Unser Fritz is quite an institution around the racetracks, and is often written up by the newspaper scribes as a terrible example of what a horse player comes to, although personally I always say that what Unser Fritz comes to is not so tough when you figure that he does not do a tap of work in all these years.

In his day, Unser Fritz is a most successful handicapper, a handicapper being a character who can dope out from the form what horses ought to win the races, and as long as his figures turn out all right, a handicapper is spoken of most respectfully by one and all, although of course when he begins missing out for any length of time as handicappers are bound to do, he is no longer spoken of respectfully, or even as a handicapper. He is spoken of as a bum.

It is a strange thing how a handicapper can go along for years doing everything right, and then all of a sudden he finds himself doing everything wrong, and this is the way it is with Unser Fritz. For a long time his figures on the horse races are considered most remarkable indeed, and as he will bet till the cows come home on his own figures, he generally has plenty of money, and a fiancée by the name of Emerald Em.

She is called Emerald Em because she has a habit of wearing a raft of emeralds in rings, and pins, and bracelets, and one thing and another, which are purchased for her by Unser Fritz to express his love, an emerald being a green stone that is considered most expressive of love, if it is big enough. It seems that Emerald Em is very fond of emeralds, especially when they are surrounded by large, coarse diamonds.

I hear the old-timers around the racetracks say that when Emerald Em is young, she is a tall, good-looking Judy with yellow hair that is by no means a phony yellow, at that, and with a shape that does not require a bustle such as most Judys always wear in those days.

But then nobody ever hears an old-timer mention any Judy that he remembers from back down the years who is not good-looking, and in fact beautiful. To hear the old-timers tell it, every pancake they ever see when they are young is a double Myrna Loy, though the chances are, figuring in the law of averages, that some of them are bound to be rutabagas, the same as now. Anyway, for years this Emerald Em is known on every racetrack from coast to coast as Unser Fritz's fiancée, and is considered quite a remarkable scene, what with her emeralds, and not requiring any bustle, and everything else.

Then one day Unser Fritz's figures run plumb out on him, and so does his dough, and so does Emerald Em, and now Unser Fritz is an old pappy guy, and it is years since he is regarded as anything but a crumbo around the race-tracks, and nobody remembers much of his story, or cares a cuss about it, for if there is anything that is a drug on the market around the tracks it is the story of a broker.

How he gets from place to place, and how he lives after he gets there, is a very great mystery to one and all, although I hear he often rides in the horsecars with the horses, when some owner or trainer happens to be feeling tenderhearted, or he hitchhikes in automobiles, and sometimes he even walks, for Unser Fritz is still fairly nimble, no matter how old he is.

He always has under his arm a bundle of newspapers that somebody throws away, and every night he sits down and handicaps the horses running the next day according to his own system, but he seldom picks any winners, and even if he does pick any winners, he seldom has anything to bet on them.

Sometimes he promotes a stranger, who does not know he is bad luck to a good hunting dog, to put down a few dibs on one of his picks, and once in a while the pick wins, and Unser Fritz gets a small stake, and sometimes an old-timer who feels sorry for him will slip him something. But whatever Unser Fritz gets hold of, he bets off right away on the next race that comes up, so naturally he never is holding anything very long.

Well, Unser Fritz stands under the elms with me awhile, speaking of this and that, and especially of the races, and I am wondering to myself if I will become as disheveled as Unser Fritz if I keep on following the races, when he gazes at the Grand Union Hotel, and says to me like this:

"It looks nice," he says. "It looks cheerylike, with the lights, and all this and that. It brings back memories to me. Emma always lives in this hotel whenever we make Saratoga for the races back in the days when I am in the money. She always has a suite of two or three rooms on this side of the hotel. Once she has four.

"I often stand here under these trees," Unser Fritz says, "watching her windows to see what time she puts out her lights, because, while I trust Emma implicitly, I know she has a restless nature, and sometimes she cannot resist returning to scenes of gaiety after I bid her good night, especially," he says, "with a party by the name of Pete Shovelin, who runs the restaurant where she once deals them off the arm."

"You mean she is a biscuit shooter?" I say.

"A waitress," Unser Fritz says. "A good waitress. She comes of a family of farm folks in this very section, although I never know much about them," he says. "Shovelin's is a little hole-in-the-wall up the street here somewhere which long since disappears. I go there for my morning java in the old days.

"I will say one thing for Shovelin," Unser Fritz says, "he always has good java. Three days after I first clap eyes on Emma, she is wearing her first emerald, and is my fiancée. Then she moves into a suite in the Grand Union. I only wish you can know Emma in those days," he says. "She is beautiful. She is a fine character. She is always on the level, and I love her dearly."

"What do you mean—always on the level?" I say. "What about this Shovelin party you just mention?"

"Ah," Unser Fritz says, "I suppose I am dull company for a squab, what with having to stay in at night to work on my figures, and Emma likes to go around and about. She is a highly nervous type, and extremely restless, and she cannot bear to hold still very long at a time. But," he says, "in those days it is not considered proper for a young Judy to go around and about without a chaperon, so she goes with Shovelin for her chaperon. Emma never goes anywhere without a chaperon," he says.

Well, it seems that early in their courtship, Unser Fritz learns that he can generally quiet her restlessness with emeralds, if they have diamonds on the side. It seems that these stones have a very soothing effect on her, and this is why he purchases them for her by the bucket.

"Yes," Unser Fritz says, "I always think of Emma whenever I am in New York City, and look down Broadway at night with the go lights on."

But it seems from what Unser Fritz tells me that even with the emeralds her restless spells come on her very bad, and especially when he finds himself running short of ready, and is unable to purchase more emeralds for her at the moment, although Unser Fritz claims this is nothing unusual. In fact, he says anybody with any experience with nervous female characters knows that it becomes very monotonous for them to be around people who are short of ready.

"But," he says, "not all of them require soothing with emeralds. Some require pearls," he says.

Well, it seems that Emma generally takes a trip without Unser Fritz to break the monotony of his running short of ready, but she never takes one of these trips without a chaperon, because she is very careful about her good name, and Unser Fritz's, too. It seems that in those days Judys have to be more careful about such matters than they do now.

He remembers that once when they are in San Francisco she takes a trip through the Yellowstone with Jockey Gus Kloobus as her chaperon, and is gone three weeks and returns much refreshed, especially as she gets back just as Unser Fritz makes a nice score and has a seidel of emeralds waiting for her. He remembers another time she goes to England with a trainer by the name of Blootz as her chaperon and comes home with an English accent that sounds right cute, to find Unser Fritz going like a house afire at Belmont.

"She takes a lot of other trips without me during the time we are engaged," Unser Fritz says, "but," he says, "I always know Emma will return to me as soon as she hears I am back in the money and can purchase more emeralds for her. In fact," he says, "this knowledge is all that keeps me struggling now."

"Look, Fritz," I say, "what do you mean, keeps you going? Do you mean you think Emma may return to you again?"

"Why, sure," Unser Fritz says. "Why, certainly, if I get my rushes again. Why not?" he says. "She knows there will be a pail of emeralds waiting for her. She knows I love her and always will," he says.

Well, I ask him when he sees Emerald Em last, and he says it is 1908 in the old Waldorf-Astoria the night he blows a hundred and sixty thousand betting on a hide called Sir Martin to win the Futurity, and it is all the dough Unser Fritz has at the moment. In fact, he is cleaner than a jaybird, and he is feeling somewhat discouraged.

It seems he is waiting on his floor for the elevator, and when it comes down Emerald Em is one of the several passengers, and when the door opens, and Unser Fritz starts to get in, she raises her foot and plants it in his stomach, and gives him a big push back out the door and the elevator goes on down without him.

"But, of course," Unser Fritz says, "Emma never likes to ride in the same elevator with me, because I am not always tidy enough to suit her in those days, what with having so much work to do on my figures, and she claims it is a knock to her socially. Anyway," he says, "this is the last I see of Emma."

"Why, Fritz," I say, "nineteen-eight is nearly thirty years back, and if she ever thinks of returning to you, she will return long before this."

"No," Unser Fritz says. "You see, I never make a scratch since then. I am never since in the money, so there is no reason for Emma to return to me. But," he says, "wait until I get going good again and you will see."

Well, I always figure Unser Fritz must be more or less of an old screwball for going on thinking there is still a chance for him around the tracks, and now I am sure of it, and I am about to bid him good evening, when he mentions that he can use about two dollars if I happen to have a deuce on me that is not working, and I will say one thing for Unser Fritz, he seldom comes right out and asks anybody for anything unless things are very desperate with him, indeed.

"I need it to pay something on account of my landlady," he says. "I room with old Mrs. Crob around the corner for over twenty years, and," he says, "she only charges me a finnif a week, so I try to keep from getting too far to the rear with her. I will return it to you the first score I make."

Well, of course I know this means practically never, but I am feeling so good about my success at the track that I slip him a deucer, and it is half an hour later before I fully realize what I do, and go looking for Fritz to get anyway half of it back. But by this time he disappears, and I think no more of the matter until the next day out at the course when I hear Unser Fritz bets two dollars on a thing by the name of Speed Cart, and it bows down at 50 to 1, so I know Mrs. Crob is still waiting for hers.

Now there is Unser Fritz with one hundred slugs, and this is undoubtedly more money than he enjoys since Hickory Slim is a two-year-old. And from here on the story becomes very interesting, and in fact remarkable, because up to the moment Speed Cart hits the wire, Unser Fritz is still nothing but a crumbo, and you can say it again, while from now on he is somebody to point out and say can you imagine such a thing happening?

He bets a hundred on a centipede called Marchesa, and down pops Marchesa like a trained pig at 20 to 1. Then old Unser Fritz bets two hundred on a caterpillar by the name of Merry Soul, at 4 to 1, and Merry Soul just laughs his way home. Unser Fritz winds up the day betting two thousand more on something called Sharp Practice, and when Sharp Practice wins by so far it looks as if he is a shoo-in, Fritz finds himself with over twelve thousand slugs, and the way the bookmakers in the betting ring are sobbing is really most distressing to hear.

Well, in a week Unser Fritz is a hundred thousand dollars in front, because the way he sends it in is quite astonishing to behold, although the old-timers tell me it is just the way he sends it when he is younger. He is betting only on horses that he personally figures out, and what happens is that Unser Fritz's figures suddenly come to life again, and he cannot do anything wrong.

He wins so much dough that he even pays off a few old touches, including my two, and he goes so far as to lend Joe Palladino three dollars on the Betsy that Solly and I hock with Joe for the pound note, as it seems that by this time Joe himself is practically on his way to the poorhouse, and while Unser Fritz has no use whatsoever for a Betsy he cannot bear to see a character such as Joe go to the poorhouse.

But with all the dough Unser Fritz carries in his pockets, and plants in a safe-deposit box in the jug downtown, he looks just the same as ever, because he claims he cannot find time from working on his figures to buy new clothes and dust himself off, and if you tell anybody who does not know who he is that this old crutch is stone rich, the chances are they will call you a liar.

In fact, on a Monday around noon, the clerk in the branch office that a big Fifth Avenue jewelry firm keeps in the lobby of the States Hotel is all ready to yell for the constables when Unser Fritz leans up against the counter and asks to see some jewelry on display in a showcase, as Unser Fritz is by no means the clerk's idea of a customer for jewelry.

I am standing in the lobby of the hotel on the off chance that some fresh money may arrive in the city on the late trains that I may be able to connect up with before the races, when I notice Unser Fritz and observe the agitation of the clerk, and presently I see Unser Fritz waving a fistful of bank notes under the clerk's beak, and the clerk starts setting out the jewelry with surprising speed.

I go over to see what is coming off, and I can see that the jewelry Unser Fritz is looking at consists of a necklace of emeralds and diamonds, with a centerpiece the size of the home plate, and some eardrops, and bracelets, and clips of same, and as I approach the scene I hear Unser Fritz ask how much for the lot as if he is dickering for a basket of fish.

"One hundred and one thousand dollars, sir," the clerk says. "You see, sir, it is a set, and one of the finest things of the kind in the country. We just got it in from our New York store to show a party here, and," he says, "she is absolutely crazy about it, but she states she cannot give us a final decision until five o'clock this afternoon. Confidentially, sir," the clerk says, "I think the real trouble is financial, and doubt that we will hear from her again. In fact," he says, "I am so strongly of this opinion that I am prepared to sell the goods without waiting on her. It is really a bargain at the price," he says.

"Dear me," Unser Fritz says to me, "this is most unfortunate as the sum mentioned is just one thousand dollars more than I possess in all this world. I have twenty thousand on my person, and eighty thousand over in the box in the jug, and not another dime. But," he says, "I will be back before five o'clock and take the lot. In fact," he says, "I will run in right after the third race and pick it up."

Well, at this the clerk starts putting the jewelry back in the case, and anybody can see that he figures he is on a lob and that he is sorry he wastes so much time, but Unser Fritz says to me like this:

"Emma is returning to me," he says.

"Emma who?" I say.

"Why," Unser Fritz says, 'my Emma. The one I tell you about not long ago. She must hear I am in the money again, and she is returning just as I always say she will."

"How do you know?" I say. "Do you hear from her, or what?"

"No," Unser Fritz says, "I do not hear from her direct, but Mrs. Crob knows some female relative of Emma's that lives at Ballston Spa a few miles from here, and this relative is in Saratoga this morning to do some shopping, and she tells Mrs. Crob and Mrs. Crob tells me. Emma will be here tonight. I will have these emeralds waiting for her."

Well, what I always say is that every guy knows his own business best, and if Unser Fritz wishes to toss his dough off on jewelry, it is none of my put-in, so all I remark is that I have no doubt Emma will be very much surprised indeed.

"No," Unser Fritz says. "She will be expecting them. She always expects emeralds when she returns to me. I love her," he says. "You have no idea how I love her. But let us hasten to the course," he says. "Cara Mia is a right good thing in the third, and I will make just one bet today to win the thousand I need to buy these emeralds."

"But, Fritz," I say, "you will have nothing left for operating expenses after you invest in the emeralds."

"I am not worrying about operating expenses now," Unser Fritz says. "The way my figures are standing up, I can run a spool of thread into a pair of pants in no time. But I can scarcely wait to see the expression on Emma's face when she sees her emeralds. I will have to make a fast trip into town after the third to get my dough out of the box in the jug and pick them up," he says.

"Who knows but what this other party that is interested in the emeralds may make her mind up before five o'clock and pop in there and nail them?"

Well, after we get to the racetrack, all Unser Fritz does is stand around waiting for the third race. He has his figures on the first two races, and ordinarily he will be betting himself a gob on them, but he says he does not wish to take the slightest chance of cutting down his capital at this time, and winding up short of enough dough to buy the emeralds.

It turns out that both of the horses Unser Fritz's figures make on top in the first and second races bow down, and Unser Fritz will have his thousand if he only bets a couple of hundred on either of them, but Unser Fritz says he is not sorry he does not bet. He says the finishes in both races are very close, and prove that there is an element of risk in these races. And Unser Fritz says he cannot afford to tamper with the element of risk at this time.

He states that there is no element of risk whatever in the third race, and what he states is very true, as everybody realizes that this mare Cara Mia is a stick-out. In fact, she is such a stick-out that it scarcely figures to be a contest. There are three other horses in the race, but it is the opinion of one and all that if the owners of these horses have any sense they will leave them in the barn and save them a lot of unnecessary lather.

The opening price offered by the bookmakers on Cara Mia is 2 to 5, which means that if you wish to wager on Cara Mia to win you will have to put up five dollars to a bookmaker's two dollars, and everybody agrees that this is a reasonable thing to do in this case unless you wish to rob the poor bookmaker.

In fact, this is considered so reasonable that everybody starts running at the bookmakers all at once, and the bookmakers can see if this keeps up they may get knocked off their stools in the betting ring and maybe seriously injured, so they make Cara Mia 1 to 6, and out, as quickly as possible to halt the rush and give them a chance to breathe.

This 1 to 6 means that if you wish to wager on Cara Mia to win, you must wager six of your own dollars to one of the bookmaker's dollars, and means that the bookies are not offering any prices whatsoever on Cara Mia running second or third. You can get almost any price you can think of right quick against any of the other horses winning the race, and place and show prices, too, but asking the bookmakers to lay against Cara Mia running second or third will be something like asking them to bet that Mr. Roosevelt is not President of the United States.

Well, I am expecting Unser Fritz to step in and partake of the 2 to 5 on Cara Mia for all the dough he has on his person the moment he is offered, because he is very high indeed on this mare, and in fact I never see anybody any higher on any horse, and it is a price Unser Fritz will not back off from when he is high on anything.

Moreover, I am pleased to think he will make such a wager, because it will give him plenty over and above the price of the emeralds, and as long as he is bound to purchase the emeralds, I wish to see him have a little surplus, because when anybody has a surplus there is always a chance for me. It is when everybody runs out of surpluses that I am handicapped no little. But instead of stepping in and partaking, Unser Fritz keeps hesitating until the opening price gets away from him, and finally he says to me like this:

"Of course," he says, "my figures show Cara Mia cannot possibly lose this race, but," he says, "to guard against any possibility whatever of her losing, I will make an absolute cinch of it. I will bet her third."

"Why, Fritz," I says, "I do not think there is anybody in this world outside of an insane asylum who will give you a price on the peek. Furthermore," I say, "I am greatly surprised at this sign of weakening on your part on your figures."

"Well," Unser Fritz says, "I cannot afford to take a chance on not having the emeralds for Emma when she arrives. Let us go through the betting ring and see what we can see," he says.

So we walk through the betting ring, and by this time it seems that many of the books are so loaded with wagers on Cara Mia to win that they will not accept any more under the circumstances, and I figure that Unser Fritz blows the biggest opportunity of his life in not grabbing the opening. The bookmakers who are loaded are now looking even sadder than somewhat, and this makes them a pitiful spectacle indeed.

Well, one of the saddest-looking is a character by the name of Slow McCool, but he is a character who will usually give you a gamble and he is still taking Cara Mia at 1 to 6, and Unser Fritz walks up to him and whispers in his ear, and what he whispers is he wishes to know if Slow McCool cares to lay him a price on Cara Mia third. But all that happens is that Slow McCool stops looking sad a minute and looks slightly perplexed, and then he shakes his head and goes on looking sad again.

Now Unser Fritz steps up to another sad-looking bookmaker by the name of Pete Phozzler and whispers in his ear, and Pete also shakes his head, and after we leave him I look back and see that Pete is standing up on his stool watching Unser Fritz and still shaking his head.

Well, Unser Fritz approaches maybe a dozen other sad-looking bookmakers, and whispers to them, and all he gets is the old headshake, but none of

them seem to become angry with Unser Fritz, and I always say that this proves
the bookmakers are better than some people think, because, personally, I claim
they have a right to get angry with Unser Fritz for insulting their intelligence,
and trying to defraud them, too, by asking a price on Cara Mia third.

Finally we come to a character by the name of Willie the Worrier, who
is called by this name because he is always worrying about something, and what
he is generally worrying about is a short bankroll, or his ever-loving wife, and
sometimes both, though mostly it is his wife. Personally, I always figure she is
something to worry about, at that, though I do not consider details necessary.

She is a redheaded Judy about half as old as Willie the Worrier, and this
alone is enough to start any guy worrying, and what is more she is easily
vexed, especially by Willie. In fact, I remember Solly telling me that she is
vexed with Willie no longer ago than about 11 A.M. this very day, and gives
him a public reprimanding about something or other in the telegraph office
downtown when Solly happens to be in there hoping maybe he will receive an
answer from a mark in Pittsfield, Mass., that he sends a tip on a horse.

Solly says the last he hears Willie the Worrier's wife say is that she will
leave him for good this time, but I just see her over on the clubhouse lawn
wearing some right classy-looking garments, so I judge she does not leave him
as yet, as the clubhouse lawn is not a place to be waiting for a train.

Well, when Unser Fritz sees that he is in front of Willie's stand, he starts
to move on, and I nudge him and motion at Willie, and ask him if he does not
notice that Willie is another bookmaker, and Unser Fritz says he notices him all
right, but that he does not care to offer him any business because Willie insults
him ten years ago. He says Willie calls him a dirty old Dutch bum, and while I
am thinking what a wonderful memory Unser Fritz has to remember insults
from bookmakers for ten years, Willie the Worrier, sitting on his stool looking
out over the crowd, spots Unser Fritz and yells at him as follows:

"Hello, Dirty Dutch," he says. "How is the soap market? What are you
looking for around here, Dirty Dutch? Santa Claus?"

Well, at this Unser Fritz pushes his way through the crowd around
Willie the Worrier's stand, and gets close to Willie, and says:

"Yes," he says, "I am looking for Santa Claus. I am looking for a show
price on number two horse, but," he says, "I do not expect to get it from the
shoemakers who are booking nowadays."

Now the chances are Willie the Worrier figures Unser Fritz is just trying to get sarcastic with him for the benefit of the crowd around his stand in
asking for such a thing as a price on Cara Mia third, and in fact the idea of anybody asking a price third on a horse that some bookmakers will not accept any

more wagers on first, or even second, is so humorous that many characters laugh right out loud.

"All right," Willie the Worrier says. "No one can ever say he comes to my store looking for a marker on anything and is turned down. I will quote you a show price, Dirty Dutch," he says. "You can have 1 to 100."

This means that Willie the Worrier is asking Unser Fritz for one hundred dollars to the book's one dollar if Unser Fritz wishes to be on Cara Mia dropping in there no worse than third, and of course Willie has no idea Unser Fritz or anybody else will ever take such a price, and the chances are if Willie is not sizzling a little at Unser Fritz, he will not offer such a price, because it sounds foolish.

Furthermore, the chances are if Unser Fritz offers Willie a comparatively small bet at this price, such as may enable him to chisel just a couple of hundred out of Willie's book, Willie will find some excuse to wiggle off, but Unser Fritz leans over and says in a low voice to Willie the Worrier:

"A hundred thousand."

Willie nods his head and turns to a clerk alongside him, and his voice is as low as Unser Fritz's as he says to the clerk:

"A thousand to a hundred thousand, Cara Mia third."

The clerk's eyes pop open and so does his mouth, but he does not say a word. He just writes something on a pad of paper in his hand, and Unser Fritz offers Willie the Worrier a package of thousand-dollar bills, and says:

"Here is twenty," he says. "The rest is in the jug."

"All right, Dutch," Willie says. "I know you have it, although," he says, "this is the first crack you give me at it. You are on, Dutch," he says. "P.S.," Willie says, "the Dirty does not go any more."

Well, you understand Unser Fritz is betting one hundred thousand dollars against a thousand dollars that Cara Mia will run in the money, and personally I consider this wager a very sound business proposition indeed, and so does everybody else, for all it amounts to is finding a thousand dollars in the street.

There is really nothing that can make Cara Mia run out of the money, the way I look at it, except what happens to her, and what happens is she steps in a hole fifty yards from the finish when she is on top by ten, and breezing, and down she goes all spread out, and of course the other three horses run on past her to the wire, and all this is quite a disaster to many members of the public, including Unser Fritz.

I am standing with him on the rise of the grandstand lawn watching the race, and it is plain to be seen that he is slightly surprised at what happens, and personally, I am practically dumbfounded because, to tell the truth, I take a nibble at the opening price of 2 to 5 on Cara Mia with a total of thirty slugs, which represents all my capital, and I am thinking what a great injustice it is for them to leave holes in the track for horses to step in, when Unser Fritz says like this:

"Well," he says, "it is horse racing."

And this is all he ever says about the matter, and then he walks down to Willie the Worrier, and tells Willie if he will send a clerk with him, he will go to the jug and get the balance of the money that is now due Willie.

'Dutch," Willie says, "it will be a pleasure to accompany you to the jug in person."

As Willie is getting down off his stool, somebody in the crowd who hears of the wager gazes at Unser Fritz, and remarks that he is really a game guy, and Willie says:

"Yes," he says, "he is a game guy at that. But," he says, "what about me?"

And he takes Unser Fritz by the arm, and they walk away together, and anybody can see that Unser Fritz picks up anyway twenty years or more, and a slight stringhalt, in the last few minutes.

Then it comes on night again in Saratoga, and I am standing out under the elms in front of the Grand Union, thinking that this world is by no means as beautiful as formerly, when I notice a big, fat old Judy with snow-white hair and spectacles standing near me, looking up and down the street. She will weigh a good two hundred pounds, and much of it is around her ankles, but she has a pleasant face, at that, and when she observes me looking at her, she comes to me, and says:

"I am trying to fix the location of a restaurant where I work many years ago," she says. "It is a place called Shovelin's. The last thing my husband tells me is to see if the old building is still here, but," she says, "it is so long since I am in Saratoga I cannot get my bearings."

"Ma'am," I say, "is your name Emma by any chance and do they ever call you Emerald Em?"

Well, at this the old Judy laughs, and says:

"Why, yes," she says. "That is what they call me when I am young and foolish. But how do you know?" she says. "I do not remember ever seeing you before in my life."

"Well," I say, "I know a party who once knows you. A party by the name of Unser Fritz."

"Unser Fritz?" she says. "Unser Fritz? Oh," she says, "I wonder if you mean a crazy Dutchman I run around with many years ago? My gracious," she says, "I just barely remember him. He is a great hand for giving me little presents such as emeralds. When I am young I think emeralds are right pretty, but," she says, "otherwise I cannot stand them."

"Then you do not come here to see him?" I say.

"Are you crazy, too?" she says. "I am on my way to Ballston Spa to see my grandchildren. I live in Macon, Georgia. If ever you are in Macon, Georgia, drop in at Shovelin's restaurant and get some real Southern fried chicken. I am Mrs. Joe Shovelin," she says. "By the way," she says, "I remember more about that crazy Dutchman. He is a horse player. I always figure he must die long ago and that the chances are he dies broke, too. I remember I hear people say all horse players die broke."

"Yes," I say, "he does all right, and he dies as you suggest, too," for it is only an hour before that they find old Unser Fritz in a vacant lot over near the railroad station with the Betsy he gets off Joe Palladino in his hand and a bullet-hole smack-dab through his pimple.

Nobody blames him much for taking this out, and in fact I am standing there thinking long after Emerald Em goes on about her business that it will be a good idea if I follow his example, only I cannot think where I can find another Betsy, when Solly comes along and stands there with me. I ask Solly if he knows anything new.

"No," Solly says, "I do not know anything new, except," he says, "I heard Willie the Worrier and his ever-loving make up again, and she is not going to leave him after all. I hear Willie takes home a squarer in the shape of a batch of emeralds and diamonds that she orders sent up here when Willie is not looking, and that they are fighting about all day. Well," Solly says, "maybe this is love."

Dreaming

BY BILL BARICH

I f, as the saying goes, there's a broken heart for every light on Broadway, there's also one for every hoofprint on a racetrack. Nevertheless, hope springs eternal, especially if you have a good young horse in the barn. Bill Barich, a first-rate sports writer, proves that point in this tour of Santa Anita.

A racetrack exists as a world apart, rich in its own mysteries and subject to laws of its own devising. When you walk through the turnstiles at Santa Anita Park, near Pasadena, you could be going back in time to an era of Hollywood glory and entering a grand Art Deco hotel of the thirties. There are curved mirrors and etched glass, imported Mexican tiles and semiformal gardens where punters sit reading the *Racing Form* in a sea of flowering bougainvillea, as if they were waiting for a bellhop to grab their luggage, or a cigarette girl to deliver some smokes. The chance of bumping into a retired movie star in the private turf club is extremely high, as is the opportunity to soak up the last fading essence of Southern California class.

I had come to Santa Anita to have a look at Snow Chief, a Cal-bred colt, who was the current morning-line favorite to win the Kentucky Derby. It was a rainy March afternoon when I arrived, and the distant San Gabriel Mountains had turned a deep and alluring shade of green. Mel Stute, the colt's trainer, was in his grandstand box, where I caught up with him and had some coffee to ward off the chill. In his many years on the backside, Stute has had only one previous Derby candidate, Bold and Rulling, so I had no problem forgiving him when he mentioned Snow Chief in the same breath as John Henry, then the leading money-winner in racing history.

Some trainers appear never to have mucked out a stall, but Stute isn't one of them. He's a hard worker whose sixtieth birthday is fast approaching.

Warm and friendly, he has the leathery face of a cowboy and seems full of energy. Around the clubhouse, he wears a tie and jacket, but I was sure he got out of the money suit as soon as humanly possible and back into his jeans. His first job in racing was rubbing horses for his older brother, Warren, but that didn't give him any edge as a trainer. Instead, he labored at such minor-league tracks as Golden Gate Fields and Portland Meadows before rising into the majors and making his reputation as a clever handler of claimers, buying and selling cheaper stock with the acumen of a poker shark.

The second race of the day was about to go off, so we quit talking to watch it. Stute had two maiden geldings entered, Bride's Advice and Lord Prevue, and when the gate snapped open, he began moving his arms back and forth in unison, as if he were skiing cross-country. I thought this must be a trick of his for attracting good fortune. Every gambler relies on such gimmicks. One friend of mine refuses to go to the track unless he has on his red socks, the way Alexander Calder, in old age, favored red flannel shirts for effect. My own trick is to never hold on to a losing ticket, for fear it will contaminate my aura and keep me from ever cashing a bet.

Anyhow, Stute was skiing for victory. It didn't help Bride's Advice, who took a misstep and threw his rider, but Lord Prevue was operating under a benign influence and finished first at a generous price of twenty-five to one. That had Stute whooping, and he let an admirer in the next box buy him a drink. His popularity around Santa Anita has never been higher—a Derby-bound colt will do that for a man. Fans came toward him in a steady stream, among them a heavyset guy in baggy trousers with a paper bag under his arm. The bag contained a sketch of Secretariat mounted on cardboard, and he gave it to Stute and stood there waiting to be appreciated.

"Why, thank you!" Stute said, handing it over to a bartender for safekeeping. "I don't know what my wife's going to say about it. She thinks we already have too many pictures of horses."

"A friend of mine did that," the man said proudly, drumming up business. "He's an artist. He used, what do you call it?"

"Charcoal?"

"No, not charcoal. Pencils. Anyway, Mel, if you ever want a drawing of Snow Chief, he'll be glad to do it for you."

Stute had been reunited with his prize colt earlier in the week, when Snow Chief returned from Gulfstream Park after winning the five-hundred-thousand-dollar Florida Derby. It was his most impressive performance to date. Breaking from the twelve hole at the outside of the field, he'd had to use up some of his speed to get to the front, but he had more than enough left over and turned the race into a convincing demonstration of his ability to cover a mile and an eighth. Snow Chief is not supposed to do such things. His breeding is unspectacular. He once raced at a cheap track in Mexico, for example, and he bucked his shins as a two-year-old. He should be an ordinary claiming type, not a potential star, but he continues to learn and grow. One of the raps against Cal-breds is that they don't travel well, but Snow Chief had no trouble in Florida and remained unfazed by the bright lights and popping flashbulbs.

Still, Stute was slow to accept the fact that Snow Chief might be special. The race that truly convinced him was the Del Mar Futurity last summer. Snow Chief came up from Agua Caliente, in Tijuana, where he'd been resting his bucked shins under the care of Wilfrido Martinez, a Mexican trainer, and Stute did not have time to condition the colt for a long race. He just blew him out around the first turn at Del Mar and hoped for the best. Although Snow Chief wound up losing the Futurity by two lengths, he lost it to Tasso, who went on to become the two-year-old champion.

In the fall, at Santa Anita, Snow Chief ran in the Norfolk Handicap and beat Louisiana Slew, a son of Seattle Slew, who'd cost almost three million dollars as a yearling. Despite the fine performance, Alex Solis, Snow Chief's regular jockey, noticed that the colt was holding something back, and suggested that Stute add some blinkers. Snow Chief has worn them in his last four races and has won all four handily, bringing his record to eight victories in twelve starts and suggesting that he is the genuine article, indeed.

The most common knock you hear against Snow Chief is that he has been racing too often. Valuable two-year-olds are usually turned out for a rest during the winter, but Stute has kept the colt in training, running him on an average of once a month. There are those who believe that such hard work ruins young horses, and that Snow Chief has already reached his peak, yet Stute doesn't believe it and plans to stick to his schedule right up to the Kentucky Derby.

The man who bred Snow Chief, Carl Grinstead, stopped by the box later that afternoon, while Stute went off to saddle a horse. Grinstead, a retired electronics engineer, used to have a factory near Santa Anita and bought his first horse, Eventuate, with a couple of friends. Of all the people around Snow Chief, he is the least surprised by the colt's talent. He had expected speed to show, because Snow Chief's dam, Miss Snowflake, had it in abundance. In Grinstead's opinion, the major test for Snow Chief will be whether or not the colt can cover the classic distances. He would like to see that happen if only to prove to the racing establishment that Cal-breds, even cheaper ones, should be granted some respect.

Grinstead has a partner in Snow Chief, Ben Rochelle, who soon joined us in the box. A former vaudeville dancer, Rochelle made his big money in real estate after he quit show biz, but he was more interested in talking about Betty Grable. He informed me that he had played the Strand and the Paramount and worked in pictures with Marion Davies. He thought I might want a photo of him and his dancing partner, so he said to Grinstead, "Carl, you've got some photos of me, haven't you?"

"I haven't got any photos of you," Grinstead replied, sounding amused.

Unperturbed, Rochelle carried on. "I saw where Snow Chief is three to one in Las Vegas to win the Derby."

"You'd be crazy to take those odds, Ben," said Grinstead. "You'll get a better price at Churchill Downs."

Grinstead and Rochelle are both in their seventies and refer to themselves as the Sunshine Boys, after the Neil Simon comedy. They are nothing like the Sunshine Boys, really, except insofar as they enjoy the limelight. When they became partners—Grinstead sold Rochelle half of his entire operation—neither of them suspected that they were closing a deal that included a million-dollar colt. In that sense, they resemble a couple who embarked on an affair and wound up committing marriage. The main thing is that both Grinstead and Rochelle are exceptionally happy to be associated with a famous horse.

"Did I tell you I'm going to be on TV in Mexico, Ben?" Grinstead asked. "I'll be talking about Snow Chief on *Tijuana: Window to the South*." He said this with a straight face.

Stute had told me that some officials from Garden State Park, in New Jersey, had urged him to run Snow Chief in the Garden State Stakes, which would qualify the colt for a million-dollar bonus. But it would also force him to interrupt his successful training schedule and compete in a race only two weeks before the Derby, so Stute refused. I was curious about Grinstead's reaction.

"I've got a little money set aside," he said, implying that he was above such temptations. "If you win in Kentucky, you go down in history. The Triple Crown races are like the Indianapolis 500 or the World Series."

"People try to buy Snow Chief," Rochelle said smugly.

"They try," his partner agreed. "And we tell them he's not for sale."

I arranged to visit Mel Stute's barn the next morning, and got up at five-thirty. The rain had stopped during the night, and now the weather was cold and clear. From the window of my motel room, I could see the crests of the San Gabriels dusted with fresh snow.

Light was just coming into the sky when I reached Santa Anita, but the backstretch was already bustling. I walked down a muddy lane between barns, dodging riders who were taking their mounts to the training track for a gallop. The barns were wooden and painted a grayish-green. I saw a sleek-feathered rooster with a brilliant-red comb parading in front of several hens on a patch of grass. Goats were hiding in the dark of shed rows. There were grooms whistling as they pitchforked straw from stalls, glad to be out in the fresh air and doing work that brought joy to the muscles. I caught a whiff of coffee and then a whiff of tobacco, and I began to feel alive myself. In fact, I *was* alive and wandering around a racetrack, and at that moment, with oxygen and sunlight flooding every cell of my body, I wouldn't have wanted to be anywhere else on earth.

Stute has Barn 97, in esteemed territory reserved for gentlemen of power. I found him in his rustic, minimalist office, where he keeps a desk, a space heater, and an armchair for visitors. I think somebody had attacked the armchair with a baseball bat. Trainers prefer such quarters, though, because they have to admit that they're involved in big business. In horse-racing circles these days, you need some basic management skills; intuition and an affection for animals aren't enough anymore. Stute has thirty-two stalls in his barn, the maximum allowed at Santa Anita, and he boards horses elsewhere as well, bringing them over by van when they're supposed to run. He has to spend a lot of time on paperwork, making certain that his owners are billed for feed, veterinary charges, and other costs. It isn't a task he enjoys.

"Well, good morning!" he roared in greeting. "Have you seen the big horse yet?" He calls Snow Chief "the big horse" for obvious reasons. He also calls Snow Chief "the little horse," because he's slightly smaller than average. Both are terms of endearment.

Stute led me down a shed row to a stall that looked no different from any other stall. Snow Chief had his head stuck out over the half door, and he was taking in the action around him. He is an alert and lively colt, who nips at his handlers a bit too hard. Almost pure black, he has a white star on his forehead. His conformation is not striking, but he has strong hindquarters and uses them to dig in when he's on a track. He never quits, and mud doesn't bother him at all. Another thing that sets him apart is his intelligence; he is eager to learn and masters his lessons quickly. Sometimes he can be lazy, gliding by on the grease of his talent. If a horse can be said to have a sense of humor, I think Snow Chief may have one.

Stute left me with the colt and his groom, Miguel Hernandez, who is known as Mena. Like everybody around Snow Chief, Mena is riding high. He got into the stall and used a currycomb on Snow Chief, applying the strokes with a firm but gentle touch. He ran a brush through the colt's mane and tail until they looked silky, while he listened to the radio news in Spanish. Mena has a broad Indian face and sparkling eyes. His English is only fair, so we conversed in smiles and one-syllable words. Yes, Mena agreed, this Snow Chief, he is a very nice kind of horse.

When the combing was done, Mena brought out Snow Chief and led him to an open area where there was a hose on the ground. The colt had worked the day before and had wraps on his front legs that needed to be washed off. Another groom held the colt while Mena sprayed his legs and peeled off the tape. "We walk him now," Mensa said. From a shed he grabbed a horse blanket, threw it over Snow Chief's back, and cinched it under his belly. He was really grinning now. "Champion!" he said, with enthusiasm. The other groom put his hands to his lips, made loose fists, and pretended to be playing a trumpet. He played the trumpet call you hear before every race, and Snow Chief's ears perked up, as if he were ready for the starting gate.

The groom took the reins from Mena and walked the colt around the shed row, following a circular path. At first, Snow Chief dogged it. He seemed to be having trouble finding a rhythm, but by the third go-round he had himself in gear. The groom was singing softly to him. Who knows what the song was about? Nights in Mexico, a deserted beach, a beautiful woman with a gardenia in her hair. Maybe Snow Chief was listening, or maybe he heard something else—the warbling of finches and the cooing of doves. He went around and around, tossing his head from side to side in a contented way. What a dizzy colt! He was suspended in his own motion, endlessly delighted, full of himself.

Stute showed up after he had finished his paperwork, and he asked me if I wanted to go stand by the rail and watch the horses gallop. It was almost eight o'clock, and the morning had become warm and mild. As we strolled along, Stute greeted friends and acquaintances, and accepted some good-natured ribbing. The gist of it was that he had finally got lucky. For years, he had been a regular guy, but now he was on the brink of something more significant, and everybody was waiting to see if he would break ranks with the democratic fraternity of the backstretch and turn into a titan of the turf, like D. Wayne Lukas, who had thoroughbreds competing in several states and ran his operation with the cool authority of a corporate C.E.O.

"If I was interested in money, I'd have picked another line of work," Stute whispered, behind a hand. "There are easier ways to be a millionaire."

I wondered if he honestly thought Snow Chief could win the Derby.

"Oh, he's got a real good chance!" He paused and shook his head. "But you just never know for sure. Every horse is a mystery."

There were trainers, jockeys, grooms, and jockeys' agents hanging around the rail in front of the grandstand. The main track was a muddy mess, so the horses were on the training track, which was quite far away. You couldn't watch them properly unless you had a pair of binoculars. Stute did some business with an agent, making arrangements for a mount, and then we bought some coffee and doughnuts at Clockers' Corner.

We sat at a table outside with Warren Stute, whom Mel refers to affectionately as "a tough old bird." Warren is sixty-four, lean and wiry, and he still rode his own horses when they went for a gallop. He had a slash of dried mud clinging to his cheek. Around Mel, he shows all the hard edges of an older brother, proud and jealous by turns.

"I remember back in 1950," Warren told us, reminiscing. "I had a horse called Great Circle, who was third in the Santa Anita Derby. That was a big race even back then. Anyway, his owner wanted to send him to Kentucky and was willing to foot the bill for an express railroad car. Mel was still working for me at the time, and he got all excited. We were going to the Derby! Well, I took him aside and asked him to cool it. 'Hell, Mel,' I said. 'After this, we'll be going to the Derby every year. We've got it made!' "

"So Great Circle ran?" I asked.

Warren laughed. "No, he didn't run, after all. And when I did go to the Derby years later, I went with a fifty-to-one shot, Field Master. He ran like he was fifty-to-one! We tried to get a cab back to the hotel after the race, and there must have been six hundred people lined up outside Churchill Downs."

"I'll be staying at the Galt House down there," Mel said. He doesn't travel much, although he did once take a vacation in New Zealand. While he was there, he bought a horse.

He saw Alex Solis sitting at another table, with his agent. Solis had his riding helmet on, and he was eating a bacon-and-egg sandwich on toast.

"Tell him about Snow Chief," Stute instructed the jockey.

"That colt's very intelligent," Solis said shyly. The egg was sliding on him, about to escape from the bread, but he grabbed after it and made the rescue.

"Alex just bought a house around the corner," the agent offered. "Where is it, Alex? Next door to Eddie Delahousaye?"

"Near Eddie. Gary Stevens lives near me, too."

I pictured a whole neighborhood of jockeys, with ceramic statues of big people on their lawns.

As we talked further, Solis lost his shyness and talked about himself. A graduate of the Panama Jockey School, he won his first race in Panama City when he was seventeen, and moved to Florida a year later, where he soon developed into a hot property. His transfer to California was relatively recent, but he was already sixth in the standings at Santa Anita and thrilled to be in the presence of such greats as Laffit Pincay and Chris McCarron. He looked on his success as a chocolate sundae and Snow Chief as the cherry on top.

"When you say he's a smart colt, Alex," I wondered, "how do you know it?"

"If we're in a race and I see a hole, I ask him to go through it," he explained. "But he doesn't move right away. Instead, he waits. And the hole, it gets bigger. Then he goes."

"A dumb horse wouldn't do that?"

"No."

The sun was higher in the sky now, and I closed my eyes for a minute and felt the heat seep into my bones. Spring was in the air. When I opened my eyes again, I said, "So Alex, you like this Snow Chief?"

"I don't like him," Solis said, with a smile. "I love him."

Was There a Horse with Wings?

BY BERYL MARKHAM

In 1936, Beryl Markham (1902–1986) became the first person to fly solo across the Atlantic from east to west, an account of which may be found in her bestselling 1942 memoir, *West Into The Night*. She was born in England but grew up in East Africa where her father bred and trained racehorses. She became, at the age of eighteen, the first woman in Africa to receive a trainer's license. After a tumultuous life that included three marriages and celebrity as an aviator and writer, she returned to Africa and her love of horses. From the late fifties to the early seventies, she was the most successful racehorse trainer in Kenya.

The black book lies on my father's desk, thick and important. Its covers are a little bent; the weight of his fingers and mine have curled back its pages, but they are not yellow. The handwriting is bold—in places it is even proud as when he has inscribed such names as these: 'Little Miller—Ormolu—Véronique.' They are all Thoroughbred mares out of stock old as boulders on an English hill.

The name 'Coquette' is inscribed more soberly, with no flourish—almost with doubt. It is as if here is a girl, pretty as any, but brought by marriage into a family of respectability beyond her birth or farthest hopes.

The brief career of Coquette is, in fact, ever so slightly chequered; her background, while not obscure, suggests something less than the dazzling gentility of her stable-mates. Still, not to be English is hardly regarded as a fatal deficiency even by the English, though grave enough to warrant sympathy. Coquette is Abyssinian. She is small and golden yellow with a pure white mane and tail.

Coquette was smuggled out of Abyssinia because Abyssinians do not permit good native mares to leave their country. I do not remember who did the smuggling, but I suppose my father condoned it, in effect, when he bought her. He must have done it with one eye shut and the other on the sweet, tidy lines of her vigorous body.

My father was, and is, a law-abiding citizen of the realm, but if ever he wanders off the path of righteousness, it will not be gold or silver that enticed him, but, more likely, I think, the irresistible contours of a fine but elusive horse.

A lovely horse is always an experience to him. It is an emotional experience of the kind that is spoiled by words. He has always talked about horses, but he has never unravelled his love of them in a skein of commonplace adjectives. At seventy, in competition with the crack trainers of South Africa, his name heads the list of winners in the high-stake racing centre of Durban. In view of this and other things, I demand forgiveness for being so obviously impressed with my own parent.

He came out of Sandhurst with such a ponderous knowledge of Greek and Latin that it would have submerged a lesser man. He might have gone down like a swimmer in the sea struggling with an Alexandrian tablet under each arm, but he never let his education get the better of him. He won what prizes there were translating Ovid and Æschylus, and then took up steeplechasing until he became one of the finest amateur riders in England. He took chances on horses and on Africa; he never regretted the losses, nor boasted about the wins.

He sometimes dreamed over the thick black book—almost as I am dreaming now, now that the names are just names, and the great-grandchildren of those elegant dams and sterling sires are dispersed, like a broken family.

But all great characters come back to life if you call them—even great horses.

Coquette, in her way, was great. She won races, though she never set the world agog, but she gave me my first foal.

It all goes back to the thick black book. And that is a long way back.

It lies there, dustless, because it is too much touched, and I am grown a little now and charged with duties inflexible as a drill sergeant's, but more pleasant. I have a corporal in Kibii, but he is often away from the farm these days, engaged in new and enigmatic offices.

My personal staff still numbers two—lean Otieno and fat, fat Toombo.

It is a morning in November. Some places in the world are grey as a northern sea in November, and colder. Some are silver with ice. But not Njoro. In November, Njoro and all the Highlands await their ration of warm soft rain tendered regularly by one or another of the Native Gods—Kikuyu, Masai, Kavirondo—or by the White Man's God, or perhaps by all known Gods, working amiably together. November is a month of benison and birth.

I open the black book and run my finger down one of its freshest pages. I come to Coquette.

The book says:

COQUETTE

Date of Service	Stallion
20/1/1917	Referee

Eleven months for a mare. Bred to Referee—small, perfect, gallant as a warrior, smooth as a coin—Coquette is due to foal in a matter of days. I close the book and call for Toombo.

He comes—rather, he appears; he is a visitation in ebony. Nothing in this world of extremes is blacker than Toombo, nothing is rounder than his belly, nothing is broader than his smile. Toombo is the good jinn—the one that never got locked in the pot. He suddenly fills the doorway as if he had been set into it like a polished stone into a trinket.

'Do you want me, Beru—or is it Otieno?'

No matter how many times the name Beryl goes in the Native or Indian ear, it emerges from the lips—Beru. No English word is so smooth that the tongue trained to Swahili cannot make it smoother.

'I want both of you, Toombo. The day for Coquette is very near. We must begin the watch.'

Toombo's grin spreads over his wide face like a ripple in a pond. To him, birth and success are synonymous; the hatching of a hen's egg is a triumph, or even the bursting of a seed. Toombo's own birth is the major success of his life. He grins until there is no more room for both the grin and his eyes, so his eyes disappear. He turns and shuffles through the doorway and I hear his deep voice bawling for Otieno.

The missionaries have already pitched their tents in the Kavirondo country, which is Otieno's home. They have jousted with the old black gods and even unhorsed a few. They have traded a tangible Bible for a handful of intangible superstitions—the Kavirondo mind is fertile ground.

Otieno's Bible (translated into Jaluo, which he reads) has made him both a Christian and a night-owl. Night after night he sits in the yellow circle of his hurricane lamp and squints over the pages. He is indefatigable, sleepless, dependable as daylight—and half a mystic. I let him undertake, with Toombo, the night-watch in Coquette's box, knowing that he never nods.

He accepts the duty with pious gravity—as indeed he should. Tall and sombre-eyed, he stands where Toombo stood. If it were not morning, and if there were no work to be done, and if it were not my father's study, Otieno would sheepishly stroke the calf of his black leg with the sole of his black foot and tell me the story of Lot's wife.

'I have been reading in the Book,' he would begin, 'about a strange happening . . .'

But something more common, though perhaps as strange, is near its happening, and Otieno leaves and I close the black book and follow him down to the stables.

Ah, Coquette! How could a creature deserving such a gay name have become so dowdy? Once she was small and pert and golden, but now she is plain and shapeless with the weight of her foal. Her thin pasterns are bent with it until her fetlocks seem ready to touch the ground; her hooves are of lead. She has seen so much—the savage hills and plains of Abyssiania, all that wild and deep country on the way to Njoro, all those different people, those different races, those different rocks and trees. Coquette has seen the world, but the bright, wise eyes are not now so bright. Soon they will be wiser.

Her foaling-box is ready. Her body-brush, her dandy-brush, and her kitamba are there. Her coat is still no other colour than gold, her mane and her tail are still white silk. The gold is tarnished; the silk lacks lustre. Coquette looks at me as she enters the box—to wait, and wait.

All of us there—Toombo, Otieno, and myself—know the secret. We know what Coquette is waiting for, but she does not. None of us can tell her.

Toombo and Otieno begin their nightly watch. And the time goes slowly.

But there are other things. Everything else goes on as it always has. Nothing is more common than birth; a million creatures are born in the time it takes to turn this page, and another million die. The symbolism is commonplace; countless dreamers have played countless tunes upon the mystery, but horse-breeders are realists and every farmer is a midwife. There is no time for mystery. There is only time for patience and care, and hope that what is born is worthy and good.

I do not know why most foals are born at night, but most of them are. This one is.

Nineteen long days pass, and on the evening of the twentieth, I make the rounds of the stables, as usual, ending at Coquette's foaling-box. Buller is at my heels. Otieno The Vigilant is there—and Toombo The Rotund.

The hurricane lamp has already been lighted inside the foaling-box. It is a large box, large as a room, with walls of cedar planking milled on the farm. The floor is earthen, covered with deep grass bedding gathered fresh from the pastures; the smell of a mowed field is gathered with it.

Coquette stands heavily under the gentle glow of the lamp, her evening feed not finished. Creating new life within her, she is herself almost lifeless. She lowers her head as if it were not the exquisitely fashioned head that it is, but an ugly and tiresome burden. She nibbles at a single leaf of lucerne, too small to be tasted, then shambles on sluggish feet across the box. To her all things are poignantly lacking—but she is incapable of desiring anything.

Otieno sighs. Toombo's face beams back at the hurricane lamp, matching its glow with his glow. Outside the box, Buller challenges the oncoming night with a softly warning growl.

I bend down and lay my head against the smooth, warm belly of the mare. The new life is there. I hear and feel it, struggling already—demanding the right to freedom and growth. I hope it is perfect; I hope it is strong. It will not, at first, be beautiful.

I turn from Coquette to Otieno. 'Watch carefully. It is near.'

The tall, thin Kavirondo looks into the face of the fat one. Toombo's face is receptive—it cannot be looked at, it can only be looked into. It is a jovial and capacious bowl, often empty, but not now. Now it is filled to the brim with expectation. 'This is a good night,' he says, 'this is a good night.' Well, perhaps he is optimistic, but it proves a busy night.

I return to my hut—my new, proud hut which my father has built for me out of cedar, with real shingles instead of thatch. In it I have my first glass window, my first wood floor—and my first mirror. I have always known what I looked like—but at fifteen-odd, I become curious to know what can be done about it. Nothing, I suppose—and who would there be to know the difference? Still, at that age, few things can provoke more wonderment than a mirror.

At eight-thirty Otieno knocks.

'Come quickly. She is lying.'

Knives, twine, disinfectant—even anæsthetic—are all ready in my foaling-kit, but the last is precaution. As an Abyssinian, Coquette should have few of the difficulties that so often attend a thoroughbred mare. Still, this is Coquette's first. First things are not always easy. I snatch the kit and hurry through the cluster of huts, some dark and asleep, some wakeful with square, yellow eyes. Otieno at my heels, I reach the stable.

Coquette is down. She is flat on her side, breathing in spasmodic jerks. Horses are not voiceless in pain. A mare in the throes of birth is almost helpless, but she is able to cry out her agony. Coquette's groans, deep, tired, and a little frightened, are not really violent. They are not hysterical, but they are infinitely expressive of suffering, because they are unanswerable.

I kneel in the grass bedding and feel her soft ears. They are limp and moist in the palm of my hand, but there is no temperature. She labours heavily, looking at nothing out of staring eyes. Or perhaps she is seeing her own pain dance before them.

The time is not yet. We cannot help, but we can watch. We three can sit cross-legged—Toombo near the manger, Otieno against the cedar planking, myself near the heavy head of Coquette—and we can talk, almost tranquilly, about other things while the little brush of flame in the hurricane lamp paints experimental pictures on the wall.

'Wa-li-hie!' says Toombo.

It is as solemn as he ever gets. At the dawning of doomsday he will say no more. A single 'Walihie!' and he has shot his philosophic bolt. Having shot it, he relaxes and grins, genially, into himself.

The labouring of Coquette ebbs and flows in methodical tides of torment. There are minutes of peace and minutes of anguish, which we all feel together, but smother, for ourselves, with words.

Otieno sighs. 'The Book talks of many strange lands,' he says. 'There is one that is filled with milk and with honey. Do you think this land would be good for a man, Beru?'

Toombo lifts his shoulders. 'For which man?' he says. 'Milk is not bad food for one man, meat is better for another, *ooji* is good for all. Myself, I do not like honey.'

Otieno's scowl is mildly withering. 'Whatever you like, you like too much, Toombo. Look at the roundness of your belly. Look at the heaviness of your legs!"

Toombo looks. 'God makes fat birds and small birds, trees that are wide and trees that are thin, like wattle. He makes big kernels and little kernels. I am a big kernel. One does not argue with God.'

The theosophism defeats Otieno; he ignores the globular Jesuit slouching unperturbed under the manger, and turns again to me.

'Perhaps you have seen this land, Beru?'

'No.' I shake my head.

But then I am not sure. My father has told me that I was four when I left England. Leicestershire. Conceivably it could be the land of milk and honey, but I do not remember it as such. I remember a ship that sailed interminably up the hill of the sea and never, never reached the top. I remember a place I was later taught to think of as Mombasa, but the name has not explained the memory. It is a simple memory made only of colours and shapes, of heat and trudging people and broad-leaved trees that looked cooler than they were. All the country I know is this country—these hills, familiar as an old wish, this veldt, this forest. Otieno knows as much.

'I have never seen such a land, Otieno. Like you, I have read about it. I do not know where it is or what it means.'

'That is a sad thing,' says Otieno; 'it sounds like a good land.'

Toombo rouses himself from the stable floor and shrugs. 'Who would walk far for a kibuyu of milk and a hive of honey? Bees live in every tenth tree, and every cow has four teats. Let us talk of better things!'

But Coquette talks first of better things. She groans suddenly from the depth of her womb, and trembles. Otieno reaches at once for the hurricane lamp and swells the flame with a twist of his black fingers. Toombo opens the foaling-kit.

'Now.' Coquette says it with her eyes and with her wordless voice. 'Now—perhaps now—'

This is the moment, and the Promised Land is the forgotten one.

I kneel over the mare waiting for her foal to make its exit from oblivion. I wait for the first glimpse of the tiny hooves, the first sight of the sheath—the cloak it will wear for its great début.

It appears, and Coquette and I work together. Otieno at one of my shoulders, Toombo at the other. No one speaks because there is nothing to say.

But there are things to wonder.

Will this be a colt or a filly? Will it be sound and well-formed? Will its new heart be strong and stubborn enough to snap the tethers of nothingness that break so grudgingly? Will it breathe when it is meant to breathe? Will it have the anger to feed and to grow and to demand its needs?

I have my hands at last on the tiny legs, on the bag encasing them. It is a strong bag, transparent and sleek. Through it I see the diminutive hooves, pointed, soft as the flesh of sprouted seeds—impotent hooves, insolent in their urgency to tread the tough earth.

Gently, gently, but strong and steady, I coax the new life into the glow of the stable lamp, and the mare strains with all she has. I renew my grip, hand over hand, waiting for her muscles to surge with my pull. The nose—the head, the whole head—at last the foal itself, slips into my arms, and the silence that follows is sharp as the crack of a Dutchman's whip—and as short.

'Walihie!' says Toombo.

Otieno smears sweat from under his eyes; Coquette sighs the last pain out of her.

I let the shining bag rest on the pad of trampled grass less than an instant, then break it, giving full freedom to the wobbly little head.

I watch the soft, mouse-coloured nostrils suck at their first taste of air. With care, I slip the whole bag away, tie the cord and cut it with the knife Otieno hands me. The old life of the mare and the new life of the foal for the last time run together in a quick christening of blood, and as I bathe the wound with disinfectant, I see that he is a colt.

He is a strong colt, hot in my hands and full of the tremor of living.

Coquette stirs. She knows now what birth is; she can cope with what she knows. She lurches to her feet without gracefulness or balance, and whinnies once—so this is mine! So this is what I have borne! Together we dry the babe.

When it is done, I stand up and turn to smile at Otieno. But it is not Otieno; it is not Toombo. My father stands beside me with the air of a man who has observed more than anyone suspected. This is a scene he has witnessed more times than he can remember; yet there is bright interest in his eyes—as if, after all these years, he has at last seen the birth of a foal!

He is not a short man nor a tall one; he is lean and tough as a riem. His eyes are dark and kind in a rugged face that can be gentle.

'So there you are,' he says—'a fine job of work and a fine colt. Shall I reward you or Coquette—or both?'

Toombo grins and Otieno respectfully scuffs the floor with his toes. I slip my arm through my father's and together we look down on the awkward, angry little bundle, fighting already to gain his feet.

'Render unto Cæsar,' says my father; 'you brought him to life. He shall be yours.'

A bank clerk handles pounds of gold—none of it his own—but if, one day, that fabulous faery everyone expects, but nobody ever meets, were to give him all this gold for himself—or even a part of it—he would be no less overjoyed because he had looked at it daily for years. He would know at once (if he hadn't known it before) that this was what he had always wanted.

For years I had handled my father's horses, fed them, ridden them, groomed them, and loved them. But I had never owned one.

Now I owned one. Without even the benefit of the good fairy, but only because my father said so, I owned one for myself. The colt was to be mine, and no one could ever touch him, or ride him, or feed him, or nurse him—no one except myself.

I do not remember thanking my father; I suppose I did, for whatever words are worth. I remember that when the foaling-box was cleaned, the light turned down again, and Otieno left to watch over the newly born, I went out and walked with Buller beyond the stables and a little way down the path that used to lead to Arab Maina's.

I thought about the new colt, Otieno's Promised Land, how big the world must be, and then about the colt again. What shall I name him?

Who doesn't look upward when searching for a name? Looking up-ward, what is there but the sky to see? And seeing it, how can the name or the hope be earthbound? Was there a horse named Pegasus that flew? Was there a horse with wings?

Yes, once there was—once, long ago, there was. And now there is again.

On Winning

BY WILLIAM STEINKRAUS

The first American to win an individual Olympic equestrian gold medal, Bill Steinkraus served as captain of the United States Equestrian Team before going on to equal distinction as a Team official, commentator and author. His best-selling *Riding and Jumping*—now *Reflections On Riding And Jumping*—has been of immense theoretical and practical value now to countless riders and trainers.

When I started riding, winning wasn't thought to be all that important. It was simply something that happened if you worked hard, tried to do what teachers demanded and chose good models to copy. *Having fun* was the important thing, and even on the Olympic level, winning was explicitly subordinated to "taking part" by the Games' founder, Baron de Coubertin.

Today all this seems to have changed. Even the traditional Olympic values seem to have shifted almost 180 degrees; winning is now *really* important, for it leads to better TV ratings and a more positive "bottom line." In fact, we have all been told for some time that winning isn't just the most important thing, it's the *only* thing. (In fairness to the legendary football coach, Vince Lombardi, who supposedly was the first to utter these words, *he* always denied them, at least out of context, maintaining that the true *only* thing was *really trying.*)

Obviously there are lots of other possible attitudes towards winning, all the way from that attributed to Lombardi to the facetious "It's not whether you win or lose, it's that your best friend fails" and "it's not whether you win or lose, it's how you *look.*" In fact, everyone has a right to place an appropriate value on winning for himself, provided that he can live with his own rationalization.

145

We have already discussed specific techniques for riding different types of competitions such as speed classes, jump-off classes and puissance competitions (see Chapter Nine). In addition to these stratagems, however, there are also various broader prescriptions that can contribute to a winning formula. A very simple one, much favored by trainers at the race track, is to have the best horse. Unfortunately, this is easier said than done and usually takes a lot of money, not to mention luck. Moreover, even if you have the best horse and don't know exactly what to do with it, there's no guarantee that you'll win. For all of this, it's obviously important to be as well mounted as you can contrive to be, and not fall into the trap of spending your life on tantalizing time-wasters who offer an interesting technical challenge. Even great riders have been known to make this mistake.

If you can't necessarily always have the best horse, you can try to be the best rider, or even better, the best horseman, for then you'll have more chances to be sitting on a superior horse as well. It's observable in the show ring (if not, perhaps, the race track) that the best riders win far more than their share of competitions even when they don't happen to be sitting on the best horses. A practical way to accomplish this is by trying to eliminate reasons why you lose, whether this is winning moves your horses haven't learned to make or unsolved technical problems of your own. A cardinal principle that I have used in teaching and judging is that if the horse isn't absolutely perfect, the rider can be seen to be making the right correction, no matter how subtly. Every rider should always have an immediate answer to the question, "what are your and your horses' main faults, and what are you doing about them?" Yet all of us have seen riders who stick so stubbornly to losing techniques and tactics that they seem almost determined to fail. (And in fact, the proportion of riders in any given competition who are actually trying to win, and capable of doing so, may be quite small; many competitors are simply hoping to get around and look respectable.)

Thus many riders "make do" for their whole careers with a swinging lower leg, an upper body that snaps open the minute a horse starts its descent over a jump, a habit of invariably "lifting" horses off the ground, a crest release that prevents them from influencing the horse's trajectory in the air or its first stride after landing, and any number of other technical weaknesses that could easily be corrected in a matter of days, weeks, or at worst, months. Oh sure, talented riders sometimes win even despite weaknesses such as these, but they could win a lot more if they overcame them. It is especially sad that so many riders stop developing technically as soon as they've started to enjoy some success. "That's just the way I ride," they say of their faults, thereby condemning themselves to making the same mistakes for the rest of their riding careers.

If you don't have the best horses and haven't yet become the best horseman, there is still another winning edge you can gain, because you control all the ingredients yourself: make yourself and your horses as fit as possible. Bertalan de Némethy, the legendary USET coach, and George Morris, the legendary trainer, are famous for their scathing comments about riders who showed up for instruction "carrying a little extra weight," and through the years I have often observed the riding benefits that can accrue from being and feeling a bit leaner and hungrier. (Indeed, I have often observed them in myself.)

I used to think that just riding a lot would make you fit enough for riding, and it's certainly true that riding fitness is not the same thing as "gym" fitness. But the opposite is also true. In my view, the fitness level that comes from normal schooling is rarely enough to enable either horse or rider to meet the aerobic demands of a maximum competitive effort; only running (for the rider) and galloping (for the horse) can provide the aerobic fitness you need. How often have you seen horses and riders start to fall apart towards the end of a big course and be blowing hard when they pull up, simply because they were starting to "run out of gas" physically? I've seen it a lot, and it comes as no surprise since so much of the entry in many kinds of equestrian competition typically consists of horses and riders who are not ideally fit for the jobs expected of them.

A key winning component that can even compensate partially for some other deficiencies is simply to have the best competitive attitude. Sports psychologists make a good living these days out of speaking, writing and counseling on this subject, and though I have no academic background in it at all, I have certainly used some of the techniques they recommend. I hasten to add that my idea of a sound competitive attitude should not be confused with the idea of "positive thinking" alone, or wishing, will make your dreams come true in the absence of other key ingredients. A lot of the riders I see who are "down on themselves" deserve to be, until they lose some weight, get really fit and learn to ride better.

For me, the essential ingredients of a sound psychological attitude are a set of realistic, progressive goals, enough maturity to cope with disappointment, and an unwillingness to give up and stop working even when things are going very badly. Most losers seem to expect to lose, and when the breaks go against them, they readily accept it. Winners, in contrast, fight adversity—they struggle to help the horse jump cleanly until the rail hits the ground, and then they struggle to jump the rest of the course cleanly and see if they can't be the fastest four-faulter.

They are equally stubborn when it comes to building a sound foundation for their horses, or correcting faults in their own riding. Musicians say that the difference between the artist and the amateur is that the amateur practices a difficult passage until he plays it correctly once; the artist practices it until he never plays it wrong. And so it is with the great riders in every discipline—they never accept just doing things right occasionally.

Less successful competitors simply can't believe how hard the really good guys are willing to work. To be sure, they get very frustrated with their own problems, and have a zillion excuses to explain them. But somehow they can't accept the fact, though they see evidence of it at every show, that they're being beaten by riders who are never too tired to put out that extra little bit of effort that will enable them to excel. I used to think that people who talked about "desire" as the key ingredient in success were talking a certain amount of hot air, but I may be saying the same thing myself in different words.

It cannot be denied that a final winning ingredient can be luck, or at least, the absence of bad luck. One tends to think of luck as being quite beyond our control, and while this may be, I have always liked the comment I first heard attributed to Ben Jones, trainer of Calumet Farm's five Kentucky Derby winners: "Of course I've been lucky; in fact; the harder I work the luckier I get."

"If it takes so much hard work to excel," one may be tempted to ask, "what happens to the fun?" Believe me, riding to win and winning are more fun than riding to lose and losing. Even better, helping horses to achieve their full potential and working to achieve your own are satisfying and fulfilling, and if you can come close to accomplishing this, winning as such will take care of itself.

Buster

BY THOMAS McGUANE

Tom McGuane and I share a passion for horses and for flyfishing. However, that's where the similarity between us ends, for he is demonstrably one of this country's great novelists and essayists. Especially when writing about horses, McGuane has an unerring eye and ear that allow him to combine wise words with a style that elevates craft into art.

Almost a decade ago, I was working in what is ponderously known as the motion picture industry, which required my presence for a long spell in Los Angeles. I spent my time in script conferences with a movie star who managed to wake up in a different world each day. Sometimes our story took place high in the mountains; other times the scene moved to the desert or to a nonexistent little town that derived its features from the star's days in movie houses, when he dreamed of working on his draw instead of on his lines. Some days the Indians won, some days the law. This was about to be one of the last cowboy movies America would put up with.

But myth was something I was still interested in. And so, in the evenings, my wife and I would drive out to Chino, where our friend Joe Heim trained cutting horses. We worked cattle under the lights, an absolute anomaly in a run-down suburb. His place was very small, a couple of acres maybe, and the horses and cows were penned wherever space could be found. I particularly remember an old oak tree where we used to hang the big festoon of bridles and martingales. Joe lived in a trailer house, did his books on a desk at one end and slept in the other. On those warm nights when cattle and horses did things that required decoding, Joe would always begin, "What Buster would do here is . . ." I had never seen Buster Welch, but his attempts to understand an ideal relationship between horsemen and cattle sent ripples anywhere that cows grazed, from Alberta to the Mexican border. It would be many years before I drove into his yard in West Texas.

Buster Welch was born and more or less raised north of Sterling City, Texas, on the divide between the Concho and Colorado rivers. His mother died shortly after he was born, and he was brought up by his grandfather, a retired peace officer, and his grandmother on a stock farm in modest self-sufficiency. Buster came from a line of people who had been in Texas since before the Civil War, Tennesseans by origin. Growing up in the Roosevelt years in a part of Texas peculiarly isolated from modern times, Buster was ideally situated to understand and convey the practices of the cowboys of an earlier age to an era rapidly leaving its own mythology. The cutting horse is a sacred link to those times, and its use and performance are closer to the Japanese martial theater than to rodeo. Originally, a cutting horse was used to separate individual cattle for branding or doctoring. From the "brag" horses of those early days has evolved the cutting horse, which refines the principles of stock handling and horsemanship for the purposes of competition.

When Buster was a young boy, his father remarried and moved his wife, her two children, and Buster to Midland and worked as a tank boss for Atlantic Richfield. Buster's separation from Sterling City and his grandparents and their own linkage to the glorious past had the net result of turning Buster into a truant from the small, poor school he attended, a boy whose dreams were triggered by the herds of cattle that were trailed past the schoolhouse to the stockyards. He became a youthful bronc buster at the stockyards and was befriended by people like Claude "Big Boy" Whatley, a man so strong he could catch a horse by the tail, take hold of a post, and instruct Buster to let the other horses out of the corral. By the time Buster reached the sixth grade, he had run away a number of times, and at thirteen he ran away for keeps. In making his departure on a cold night, he led a foul old horse named Handsome Harry well away from the house so his family wouldn't hear the horse bawling when it bucked. He climbed on the horse and rode away. From there he went to work for Foy and Leonard Proctor, upright and industrious cowmen who handled as many as thirty thousand head of cattle a year. Buster began by breaking broncs, grubbing prickly pear, chopping firewood, wrangling horses, and holding the cut when a big herd was being worked, a lowly job where much can be learned.

When you see Buster's old-time herd work under the lights in Will Rogers coliseum or at the Astrodome in Houston, that is where it began. The Proctors are still alive, revered men in their nineties, descendants of trail drovers and Indian fighters. From them, Buster learned to shape large herds of cattle and began the perfection of his minimalist style of cutting horsemanship and cattle ranching in general. He worked with horses that "weren't the kind a man liked to get on." But in those early days, he was around some horses that "went on," including Jesse James, who became the world champion cutting horse. Nevertheless, he probably spent more time applying 62 Smear, a chloroform-based screwworm concoction, to afflicted cattle than to anything more obviously bound for glory.

Buster rode the rough string for the storied Four Sixes Ranch at and around Guthrie. One of the horses had been through the bronc pen two or three times and was so unrepentant that you had to ride him all day after you topped him off in the morning, relieving yourself down the horse's shoulder rather than getting off, and at the end of the day, buck down to the end of the reins, turn around, and scare the horse back before he could paw and strike you. But this was an opportunity to be around those good and important cowmen and to work cattle out with the chuck wagon or from the permanent camps on that big ranch. Buster is remembered for his white shirts and for being the only man able to ride the rough string and stay clean. Hands circulated from the Four Sixes to the Matador and the Pitchfork in what amounted to graduate schools for cowboys. Off and on in that period, Buster rode saddle broncs at the casual rodeos of the day, where the prospects for injury far outweighed the opportunity for remuneration. There was certainly in Buster's life a drive or individuality in his work that might have been realized earlier if someone had been good enough to leave him a ranch. Even by then ranches were in the hands of "sons, sons-in-law, and sons of bitches." To this day, he sees himself primarily as a rancher. But until recently, a cutting horse was an essential part of a rancher's life. Now it is quite possible for a cutting horse to never see open country; too many of them live the lives of caged birds, with an iron routine from box stall to training pen to hot walker to box stall, moving through the seasons of big-purse events to long retirement in breeding programs.

By the time Buster Welch began to establish himself as a horseman, beyond someone who could get the early saddlings on rough stock and bring a horse to some degree of finish and refinement, the cutting horse began to come into its own as a contest animal. The adversity of the Texas cattle business had a lot to do with Welch's career. His plan had always been to use his advantages in training the cutting horse to establish himself in the cow business. And he was well on his way to making that happen in the fifties, running eight hundred cows on leased land, when the drought struck. Ranches big and small, including some that had survived from the days of the frontier, vanished forever. It ruined many a stouter operator than Buster Welch. In those tough times a horse called Marion's Girl came into Buster's life. The weather focused his options, and the mare focused his talent. Buster went on the road with Marion's Girl and made her the world champion cutting horse that year, 1954. If he ever looked back, he never said so.

I spent one winter in the Deep South, working and going to weekend cuttings. I had been staying mainly in Alabama and by April was getting ready to go home to Montana. I had managed to catch a ride for my horses from Hernando, Mississippi, to Amarillo, where I wanted to make a cutting, then go on home. This all seemed ideal for paying a visit to Buster at Merkel en route.

Buster greeted me from the screen door of the bunkhouse. The ranch buildings were set among the steadily ascending hills that drew your mind forever outward into the distance. I began to understand how Buster has been able to refuel his imagination while the competition has burned out and fallen behind. There was a hum of purpose here. It was a horseman's experimental station right in the heart of the range cattle industry.

Buster and I rode the buckboard over the ranch, taking in Texas at this remote end of the Edwards Plateau. Was this the West? The South? The groves of oak trees and small springs, the sparse distribution of cattle on hillsides that seemed bountiful in a restrained sort of way, the deep wagon grooves in rock. We clattered through a dry wash in this Texas desert, where cactus and blue quail seem to belong and where one sensed that man's occupancy must be conducted delicately if it was to last.

"Nobody can ranch as cheap as I can," said Buster, leaning out over the team to scrutinize it for adjustment, the heavy latigo reins draped familiarly in his hands. "If I have to." But when we passed an old gouge in the ground, he stopped and said ruefully, "It took the old man that had this place first a lifetime to fill that trash hole up. We haul more than that away every week." Each year Buster and his wife, Sheila, win hundreds of thousands of dollars riding cutting horses but there was something about this prosperity with which he was uncomfortable.

Of the hands working on Buster's ranch, hailing from Texas, Washington, and Australia, there was an array of talent in general cow work. But so far as I could discern, nobody didn't want to be a cutting-horse trainer. There is considerable competition and activity for people interested in cutting horses in Australia, but the country is so vast, especially the cattle country, that well-educated hands go home and basically dry up for lack of seeing one another or for being unable to cope with the mileage necessary to get to cuttings. Nevertheless, such as the situation is, much of the talent in Australia grew up under

Buster's tutelage. Buster is very fond of his Australians and thinks they are like the old-time Texans who took forever to fill the trash hole behind the house. Buster has said to me several times that he would like to have lived in Australia.

Cowboys have their well-known high spirits, but under Buster's guidance they are quiet and polite. At meals, they rise, introduce themselves, shake hands, and try to be helpful. In their limited spare time these cowboys make the Saturday night run to town, or they attend Bible classes, or they hole up in the bunkhouse to listen to heavy metal on their boom boxes. Buster finds something to like in each of them: one is industrious, another is handy with machinery, another has light hands with a colt, and so on. Every time he works his horse, they watch him studiously, reminding me of the advantages of apprenticeship: there was a sharp contrast between these vigilant young men and the barely awake denizens of a college lecture hall.

Buster has been blessed by continuity and by an enormous pride in his heritage. One of his forebears rode with Fitzhugh Lee and, refusing to surrender when the Confederacy fell, was never heard from again; another fought to defend Vicksburg. Buster's grandfather was a sheriff in West Texas, still remembered with respect. There are a lot of pictures of his ancestors around the place, weathered, unsmiling Scotch-Irish faces. Buster doesn't smile for pictures either, though he spends a lot of time smiling or grinning at the idea of it all, the peculiar, delightful purposefulness of life and horses, the rightness of cattle and West Texas, but above all, the perfection and opportunity of today, the very day we have right here.

By poking around and prying among the help, I was able to determine that the orderly world I perceived as Buster's camp was something of an illusion and that there were many days that began quite unpredictably. In fact, there was the usual disarray of any artist's mise-en-scène, though we had here, instead of a squalid Parisian atelier, a cattle ranch. But I never questioned that this was an artist's place, one which moved more to inspiration than routine.

For example, the round pen. Buster invented its present use. Heretofore, cutting horses not trained on the open range—and those had become exceedingly rare—were trained in square arenas. Buster trained that way. But one day a song insistently went through his head, a song about "a string with no end," and Buster realized that that was what he was looking for, a place where the logic of a cow horse's motion and stops could go on in continuity as it once did on the open range, a place where walls and corners could never eat a horse and its rider and stop the flow. By moving from a square place of training to a circular one, Buster achieved a more accurate simulation of the range. A horse could be worked in a round place without getting mentally "burned" by tedious interruptions (corners); the same applied to the rider, and since horse and rider in cutting are almost the same thing, what applied to the goose applied to the gander. The round pen made the world of cutting better; even the cattle kept their vitality and inventiveness longer. But Buster's search for a place where the movement could be uninterrupted was something of a search for eternity, at least his eternity, which inevitably depends on a horseman tending stock. Just as the Plains Indians might memorialize the buffalo hunt in the beauty of their dancing, the rider on a cutting horse can celebrate the life of the open range forever.

Buster Welch's horses have a "look," and this matter of look, of style, is important. The National Cutting Horse Association book on judging cutting horses makes no mention of this; but it is a life-and-death factor. There are "plain" horses, or "vanilla" horses, and there are "good-moving" horses, or "scorpions." Interestingly enough, if categorization were necessary, Buster's horses tend to be plain. It is said that it takes a lot of cow to make one of his horses win a big cutting. On the other hand, his cutting horses are plain in the way that Shaker furniture is plain. They are so direct and purposeful that their eloquence of motion can be missed. Furthermore, we may be in the age of the baroque horse, the spectacular, motion-wasteful products of training pens and indoor arenas. Almost no one has the open range background of Buster Welch anymore.

Those who worked cattle for a long time on the open range learned a number of things about the motion of cow horses. A herd of cattle is a tremulous, exploding thing, as anxious to change shapes as a school of fish is. Control is a delicate matter. A horse that runs straight and stops straight doesn't scare cattle. And a straight-stopping horse won't fall with you either. Buster Welch's horses run straight and stop straight. They're heads-up, alert horses, unlikely to splay out on the floor of the arena and do something meretricious for the tourists. They are horses inspired by the job to be done and not by the ambitions of the rider. Buster has remarked that he would like to win the world championship without ever getting his horse out of a trot. That would make a bleak day for the Fort Worth Chamber of Commerce but a bright one for the connoisseur.

There were three or four people hanging around the bunkhouse when we got back from taking in the ranch. One was the daughter of a friend of mine in the Oklahoma panhandle, there with her new husband. They had all just been to a horse sale in Abilene, where they ran some young horses through. They were in shock. They just sprawled out on the benches in the dogtrot, which was a kind of breezeway, and took in what a rude surprise the price of horses had gotten to be. "Look at it this way," said Buster. "You don't have to feed those suckers anymore." He looked around at the faces. "You are the winners," he added for emphasis. There was no reaction from the "winners."

Buster is practical. He helped start the futurity for three-year-old horses because the good, broke, open horses lasted so long; the need for trainers was small and even shrinking. He thought it might be good to steal a notion from the automobile industry and build some planned obsolescence into the western cow horse. He may have underestimated our hunger for novelty.

The boom in cutting, the millions in prize money given away annually, is largely spent on the young horses, especially three- and four-year-olds. Syndicates have proliferated, and certified public accountants lead shareholders past the stalls of the assets. This year's horses spring up and vanish like Cabbage Patch dolls, and the down-the-road open horse is in danger of becoming a thing of the past, an object of salvage. If the finished open horse doesn't regain its former stature, the ironic effect of large purses for young horses and the concentration of those events in Texas will be to deprive cutting of its national character and to consign it to the minor leagues.

One of the best horses Buster ever trained is a stud named Haida's Little Pep. When Buster asked me if there was any horse in particular I wanted to ride, I said Haida's Little Pep. Buster sent a stock trailer over to Sterling City, where the horse was consorting with seventy mostly accepting mares. I couldn't wait to see the horse whose desire and ability, it had been said, had forced Buster to change his training methods. (He actually leaks some of these rumors himself.) Buster watched the men unload the stallion, in his characteristic stance: elbows back, hands slightly clenched, like a man preparing to jump into a swimming pool. Haida's Little Pep stepped from the trailer and gazed coolly around at us, a thickset sorrel stud with a demeanor of quiet confidence.

We saddled him and went into the arena. "Go ahead and cut you a cow," said Buster. Two cowboys held a small herd of cattle at one end. My thought was, What? No last-minute instructions?

I climbed aboard. Here I had a different view of this famous beast: muscle, compact horse muscle; in particular a powerful neck that developed from behind the ears, expanding back toward the saddle to disappear between my knees. The stud stood awaiting some request from me. I didn't know if, when I touched him with a spur, he was going to squeal and run through the cedar walls of the pen or just hump his back, put his head between his legs, and send me back to Montana. But he just moved off, broke but not broke to death; the cues seemed to mean enough to get him where you were going but with none of the death-defying spins of the ride-'em-and-slide-'em school. Haida's Little Pep, thus far, felt like a mannerly ranch horse. I headed for the herd.

Once among the cattle, I had a pleasant sensation of the horse moving as requested but not bobbing around trying to pick cattle himself. His deferring to me made me wonder if he was really cooperating in this enterprise at all. As I sorted a last individual, he stood so flat-footed and quiet that I asked myself if he had mentally returned from the stallion station. I put the reins down. The crossbred steer gazed back at the herd, and when he turned to look at us, Haida's Little Pep sank slowly on his hocks. When the steer bolted, the horse moved at a speed slightly more rapid than the ability of cattle to think and in four turns removed the steer's willpower and stopped him. The horse's movements were hard and sudden but so unwasteful and accurate that he was easy to ride. Because of the way this horse was broke, I began thinking about the problems of working these cattle. I immediately sensed that the horse and I had the same purpose. I've been on many other horses that produced no such feeling. There was too much discrepancy between our intentions. We wanted to cut different cattle. They didn't want to hold and handle cattle; they wanted to chase them. They didn't want to stop straight; they wanted to round their turns and throw me onto the saddle horn. But this high-powered little stud was correct, flat natural, well intentioned, and extremely easy to ride.

We looked at some old films in Buster's living room. They were of Marion's Girl, whom Buster had trained in the fifties, the mare who had done a lot to change the rest of his life. I had long heard about her, but I remember Buster describing her to me for the first time at a cutting on Sweet Grass Creek in Montana. The ranch there was surrounded by a tall, steep bluff covered with bunchgrass and prickly pear; it was maybe a thousand feet high and came down to the floor of the valley at a steep angle. Buster had said that Marion's Girl would run straight down something like that to head a cow, stop on her rear end, and slide halfway to the bottom before turning around to drive the cow. As all great trainers feel about all great horses, Buster felt that Marion's Girl had trained him; more explicitly, she had trained him to train the modern cutting horse. At that time most cutting horses kind of ran sideways and never stopped quite straight. Buster considered that to be a degraded period during which the proper practices of the open range were forgotten. Marion's Girl, like some avatar from the past, ran hard, stopped straight, and turned through herself without losing ground to cattle.

As I watched the old film, I could see this energetic and passionate mare working in what looked like an old corral. Though she has been dead for many years, the essence of the modern cow horse was there, move after move. In the film Buster looked like a youngster, but he bustled familiarly around with his elbows cocked, ready to dive into the pool.

"Are horses smart or dumb?" I asked Buster.

"They are very smart," he said with conviction. "Very intelligent. And if you ask one to do something he was going to do anyway, you hurt his feelings, you insult his intelligence."

Everyone wants to know what Buster Welch's secret in training horses is; and that's it. Only it's not a secret. All you need to know is what the horse was going to do anyway. But to understand that, it may be necessary to go back forty years and sit next to your bedroll in front of the Scharbauer Hotel in Midland, waiting for some cowman to come pick you up. If you got a day's work, it might be on a horse that would just love to kill you. It was a far cry from the National Cutting Horse Association Futurity, but it was the sort of thing Buster began with, and it lies at the origins of his education as to what horses are going to do anyway.

I stayed in the living room to talk to Sheila Welch while, outside the picture window, horses warmed up in the cedar pen. Sheila is a cool beauty, a fine-boned blonde from Wolf Point, Montana, and a leading interpreter, through her refined horsemanship, of Buster's training. She is capable of looking better on Buster's horses than he does and certainly could train a horse herself. Cutting horses move hard and fast enough to make rag dolls of ordinary horsemen, but Sheila goes beyond poise to a kind of serenity. A little bit later, Sheila stood in the pen waiting for someone to give her the big sorrel horse she has used to dispirit the competition for years. When he was brought up, she slipped up into the saddle, eased into the herd, and imperceptibly isolated a single cow in front of her. The horse worked the cow with the signature speed and hard stops; Sheila seemed to float along cooperatively and forcefully at once. But I noticed that in the stops, those places where it is instinctive to grip with one's leg and where it is preferable not to touch the horse at all, there was a vague jingling sound. What was that vague jingling sound? It was the sound of iron stirrups rattling on Sheila's boots.

At its best, the poetry of the open range remains, not in the scared, melodramatic antics of the stunt horses but in the precision of that minority singled out as "cow horses," sometimes lost in the artificial atmosphere of the big events.

For years, I have tried to understand Buster's way of training horses. In the age of proliferating horse whisperers, his methods are direct, based on reaching an understanding with the horse that there is a job to be done. In this sense, he is not seeking companionship with horses, though his relationship with horses he likes, such as his all-around using horse Enchilada, is equivalent to the consistent respect one accords an esteemed co-worker. In the beginning of training a cow horse, the horseman knows the job and the horse does not. Therefore, a progression of steps toward wider understanding is devised: trailing a cow, driving a cow, anticipating a cow, and so on. This part can be fairly easily understood by one undertaking the training of a cow horse. Less easy is knowing horses well enough to know the rate at which the horse can absorb the learning, and knowing when the learning has stuck sufficiently that interdependent further steps may be taken. Timing is also critical; one is inclined to say that it is everything, except that some trainers with good principles, good consistency, good work habits, and good understanding of the horse get along quite well with merely adequate timing. That is, their sense of timing is sufficient to take the horse to the level at which the trainer may gracefully retire from suggestion making and let the horse's own timing rise to the fore. This is known as "getting out of the way" or, more to the point, "letting the cow train the horse." Once this stage has been reached, the most important issue is riding the horse correctly. I once gave Eugen Herrigel's little masterpiece *Zen in the Art of Archery* to Buster to read and he concluded that its application to horsemanship was that if you are thinking about your riding you are interfering with your horse.

Interfering with your horse. Therein lies the core of respect Buster Welch has for horses. A rider may train a horse to understand the basic parameters of cow work but then the opportunity must exist for the horse to make his contribution. The great Canadian trainer Dave MacGregor told me that years ago when they would drive four- and five-year-old wild horses from the open range in Alberta into the corral where they were to be trained, these unbroke horses ran full tilt and made long sliding, straight stops of the kind trainers tear their hair out trying to produce in their mounts. His point, like Buster's, is that a horse can already do many of the things we require of it, if we would just get out of the way and let them do it. Avoiding this redundancy is at the heart of Buster's training. Therefore, when a horse is working as he should, it is essential that the rider take a light and relaxed seat in the saddle, with a rein hand that is assuredly down on the horse's neck and with eyes focused on the same thing the horse is watching, the cow. If no training is required, the rider's body, in Buster's words, "should have no opinion." If it becomes necessary to "call on" the horse, that is, ask him to do something more, the rider shouldn't overspecify the request by special leg pressure or fancy spurring but merely "knock" the horse, a kind of reminder in the form of a light kick, which instead of offering specific instruction to the horse honors the horse by saying, "Come on, you know what I'm talking about." These sorts of communications in which the horse is treated as knowing a great deal about the job to be done have the result of leaving the brightness and originality of the horse, its indelible spirit and vigor, there for all to see, rather than that spectacle of obedience, of compliance, in an animal that is all too trained. Buster has isolated the irreducible basics of cow work, the straight run, the hard stop, "rating," or the quick estimation of the cow's speed, and made them the ABC's of training. Within these requirements, the horse may indulge the intricacies of his own ideas of how things are to be done. It is here that we see with delight how different one horse is from another.

I am sometimes concerned that the kind of cutting horse that Buster Welch advocates is becoming a thing of the past but there are enough good hands who feel as I do that the day may be long in coming. I recall watching a spectacular horse at the Augusta Futurity, a real crowd pleaser, who sat way down onto the root of his tail getting turned, or spun around, in effect overreacting to the cow, whose danger to him was greatly emphasized by much spurring. Buster watched bemusedly and said, "I don't know any situation, indoors or out, where that is a good way to handle a cow." Yet, it was a winning look. Later, we watched Miss Silver Pistol at a cutting in Amarillo. Here again was a belly crawling, overrevved, thoroughly passionate horse, one of the great winners of modern times. I sat watching with an Englishman, a literary man, who had never seen a cow horse before and had just watched about a hundred of them; yet, he was startled into attention by this mare. Buster commented, "This cuttin's gettin' to be more and more like professional wrestling but *damn* that Miss Silver Pistol can moan and pound the mat!" He has stated that today's horses break so far in heading a cow that you wonder if the cow will ever *catch* the horse.

There is a kind of sweet spot on a cow when you are running across the ground trying to hold her. You basically try to keep the nose of your horse at the juncture of the cow's neck and shoulder. This generally, in a stride or two, will turn the cow. Of course it can transpire at blazing speed. In the classic style, the horse, through swiftness, quick stops, and general agility, maintains this position. A riskier and more spectacular way of stopping a cow is by simply heading it; that is, driving the horse far enough past the cow that the cow turns to go the other way. This results in broader and more extreme movements, left and right, in stopping the cow. Stopping cattle as close to immediately as possible is the contemporary style. Since cattle are unpredictable this style often results in the abandoned, crowd-pleasing runs that win today's cuttings. "To win," says one top modern trainer, "your horse needs to be ginnin' around."

Buster's dream of winning the world without getting his horse out of a trot does not fit this approach.

In the modern method, a horse does not simply rate and stop with a cow. After the cow and horse have stopped, the trainer may "take the horse across" the cow, bringing the horse to a position whereby it faces in the opposite direction of the cow, then returning the horse to the center of the cow. As this becomes muscle memory, a horse runs and stops with the cow, then immediately jumps up into the middle of the cow. Instead of a neat and finished movement, one is presented with a quick, synchronized double motion that suggests that the job of the cutting horse is not so much to control the cow but to challenge it. When properly accomplished it is a glorious thing to observe, attesting to heightened athleticism and a kind of glittering commentary on the idea of cow work. Indeed, the creative side of a horse's nature may be more visible in this style, as it is considerably less restrained.

On the other hand, it is very far from the work of the ranch and while this latest version of the cutting horse is a delight to present to a judge on the cultivated footing of a modern arena, this same horse would be an absolute nightmare with which to work cattle on the open range. The rider, though moving few cattle to their objectives, would end the day with raw buttocks and an enhanced sense of futility. Without a sanctioned judge to reward him, he might feel that quieter sports beckoned.

In training horses, Buster's advantage is a broader base of knowledge from which to draw. He frequently starts out under a tree at daybreak with a cup of coffee, reading history, fiction, politics, anything that seems to expand his sense of the world he lives in. This may be a compensatory habit from his abbreviated formal education, and it may be an echo of his revered grandfather's own love of books. In any event, Buster has made of himself far and away the most educated cutting-horse trainer there is. In any serious sense, he is vastly more learned than many of his clients, however exalted their stations in life. And apart from the intrinsic merits of his knowledge, there is a place for it in Buster's work; because an unbroke horse is original unmodeled clay that can be brought to a level of great beauty or else remain in its original muddy form, dully consuming protein with the great mass of living creatures on the planet, but a cutting horse is a work of art. Buster Welch once described his great champion Little Peppy as "the clearest-minded horse that ever looked through a bridle."

I think Buster was looking through the same bridle.

All Things Bright and Beautiful

BY JAMES HERRIOT

J ames Herriot's accounts of life as a Yorkshire veterinarian made his four "All Creatures" books perennial best sellers. They deserved all their success, as shown by this selection from *All Things Bright and Beautiful* on the decline of the draft horse in rural North of England agriculture.

Probably the most dramatic occurrence in the history of veterinary practice was the disappearance of the draught horse. It is an almost incredible fact that this glory and mainstay of the profession just melted quietly away within a few years. And I was one of those who were there to see it happen.

When I first came to Darrowby the tractor had already begun to take over, but tradition dies hard in the agricultural world and there were still a lot of horses around. Which was just as well because my veterinary education had been geared to things equine with everything else a poor second. It had been a good scientific education in many respects but at times I wondered if the people who designed it still had a mental picture of the horse doctor with his top hat and frock coat busying himself in a world of horse-drawn trams and brewers' drays.

We learned the anatomy of the horse in great detail, then that of the other animals much more superficially. It was the same with the other subjects; from animal husbandry with such insistence on a thorough knowledge of shoeing that we developed into amateur blacksmiths—right up to medicine and surgery where it was much more important to know about glanders and strangles than canine distemper. Even as we were learning, we youngsters knew it was ridiculous, with the draught horse already cast as a museum piece and the obvious potential of cattle and small animal work.

Still, as I say, after we had absorbed a vast store of equine lore it was a certain comfort that there were still a lot of patients on which we could try it out. I should think in my first two years I treated farm horses nearly every day and though I never was and never will be an equine expert there was a strange thrill in meeting with the age-old conditions whose names rang down almost from mediaeval times. Quittor, fistulous withers, poll evil, thrush, shoulder slip—vets had been wrestling with them for hundreds of years using very much the same drugs and procedures as myself. Armed with my firing iron and box of blister I plunged determinedly into what had always been the surging mainstream of veterinary life.

And now, in less than three years the stream had dwindled, not exactly to a trickle but certainly to the stage where the final dry-up was in sight. This meant, in a way, a lessening of the pressures on the veterinary surgeon because there is no doubt that horse work was the roughest and most arduous part of our life.

So that today, as I looked at the three year old gelding it occurred to me that this sort of thing wasn't happening as often as it did. He had a long tear in his flank where he had caught himself on barbed wire and it gaped open whenever he moved. There was no getting away from the fact that it had to be stitched.

The horse was tied by the head in his stall, his right side against the tall wooden partition. One of the farm men, a hefty six footer, took a tight hold of the head collar and leaned back against the manger as I puffed some iodoform into the wound. The horse didn't seem to mind, which was a comfort because he was a massive animal emanating an almost tangible vitality and power. I threaded my needle with a length of silk, lifted one of the lips of the wound and passed it through. This was going to be no trouble, I thought as I lifted the flap at the other side and pierced it, but as I was drawing the needle through, the gelding made a convulsive leap and I felt as though a great wind had whistled across the front of my body. Then, strangely, he was standing there against the wooden boards as if nothing had happened.

On the occasions when I have been kicked I have never seen it coming. It is surprising how quickly those great muscular legs can whip out. But there was no doubt he had had a good go at me because my needle and silk were nowhere to be seen, the big man at the head was staring at me with wide eyes in a chalk white face and the front of my clothing was in an extraordinary state. I was wearing a 'gaberdine mac' and it looked as if somebody had taken a razor blade and painstakingly cut the material into narrow strips which hung down in ragged strips to ground level. The great iron-shod hoof had missed my legs by an inch or two but my mac was a write-off.

I was standing there looking around me in a kind of stupor when I heard a cheerful hail from the doorway.

'Now then, Mr. Herriot, what's he done at you?' Cliff Tyreman, the old horseman, looked me up and down with a mixture of amusement and asperity.

'He's nearly put me in hospital, Cliff,' I replied shakily. 'About the closest near miss I've ever had. I just felt the wind of it.'

'What were you tryin' to do?'

'Stitch that wound, but I'm not going to try any more. I'm off to the surgery to get a chloroform muzzle.'

The little man looked shocked. 'You don't need no chloroform. I'll haul him and you'll have no trouble.'

'I'm sorry, Cliff.' I began to put away my suture materials, scissors and powder. 'You're a good bloke, I know, but he's had one go at me and he's not getting another chance. I don't want to be lame for the rest of my life.'

The horseman's small, wiry frame seemed to bunch into a ball of aggression. He thrust forward his head in a characteristic posture and glared at me. 'I've never heard owt as daft in me life.' Then he swung round on the big man who was still hanging on to the horse's head, the ghastly pallor of his face now tinged with a delicate green. 'Come on out o' there, Bob! You're that bloody scared you're upsetting t'oss. Come on out of it and let me have 'im!'

Bob gratefully left the head and, grinning sheepishly moved with care along the side of the horse. He passed Cliff on the way and the little man's head didn't reach his shoulder.

Cliff seemed thoroughly insulted by the whole business. He took hold of the head collar and regarded the big animal with the disapproving stare of a schoolmaster at a naughty child. The horse, still in the mood for trouble, laid back his ears and began to plunge about the stall, his huge feet clattering ominously on the stone floor, but he came to rest quickly as the little man upper-cutted him furiously in the ribs.

'Get stood up straight there, ye big bugger. What's the matter with ye?' Cliff barked and again he planted his tiny fist against the swelling barrel of the chest, a puny blow which the animal could scarcely have felt but which reduced him to quivering submission. 'Try to kick, would you, eh? I'll bloody fettle you!' He shook the head collar and fixed the horse with a hypnotic stare as he spoke. Then he turned to me. 'You can come and do your job, Mr Herriot, he won't hurt tha.'

I looked irresolutely at the huge, lethal animal. Stepping open-eyed into dangerous situations is something vets are called upon regularly to do and I suppose we all react differently. I know there were times when an over-vivid imagination made me acutely aware of the dire possibilities and now my mind seemed to be dwelling voluptuously on the frightful power in those enormous shining quarters, on the unyielding flintiness of the spatulate feet with their rim of metal. Cliff's voice cut into my musings.

'Come on, Mr Herriot, I tell ye he won't hurt tha.'

I reopened my box and tremblingly threaded another needle. I didn't seem to have much option; the little man wasn't asking me, he was telling me. I'd have to try again.

I couldn't have been a very impressive sight as I shuffled forwards, almost tripping over the tattered hula-hula skirt which dangled in front of me, my shaking hands reaching out once more for the wound, my heart thundering in my ears. But I needn't have worried. It was just as the little man had said; he didn't hurt me. In fact he never moved. He seemed to be listening attentively to the muttering which Cliff was directing into his face from a few inches' range. I powdered and stitched and clipped as though working on an anatomical specimen. Chloroform couldn't have done it any better.

As I retreated thankfully from the stall and began again to put away my instruments the monologue at the horse's head began to change its character. The menacing growl was replaced by a wheedling, teasing chuckle.

'Well, ye see, you're just a daft awd bugger, getting yourself all airigated over nowt. You're a good lad, really, aren't ye, a real good lad.' Cliff's hand ran caressingly over the neck and the towering animal began to nuzzle his cheek, as completely in his sway as any Labrador puppy.

When he had finished he came slowly from the stall, stroking the back, ribs, belly and quarters, even giving a playful tweak at the tail on parting while what had been a few minutes ago an explosive mountain of bone and muscle submitted happily.

I pulled a packet of Gold Flake from my pocket. 'Cliff, you're a marvel. Will you have a cigarette?'

'It 'ud be like givin' a pig a strawberry,' the little man replied, then he thrust forth his tongue on which reposed a half-chewed gobbet of tobacco. 'It's allus there. Ah push it in fust thing every mornin' soon as I get out of bed and there it stays. You'd never know, would you?'

I must have looked comically surprised because the dark eyes gleamed and the rugged little face split into a delighted grin. I looked at that grin—boyish, invincible—and reflected on the phenomenon that was Cliff Tyreman.

In a community in which toughness and durability was the norm he stood out as something exceptional. When I had first seen him nearly three years ago barging among cattle, grabbing their noses and hanging on effortlessly, I had put him down as an unusually fit middle-aged man; but he was in fact nearly seventy. There wasn't much of him but he was formidable; with his long arms swinging, his stumping, pigeon-toed gait and his lowered head he seemed always to be butting his way through life.

'I didn't expect to see you today,' I said. 'I heard you had pneumonia.'

He shrugged. 'Aye, summat of t'sort. First time I've ever been off work since I was a lad.'

'And you should be in your bed now, I should say.' I looked at the heaving chest and partly open mouth. 'I could hear you wheezing away when you were at the horse's head.'

'Nay, I can't stick that nohow. I'll be right in a day or two.' He seized a shovel and began busily clearing away the heap of manure behind the horse, his breathing loud and sterterous in the silence.

Harland Grange was a large, mainly arable farm in the low country at the foot of the Dale, and there had been a time when this stable had had a horse standing in every one of the long row of stalls. There had been over twenty with at least twelve regularly at work, but now there were only two, the young horse I had been treating and an ancient grey called Badger.

Cliff had been head horseman and when the revolution came he turned to tractoring and other jobs around the farm with no fuss at all. This was typical of the reaction of thousands of other farm workers throughout the country; they didn't set up a howl at having to abandon the skills of a lifetime and start anew—they just got on with it. In fact, the younger men seized avidly upon the new machines and proved themselves natural mechanics.

But to the old experts like Cliff, something had gone. He would say: 'It's a bloody sight easier sitting on a tractor—it used to play 'ell with me feet walking up and down them fields all day.' But he couldn't lose his love of horses; the fellow feeling between working man and working beast which had grown in him since childhood and was in his blood forever.

My next visit to the farm was to see a fat bullock with a piece of turnip stuck in his throat but while I was there, the farmer, Mr Gilling, asked me to have a look at old Badger.

'He's had a bit of a cough lately. Maybe it's just his age, but see what you think.'

The old horse was the sole occupant of the stable now. 'I've sold the three year old,' Mr Gilling said. 'But I'll still keep the old 'un—he'll be useful for a bit of light carting.'

I glanced sideways at the farmer's granite features. He looked the least sentimental of men but I knew why he was keeping the old horse. It was for Cliff.

'Cliff will be pleased, anyway,' I said.

Mr Gilling nodded. 'Aye, I never knew such a feller for 'osses. He was never happier than when he was with them.' He gave a short laugh. 'Do you know, I can remember years ago when he used to fall out with his missus he'd come down to this stable of a night and sit among his 'osses. Just sit here for hours on end looking at 'em and smoking. That was before he started chewing tobacco.'

'And did you have Badger in those days?'

'Aye, we bred him. Cliff helped at his foaling—I remember the little beggar came arse first and we had a bit of a job pullin' him out.' He smiled again. 'Maybe that's why he was always Cliff's favourite. He always worked Badger himself—year in year out—and he was that proud of 'im that if he had to take him into the town for any reason he'd plait ribbons into his mane and hang all his brasses on him first.' He shook his head reminiscently.

The old horse looked round with mild interest as I went up to him. He was in his late twenties and everything about him suggested serene old age; the gaunt projection of the pelvic bones, the whiteness of face and muzzle, the sunken eye with its benign expression. As I was about to take his temperature he gave a sharp, barking cough and it gave me the first clue to his ailment. I watched the rise and fall of his breathing for a minute or two and the second clue was there to be seen; further examination was unnecessary.

'He's broken winded, Mr Gilling,' I said. 'Or he's got pulmonary emphysema to give it its proper name. Do you see that double lift of the abdomen as he breathes out? That's because his lungs have lost their elasticity and need an extra effort to force the air out.'

'What's caused it, then?'

'Well it's to do with his age, but he's got a bit of cold on him at the moment and that's brought it out.'

'Will he get rid of it in time?' the farmer asked.

'He'll be a bit better when he gets over his cold, but I'm afraid he'll never be quite right. I'll give you some medicine to put in his drinking water which will alleviate his symptoms.' I went out to the car for a bottle of the arsenical expectorant mixture which we used then.

It was about six weeks later that I heard from Mr Gilling again. He rang me about seven o'clock one evening.

'I'd like you to come out and have a look at old Badger,' he said.

'What's wrong? Is it his broken wind again?'

'No, it's not that. He's still got the cough but it doesn't seem to bother him much. No, I think he's got a touch of colic. I've got to go out but Cliff will attend to you.'

The little man was waiting for me in the yard. He was carrying an oil lamp. As I came up to him I exclaimed in horror.

'Good God, Cliff, what have you been doing to yourself?' His face was a patchwork of cuts and scratches and his nose, almost without skin, jutted from between two black eyes.

He grinned through the wounds, his eyes dancing with merriment. 'Came off me bike t'other day. Hit a stone and went right over handlebars, arse over tip.' He burst out laughing at the very thought.

'But damn it, man, haven't you been a doctor? You're not fit to be out in that state.'

'Doctor? Nay, there's no need to bother them fellers. It's nowt much.' He fingered a gash on his jaw. 'Ah lapped me chin up for a day in a bit o' bandage, but it's right enough now.'

I shook my head as I followed him into the stable. He hung up the oil lamp then went over to the horse.

'Can't reckon t'awd feller up,' he said. 'You'd think there wasn't much ailing him but there's summat.'

There were no signs of violent pain but the animal kept transferring his weight from one hind foot to the other as if he did have a little abdominal discomfort. His temperature was normal and he didn't show symptoms of anything else.

I looked at him doubtfully. 'Maybe he has a bit of colic. There's nothing else to see, anyway. I'll give him an injection to settle him down.'

'Right you are, maister, that's good.' Cliff watched me get my syringe out then he looked around him into the shadows at the far end of the stable.

'Funny seeing only one 'oss standing here. I remember when there was a great long row of 'em and the barfins and bridles hangin' there on the stalls and the rest of the harness behind them all shinin' on t'wall.' He transferred his plug of tobacco to the other side of his mouth and smiled. 'By gaw, I were in here at six o'clock every morning feedin' them and gettin' them ready for work and ah'll tell you it was a sight to see us all goin' off ploughing at the start o' the day. Maybe six pairs of 'osses setting off with their harness jinglin' and the ploughmen sittin' sideways on their backs. Like a regular procession it was.'

I smiled. 'It was an early start, Cliff.'

'Aye, by Gaw, and a late finish. We'd bring the 'osses home at night and give 'em a light feed and take their harness off, then we'd go and have our own teas and we'd be back 'ere again afterwards, curry-combing and dandy-brushin' all the sweat and dirt off 'em. Then we'd give them a right good stiff feed of chop and oats and hay to set 'em up for the next day.'

'There wouldn't be much left of the evening then, was there?'

'Nay, there wasn't. It was about like work and bed, I reckon, but it never bothered us.'

I stepped forward to give Badger the injection, then paused. The old horse had undergone a slight spasm, a barely perceptible stiffening of the muscles, and as I looked at him he cocked his tail for a second then lowered it.

'There's something else here,' I said. 'Will you bring him out of his stall, Cliff, and let me see him walk across the yard.'

And watching him clop over the cobbles I saw it again; the stiffness, the raising of the tail. Something clicked in my mind. I walked over and rapped him under the chin and as the membrana nictitans flicked across his eye then slid slowly back I knew.

I paused for a moment. My casual little visit had suddenly become charged with doom.

'Cliff,' I said. 'I'm afraid he's got tetanus.'

'Lockjaw, you mean?'

'That's right. I'm sorry, but there's no doubt about it. Has he had any wounds lately—especially in his feet?'

'Well he were dead lame about a fortnight ago and blacksmith let some matter out of his hoof. Made a right big 'ole.'

There it was. 'It's a pity he didn't get an anti-tetanus shot at the time,' I said. I put my hand into the animal's mouth and tried to prise it open but the jaws were clamped tightly together. 'I don't suppose he's been able to eat today.'

'He had a bit this morning but nowt tonight. What's the lookout for him, Mr Herriot?'

What indeed? If Cliff had asked me the same question today I would have been just as troubled to give him an answer. The facts are that seventy to eighty per cent of tetanus cases die and whatever you do to them in the way of treatment doesn't seem to make a whit of difference to those figures. But I didn't want to sound entirely defeatist.

'It's a very serious condition as you know, Cliff, but I'll do all I can. I've got some antitoxin in the car and I'll inject that into his vein and if the spasms get very bad I'll give him a sedative. As long as he can drink there's a chance for him because he'll have to live on fluids—gruel would be fine.'

For a few days Badger didn't get any worse and I began to hope. I've seen tetanus horses recover and it is a wonderful experience to come in one day and find that the jaws have relaxed and the hungry animal can once more draw food into its mouth.

But it didn't happen with Badger. They had got the old horse into a big loose box where he could move around in comfort and each day as I looked over the half door I felt myself willing him to show some little sign of improvement; but instead, after that first few days he began to deteriorate. A sudden movement or the approach of any person would throw him into a violent spasm so that he would stagger stiff-legged round the box like a big wooden toy, his eyes terrified, saliva drooling from between his fiercely clenched teeth. One morning I was sure he would fall and I suggested putting him in slings. I had to go back to the surgery for the slings and it was just as I was entering Skeldale House that the phone rang.

It was Mr Gilling. 'He's beat us to it, I'm afraid. He's flat out on the floor and I doubt it's a bad job, Mr Herriot. We'll have to put him down, won't we?'

'I'm afraid so.'

'There's just one thing. Mallock will be taking him away but old Cliff says he doesn't want Mallock to shoot 'im. Wants you to do it. Will you come?'

I got out the humane killer and drove back to the farm, wondering at the fact that the old man should find the idea of my bullet less repugnant than the knacker man's. Mr Gilling was waiting in the box and by his side Cliff, shoulders hunched, hands deep in his pockets. He turned to me with a strange smile.

'I was just saying to t'boss how grand t'awd lad used to look when I got 'im up for a show. By Gaw you should have seen him with 'is coat polished and the feathers on his legs scrubbed as white as snow and a big blue ribbon round his tail.'

'I can imagine it, Cliff,' I said. 'Nobody could have looked after him better.'

He took his hands from his pockets, crouched by the prostrate animal and for a few minutes stroked the white-flecked neck and pulled at the ears while the old sunken eye looked at him impassively.

He began to speak softly to the old horse but his voice was steady, almost conversational, as though he was chatting to a friend.

'Many's the thousand miles I've walked after you, awd lad, and many's the talk we've had together. But I didn't have to say much to tha, did I? I reckon you knew every move I made, everything I said. Just one little word and you always did what ah wanted you to do.'

He rose to his feet. 'I'll get on with me work now, boss,' he said firmly, and strode out of the box.

I waited awhile so that he would not hear the bang which signaled the end of Badger, the end of the horses of Harland Grange and the end of the sweet core of Cliff Tyreman's life.

As I was leaving I saw the little man again. He was mounting the iron seat of a roaring tractor and I shouted to him above the noise.

'The boss says he's going to get some sheep in and you'll be doing a bit of shepherding. I think you'll enjoy that.'

Cliff's undefeated grin flashed out as he called back to me.

'Aye, I don't mind learnin' summat new. I'm nobbut a lad yet.'

Tips on Horses

BY RING LARDNER

No horse anthology would be complete without at least one dour view of the species. The columnist Ring Lardner (1885–1933) trains his cynical—some might say realistic—sights on the subject in this pithy yet trenchant essay.

Once in every so often the undersized receives a circular from the Horse Breeders assn. of America or something along with a request to give same all possible publicity to the end that peoples' interest in horses will be revived and roused up and not allow the genus equine to become extinct in our land from lack of attention. And just as often as one of these literary broadsides hits my happy home just so often do I feel it incumbrance upon myself to come out flat-footed and open and above the boards and state my attitude towards what is known in exclusive livery stable circles as his highness le Horse.

Children, dogs and horses is regarded in this country as sacred items and it is considered pretty close to a felony to even make a face when any of the 3 is mentioned. Well, I am fond of children, well at least 4 of them and can tolerate a few dogs provided they can keep their mouth shut and ain't over a ft. high. But irregardless and less majesty and the deuce with same, I can't help from admitting at this junction that the bear mention of a horse has the same effect on me like red flags to a bull or ginger ale to a Elk.

A horse is the most overestimated animal in the world with the possible exception of a police dog. For every incidence where a horse has saved a human life I can dig you up a 100 incidents where they have killed people by falling off them or trampling them down or both. Personly, the only horse who

I ever set on their back throwed me off on my bosom before I had road him 20 ft. and did the horse wait to see if I was hurt, no.

Devotees of horse flesh is wont to point out that King Richard III once offered his kingdom for one of them, but in the first place he was not the kind of a person who I would pin any faith on his judgment of values and in the second place the kingdom had been acquired by a couple of mild little murders and it was a case of easy come, easy go.

A study of some of the expressions in usage at the present day will serve to throw light on the real personality of the horse. Take for example the phrase "eat like a horse." The picture you get from these phrases is the picture of anybody eating without no regard to ethics or good manners, the picture of a person who you would as leaf have at the table as they.

Or take "horse laugh." This indicates the coarsest, roughest kind of a laugh and a person of breeding and refinement would pretty near as soon have their friends give them a head cold as the horse laugh. Or "horse play." How often do you hear theatre-goers complain that such and such a comedy has got too much horse play or observe parents order their kiddies to cut out the horse play. The answer is that a horse can't play nice like kittens or oxen or even wolfs, but has got to be ribald and rough in their sports as in everything else.

Defenders of le Horse will no doubt point to the term "good, common horse sense," or the simile "work like a horse," as being proof of the beast's virtues, but if a horse has got such good common sense, why do they always have to have a jockey show them the way round a fenced in race track where you couldn't possibly go wrong unless you was dumb as for working like a horse, I never met a horse who worked because he thought it was funny. They work for the same reason the rest of us works.

I will pass over to what different horses has done to me in places like Saratoga, Belmont, Havana and New Orleans. Suffice it to say that none of them ever lived up to what I had been led to believe. And one day just last month I had to walk across 34th street in N.Y. city and dodged my way amongst taxi cabs, motor trucks, and street cars and was just congratulating myself on making the trip unscathed when a horse reached out and snapped at me, a stranger.

Horses ain't been no good in battle since trench warfare come into its own and besides you never heard of a horse volunteering for a army. And do you think Paul Revere even would of looked at a horse if all the taxis hadn't been engaged with the theatre crowds that night?

Last but not lease, have you ever been bit by a horse fly, which never would of been thought of only for his highness le Horse.

The Champion

BY GENE SMITH

Gene Smith was much acclaimed in American history circles for his scrupulously researched and well written biographies, including *When the Cheering Stopped*. Smith's passion for horse racing was revealed in his account of becoming an owner, *The Champion*. The title is somewhat ironic, as the animal he owned never lived up to its turf potential. Nevertheless, as this selection from the book shows, a Thoroughbred needn't cross the finish line first to demonstrate a great and generous heart.

The horse professional Diane Schoonmaker represented the eleventh generation of her family to live on their farm near New Paltz, New York. The first owner, her ancestor, had bought the place in 1680. For years and years they had dairy herds; then they shifted to vegetable production. As a young child she had no interest in horses, but when she was twelve a girl friend got her involved. She went on to a degree in equine studies at Cazenovia College near Syracuse, came back home, got married, gave birth. She set up as a teaching professional specializing in children. She had about a dozen or so regular students. In the fall of 1984 when not working with the kids, she drilled Owen Smith.

It seemed to her that the choppiness of his trot was related to the injuries he had sustained in our barn. He would go to push off on his damaged rear left leg, what is called the strike-off leg, would find it difficult and would shift to his right. But he could not do that if he were to carry handicapped children; he would throw their balance completely off. He had to keep going in a regular rhythm uninterrupted by a sudden jounce. So she worked with him to keep him going on one lead. Each day he got better. "I never saw a horse who would progress so every day. And every day he seemed to say, 'What're we doing today, what can I do for you?'"

173

She taught him to keep on one lead and to strengthen his stride so as to tone down the up-and-down action of his trot. He learned to balance himself, to find his balance and to work into it. She asked a little more each day, never too much. When after a workout she unsaddled him, she let him roam free about an unfenced field. She sensed he would not run off, that there was no need to confine him. "He seemed content to stick around," she told us later. "He didn't seem likely to want to escape the scene. He knew I trusted him to relax and stay."

That was what he was doing the morning we arrived, a month after we gave him to her. Free, untethered, unhobbled, he was munching grass outside her riding ring.

"This *is* embarrassing!" Jayne said to me. "The owners come and find their horse escaped and running around loose. I feel for Diane."

But when she saw us, she came unconcernedly strolling up and explained he was free by her permission. It was a shocker to us. We had been raising Thoroughbreds for ten years, and like all breeders our first rule was that an entry or exitway is never left open. Once a kid who worked for us left a courtyard gate swinging. Beyond the courtyard were our fields with eight horses grazing in them. Jayne told the kid it must never happen again. A day later I glanced through the kitchen window and saw that the gate was open. I went out. "Kevin," I said, "you are discharged." Years later I ran into him in town. He had gone on to be a truck mechanic, went to school for that. "I was bitter against you for a long time," he said, "but I came to realize you had to do what you did." "Kevin," I said, "how about you come out and take a look at my truck, it runs funny."

Now here was Owen Smith quite free. There aren't many horses you could do that with. We reclaimed our trailer, which we had left with Diane that first time we had gone to see Virginia Martin, and prepared to load Owen Smith. Virginia had indicated she wanted to look at him before cold weather set in. "Could I get a picture?" Diane asked, and went to get a camera. She asked me to take one of herself with him, and we drove away, she thinking, so later she told me, of how far he could have gone had she the opportunity to work some more with him, that as a performance horse he could have gone very far indeed. It seemed to me that there was a somber look on her face as she watched us take him away, and I read in that face a feeling that she would miss him.

We arrived at Virginia's and unloaded him. Jayne led him to the arena. Some teen-aged girls in riding gear were coming out—normal undisabled girls just finished with a class. "Is that the new horse?" one asked. "We're the welcoming committee," another said. At once I started talking about his brilliant background, Grandpa licked Kelso, Damascus. He was put into a stall. We left.

Months went by. We didn't want to bug Virginia Martin and called only occasionally. When we got her, she said he was coming along. She was having various capable riders work him every day. The most frequent of these riders, we learned, was one Aleen Thomas. She was a New York City woman who worked for a film company and stabled her horse, Drummer, at Borderland Farm. Drummer's stall was next to that of Owen Smith, and Miss Thomas struck up an acquaintance with him when she saw his head hanging out over the half-door. Pretty soon she was up on him trying to make his gaits even steadier than they were.

"He was very green," she told me later. "But he was spook-proof. He was extremely handle-able, you could do anything with him, you could play under his legs and he'd stand. I wanted to get his front and haunches built up by stretching and shifting him. I saw he could be quite something at dressage and so I concentrated on that—it would round him out." That translated into making him get his legs under him and getting him muscled up and firmed up so that the sway-back would round out somewhat and make his way of going more smooth.

"He's a very giving horse," she told me, "very adaptive and affectionate. He likes people. He likes having the bottom of his face stroked. This is the first Thoroughbred I ever rode with consistency. It was fascinating to see him develop." Pretty soon she took him into a New Jersey dressage show. They came in third out of twenty in the class.

"Not bad!" I said.

"I wish my own horse were half as good," she said. By then she had asked Virginia Martin if the owner would pop for a new saddle and a special foam pad that would help compensate for the sway-back. Virginia called me, and I said I'd pop for anything. With his new equipment Owen Smith went on with Aleen Thomas. "I have never really galloped him," she told me, "because I don't want him really running loose. In company out on the trail, he canters in place when he's behind. He can't be doing that and then really opening up with handicapped kids on board."

"No, of course not," I said. No. He mustn't try to be first. We had lost that, he and I. That was for the horse he might have been.

In late May of 1985, seven months after we had delivered Owen Smith to Virginia, she called me. "I think you might like to come over on Memorial Day," she said.

I drove down. The weather was magnificent, sunny and warm. My garden was planted and I'd had peas from my vines. I arrived and Virginia introduced me to Barbara Glasow. "Our chief therapist," Virginia said.

"I've read some of your writings," I said. They had been reprinted in various Winslow bulletins Virginia had sent us. Mostly they had been incomprehensible to me—too scientific. "How you get into this horse business?" I asked, and she told me that hers was the familiar tale of the horse-crazy little girl. She was from Rochester's suburbs where there was no possibility of owning a nag, but she had a cousin in Connecticut who had one. Each summer she and her parents drove down to visit the cousin and cousin's parents, and Barbara as a child spent every possible minute on the cousin's horse. When she got older, she begged to stay longer in Connecticut than her parents' vacation plans permitted, but they consented, provided she earned enough money to pay for her own transportation back to Rochester. Every penny she could lay her hands on for months before the visit was put away to pay that transportation, for years.

Barbara as a child had been, she said, a tomboy type, but with a bad back that got worse. She found herself put under the care of a physical therapist who worked long hours, long years, with her. She decided in high school that she was going to be like her therapist. At Ithaca College in upstate New York, she majored in her chosen field but in fact spent more time at her outside job than in class. The job was taking care of some twenty horses in a riding stable. She did it along with another girl who also majored in physical therapy. They were juniors in 1973 when somehow they heard there was going to be a lecture in Toronto on horseback riding for the disabled. It was Christmas week. They got leave from their job and drove up to find a Santa Claus parade wending its way through the center of the city. They got caught up in it while they battled the marchers and the unfamiliar streets and got to the lecture only in time to hear the concluding words.

But Barbara had found her destiny. She went back to Ithaca and, through her final year at school, worked on her senior project: a study of what horses could do for the disabled. There wasn't much to go on, she found. In all of the United States there were maybe half a dozen places working on it. The people at those places were local therapists. There was no communicating with others on what they had picked up or figured out. Barbara borrowed a movie camera and as her senior project made a film analyzing a normal person's interaction with a horse at the sitting trot, how the horse's movements affected the rider, what kind of strengths the riding produced, what movement in what joints. She tied it all in to what riding might do for the disabled.

"With a cerebral palsy child," she told me, "things are likely to be all out of alignment. The back is round, the shoulders are bent, the hips don't line up right. The skeleton's not right anymore. But the walk of a horse, the right horse, that motion, forces the child, pushes the child, to move his body correctly. The hips and everything, just as if he were walking himself. The horse's movement makes him move correctly. It's not static like a chair. That horse motion teaches the child balance reaction and to lean and to have the freedom to bring the arms forward and back. That motion encourages the movement of the arms and brings out the child's balance.

"There is something else. Classically, the disabled are not in charge of anything. They are not expected to be responsible. Their parents don't make them do chores. Friends carry their books at school. But such a child has to learn he is not the center of the world; he exists in a family structure, a class structure. Riding teaches him self-esteem and control of himself and of something else—this animal. He must learn responsibility. What I teach is not recreational riding. I make a child feel what normal is, normal movement, through what the horse makes the child do and what he makes the horse do. The child ought to say, Oh, this is what normal feels like, this motion. Then the child matches it, his body matches it. He knows what normal is then.

"Now, do you see that boy there?" I looked. I saw a kid in blue jeans and sneakers. He wore a red shirt. He balanced himself with aluminum crutches holding his forearms and clutched in his fists. Barbara Glasow said to me that she had worked with him for a long time in her capacity as a contract specialist for the local school system. For she had gone on from Ithaca College to a community hospital doing physical therapy and then to public health agencies and then finally into private practice in Warwick where mostly on school contracts she worked exclusively with children. "I heard about Virginia Martin and Winslow a couple of years ago," she explained. She had found that while Virginia had no formal training in the new science of hippotherapy, she had good instincts. I gathered that Virginia's personality was right also. Sheltered workshop, sheltered homes, would never have attracted Virginia. She was the kind of person who hired as stable help those unlikely to be taken on elsewhere: boys in trouble with the law for joyriding in someone else's automobile; people with learning disabilities. "They got a problem, what's their problem?" seemed to be her way of looking at things.

"Now," Barbara was saying, "that boy is highly intelligent. He needs a challenge. He doesn't need a horse who's just going to follow other horses. He'll daydream. You daydream when someone else is responsible. So you can't just be a passenger, you have to plan ahead, ask, 'What do I do now?' And give you a horse who doesn't move real big, that horse'll tell you nothing. I need a horse with a big stride for that kid, a horse who'll make him put out, make him work. Owen Smith is the horse for Steven. That's Steven Jacobetz."

I looked at the kid. He was slowly limping away on his crutches, his legs dragging along the ground. His head hung to one side. He turned to look at something, and I saw that his mouth was partly open. It looked like he was half-laughing, but I couldn't be sure. He went down a stable aisle with his dragging walk and vanished. "He'll be riding in a few minutes," Barbara said. Here was a rider for Owen Smith in place of Cordero, Jorge Velasquez, Maple, Eddie Delahoussaye, Jacinto Vasquez.

I went to my horse. He was tacked up and groomed. A volunteer had just left him. I looked into his eyes. The memory of his birth and that kick came into my mind. "Been a long time," I said. Six years. I thought back to that day Gail Jones found him trapped and permanently crippled, my dear horse I loved and would always love above all others. There was a scraping sound to my right. Steven Jacobetz was coming back. "Owen Smith," I whispered. "For God's sake, be careful."

A young woman came up and stood next to me. "Talking to Owen, are you?"

"Yes."

"He's a Thoroughbred, you know," she said.

She was telling me.

"This is some horse," she said.

"He is? Why?"

"Well, this horse, he's eager, he's willing. He's straightforward and honest, you know. You ask him something and he understands. He's willing to work with you."

I told her who I was, or rather, what I was: his owner. She introduced herself as Ellie Celeste, an area woman who stabled her horse at Borderland Farm and was a Winslow volunteer. As we talked another volunteer came and opened the stall gate and led Owen Smith out. As he went by I held out my hand and it passed over the length of him from the neck to the withers and the side and to the haunches over the legs leading down to those terrible wounds made so long ago and never to vanish in this life.

He went with the volunteer into Virginia Martin's riding arena. There was a large round wooden platform in the center, perhaps fifteen feet in diameter, with a ramp for people in wheelchairs. Coming up, leaning on his mother's arm, his crutches left below, was Steven Jacobetz. There was a kid's hockey helmet on his head, strapped under his chin.

Below, on the tanbark, Barbara Glasow stood with three Winslow volunteers. Virginia Martin was on the platform with Linda Jacobetz. Owen Smith was led up to the platform. In front of it and perhaps two feet away was a shoulder-high wooden wall; it formed a kind of open-ended alleyway that would make it impossible for a horse to move sideways when a rider was getting on board. Owen Smith walked forward and into it and stood still.

Linda Jacobetz took her son's arm and moved him forward. A volunteer joined her and slowly they got Steven on board. *Riders up,* I thought to myself. They let him move his right leg over the saddle by himself. He took up the reins. He held them level with his nose. His slight body sagged to the left. His head lolled in that direction. His mouth was open and the helmet unevenly slanted sideways.

A volunteer held Owen Smith by a lead rein, not a nose chain but just a lead hooked to the bridle. The books say never lead a Thoroughbred without that chain over his nose so you can pull him down sharply and really rap him, and I have heard Louise Meryman, the chief instructor at the burnt Millbrook Combined Training Center and later at the Millbrook Equestrian Center, tell her students they should never even lead a Thoroughbred across a courtyard without a metal chain on his nose. Once an employee of ours left a nose chain off Beau Blaze, Owen Smith's brother, and he went up in the air and put her in the emergency room. The volunteer moved Owen Smith a couple of steps forward out of the alleyway formed by the wall and the side of the raised platform. Two more volunteers came forward, one on each side, to take hold of each of Steven's heels with one hand.

"Move out, Steven," Barbara Glasow ordered. The boy pushed at the horse with the heels held in the volunteers' hands, and they, the rider and the horse and the sidewalkers, got into motion. They began slowly to circle the arena, the volunteer in front holding Owen Smith by the lead rein, the other two holding Steven's heels. Mrs. Jacobetz and Virginia stood together on the wooden platform.

They went past a large mirror, the type every riding arena has, and then along the wall. "Get him closer to the wall," Barbara called, walking along behind. Steven tugged on the right rein and Owen Smith altered course. The horse's motion, and suddenly he appeared enormous to me, gigantic, was jolting the boy forward and then back; and before my eyes, in a matter of perhaps thirty or forty seconds, a minute at the most, Steven's bent body was being pushed up straight. He stopped sagging to the left and sat upright. Within two minutes his head had ceased lolling and was sitting straight on his neck.

They came past the wooden platform in that flow stately manner, the horse, the boy, the sidewalker-volunteers. "He certainly doesn't look scared," I remarked.

"We never use that word," Virginia said in a reprimanding tone.

They circled the arena twice. "Unhook him," Barbara called, and the lead volunteer did so and stepped away. Steven Jacobetz, unafraid, was in full command. "You can let go," Barbara said to one of the heel-holding volunteers, and the boy was alone with only one sidewalker holding his left heel.

"Steven," Barbara called sharply, "ask him to go on. Wake up! Now turn him left. Left! Let him know what you want. Never let the signal wander with your hands. Don't be sloppy!"

She stepped forward into the center of the arena, directly before the boy and the horse. "Now I want you to make a circle around me," she said. "To your right. Go ahead. Do it." He pulled on the rein and slowly he circled her. "Now circle to your left and come back and make a left circle around me," she called. He came at her. "Don't run me over," she added. Everyone laughed, Linda, Virginia, the watching volunteers. He did as she had ordered.

And God took a handful of southerly wind, blew His breath over it and created the horse, the Bedouin saying goes; and among horses the Thoroughbred is second to none. Slowly this Thoroughbred, beautiful in my eyes, went on with his brave and willing rider. *And they shall be mine, saith the Lord of hosts, in that day when I make up my jewels.*

Ellie Celeste stood beside me. "This must be a very beautiful moment for you," she said gently.

I forced a smile. "My wife didn't come because she knew she'd cry," I said.

"Steven," Barbara was calling. "Go to A, turn around to the right and cross to R and turn left." He headed to the letter tacked on the wall and did as she had ordered. The volunteer walking alongside lightly holding his heel said something—a tall, young, local fellow who liked to come over and be with the horses and kids, I'd been told—and Steven ripped out a peal of laughter. He looked over to his mother standing with Virginia up on the wooden platform. His hands were no longer up at his nose's level but down in front of him where they should have been, where a horseman's hands are supposed to be.

"You see how he's rotating through the trunk?" Barbara asked me. "You see how the horse unites everything from the hip to the shoulder? He's stretching Steven, he's putting him together."

"Yes, I see," I got out. God knows this wasn't what I had dreamed for Owen Smith long ago. I had created him, to be brutally frank, to be egotistic, to reveal myself as someone who had dreamed only of my glory and my gold, as surely as the farmer creates corn by sowing the seed. My money had made him, my money bought his mother and his sire's semen; and I had nurtured her and him for eleven months of pregnancy. And I had kept him alive with Jayne and Gail and everyone else—and again I freely admit they know horses a hundred times better than I do—thought he should be put down. For this? For a crippled boy on a crippled horse?

No, never! I said to myself, watching him circle the arena with Steven directing him where to go and when to do it. I created him to go around different ovals: that great reaching one which is Belmont Park, that one which is reached by passing under Saratoga's noble trees, Aqueduct, Churchill Downs on the first Saturday of May these hundred and more years past, Santa Anita.

"Halt him, Steven," Barbara called. Steven tugged back, raising his hands much too high and losing all leverage. Owen Smith kept going. Barbara stepped forward and stopped him. It had been too much for the boy—this time.

"I can make him go forward but I can't stop him," Steven said. The words were indistinct, but understandable.

"You've got work to do, Steven," Barbara said. She looked up at him as he sat, quite straight. Like a horseman. "You have to work with this horse. This is your horse, Steven. You're going to work with him this summer and you're going to go in shows, you understand, you're going to go in shows through obstacle courses and you're going to trot him over cavalletti poles. Do you understand me?"

"Yes."

I turned away. I had dreamed great dreams. They were gone. There would never be another racehorse born in our barn. My picture with Jayne would never be in the corridor outside Belmont's Trustees' Room with that of old Mr. Woodward with Gallant Fox and young Mr. Woodward with Nashua, with Martha Gerry with Forego and Penny Chenery with Secretariat, with Vanderbilt with Native Dancer and Whitney with Tom Fool, with the owners of Seattle Slew and Spectacular Bid.

But what they had, *he* had. That desire to win, to do, to go on, to achieve, that drive and that something unknown, he had translated it into this, that beyond pain and above injury, he would do for this boy and for the others, the Down's syndrome kids, the blind, the riders with no arms or one leg—he would do what he could. Virginia had said to me once that it was her experience that horses who worked long years for her stayed healthy. When she retired them, she said, they sickened and died. They wanted, the good ones, to do things. "What's long years?" I had asked. "I've had horses working with kids who've been doing it twenty years," she said.

Twenty years? In twenty years I will be dead or very old. Jessica will be in her mid-thirties then, a mature woman. Perhaps now and then she will stop by Warwick, New York, to see the last of our horses, who never won a race, who never even ran. Who then, twenty years into the future, will remember that Cold Spring once paid forty dollars to win, or that Brave Gleam made up nearly thirty lengths from last to be up in a photo? But Owen Smith would be on helping those who needed him. And when he died, if I were still alive, or Jayne were still alive, or if Jessica still owned our place, he would come home to lie by little Birthday Girl, the playmate of his youth. We had made that clear to Virginia, and she had said she entirely understood.

"Go to C and turn to the left and go to M," Barbara was saying. Steven pushed with his heels, sitting straight, the hands right. Owen Smith went forward. I turned away and walked from the arena and down the stall aisle and outside to where my car was. Behind me the handicapped kid on the handicapped horse went on. I got to the car and started it and drove away. Behind me they went on with their work.

I had seen a hero riding a hero.

My horse was a winner, the victor, a great horse—the champion.

School Horses, the Most Important
Assistants of the Instructor

BY COLONEL ALOIS PODHAJSKY

Colonel Alois Podhajsky served as director of Vienna's Spanish Riding School from 1936 to 1965. Responsible for saving the School's celebrated Lipizzaners during World War Two, he thus helped preserve the classical dressage tradition that has been nurtured and exhibited at the School since 1572. This selection from Podhajsky's *My Horses, My Teachers* offers advice that applies equally well to any breed or discipline.

During my period at the Cavalry School I had to ride the horses I have mentioned and also remounts, that is, young horses that had to be broken in. Besides, there were the school horses on which I was given one or two lessons daily and which helped me to understand even better how important the training of dressage is for every type of riding horse. In general a horse may be called a school horse if his training in dressage has reached such a degree that he is able to convey to the pupil the correct feeling for movement and balance and the subtlety of the aids. No instructor is capable of teaching this delicate language between rider and horse without the willing assistance of the horse. The young rider, eager to learn, may rely on his four-legged teacher whose importance sometimes even rises above that of the two-legged one. The privilege of learning on a school horse is an invaluable help for the rest of the rider's life. I will be forever grateful to my school horses, for I continued to learn from them when I was given no more lessons and was working on my own and also when I was instructing other riders.

A teacher will be successful with his teaching when he is understood and respected by his pupils. In much the same way a horseman will be able to learn from his horse only when he respects him as a creature and has affection for him. Since the horse cannot speak the rider must endeavor to guess his thoughts and to interpret his reactions and draw conclusions from his behaviour. Mutual understanding will also depend on how two creatures take to each other, which may be even more important between horse and rider than between human beings. Therefore the selection of a horse is a vital point in the future relationship. This knowledge, which I gained at the Cavalry School, was further extended at the Spanish Riding School.

There are horses who appeal to the rider immediately, whom he understands easily and likes in a short time. In such a case it is easy to adjust to each other; work becomes a pleasure; and success is certain to follow. But now and then a rider comes across a horse who is alien to him and whose reactions he cannot understand. He is quickly annoyed by repeated faults and naughtiness and often an aversion develops which compromises progress and success. Such an inexplicable aversion does not appear only in the rider but certainly also in the horse. This is why some horses who give nothing but trouble to one rider change completely with a new master and work with him in full harmony. The reason does not lie in the better abilities of the new rider and, therefore, must not be taken as a gauge of standards. It is the magnetism between two creatures, which cannot be explained by the intellect.

Matching horse and rider is an art founded on a profound knowledge first of all of the physical conformation, of the habits, and last but not least, of the characters of both partners. The stable masters at the royal courts of bygone days had to possess this knowledge to a high degree, for they had to choose and prepare the horses for their "highnesses." A prince had to be superior also in mastering his horse and it was unthinkable that he fight with him or lose his dignity and reputation by falling off in public. Therefore the books that the reputable riding and stable masters of old have left to us—there are only very few because not every good rider is a good writer and vice versa—are still of great value for us today. The horse still moves in the same way as always; he thinks and feels in the same fashion; and the conformation of his body is unaltered. He is the wonderful creature of nature as extolled in the Koran. The riding masters who attained such high and responsible positions had the duty and the leisure to study this product of nature profoundly. In every book on riding of those days there are detailed instructions about the horse's body and its functions, about stable management and saddles and bridles.

Today, however, few riders know their horses and the causes of their behaviour. Everything has become superficial nowadays, except technology. With machines the physical laws may not be disregarded as we often disregard the laws of nature with our animals. The well-founded doctrines of the old riding masters are frequently rejected today with the remark that these methods are old-fashioned and not applicable in our present times, which demand quick success. And what is the result of this fast training? The standard has declined until the once so beautiful movements have become caricatures of what they were. And yet a performance of the highest standard must be built up step by step and on a well-founded basis. I have learned by experience that today's riders may indeed rely upon the teachings of our predecessors, for they are of invaluable help in the reasonable development of this sport. If a rider thinks that he has found a new method he may be sure that if it is any good he has come upon it by instinct or by chance and that it was practiced long ago by the old masters.

Speed at the cost of quality is always wrong, not only in riding. When the famous New York City Ballet performed in Vienna I asked the ballet master George Balanchine whether he would take the so-called modern conception into consideration when training his dancers and shorten the time of their education. Excitedly Balanchine jumped off his seat and exclaimed: "How could I? The human body is still the same as always. The old schools of ballet demanded a certain amount of time and they were right. Did they not achieve perfection and have they not been our ideals for hundreds of years? Why should we change?" It is exactly the same with equitation if it pretends to be an art.

But let us go back to a small part of this art, to the choice of the right horse for the right rider, which is a sort of matchmaking between the two creatures, and should be one of the most important concerns of any good riding instructor. Unfortunately only a few of my instructors possessed this tact. In most cases the horses were allotted in a rather superficial way. Very frequently the horses were exchanged in accordance with the obvious principle of giving the difficult horse to the more accomplished rider, which would have been the correct method had it not been for the fact that as soon as the difficult horse had been somewhat retrained by the good rider, he was returned to a weaker one. In a short time there were new difficulties and the vicious circle began again. This method made the riders lose interest and pleasure in their work and did not allow a friendship to grow between horse and rider. The horse as a teacher did not come into action.

Because of these frequent changes I remember only a few school horses from my time at the Cavalry School. My first experience was a negative one and rather discouraging. From the chestnut mare Fanny I learned how vital it is for successful cooperation that the two partners be sympathetic to each other and how dismal may be the daily lesson if horse and rider do not meet in friendship. As with every school horse, I had to ride her without stir-rups for several months. I did not succeed, however, in finding contact with her and my vexation grew when, every day, she gave me trouble, unseating me by sudden leaps and starts at the most unexpected moment and at the slightest provocation. I could not discover the reason for her behaviour or bring about a change by calming her or administering punishment. With every new day it became harder to remain patient. Eventually I took such a dislike to her that I began to be annoyed the very moment she was brought into the arena. Very probably she disliked me as much as I did her; there was just no getting along with each other. And Fanny of all horses I had to keep for such a long time! But even those nerve-wracking fights had a positive result. I learned that the willing cooperation of our horses is not to be taken for granted and began to pay greater attention to the psychological relationship between horse and rider. This approach has been of great help to me in my later career as a rider as well as an instructor.

Even though I was not able to get along with Fanny I grew conscious of the fact that horses cannot all be trained after the same set pattern. The phlegmatic horse should be taken with a firmer hand and the willing horse, in-clined to nervousness, should be treated more leniently. Between the two there are a number of nuances, of course, and I realized these contrasts especially when changing from a lazy horse to a temperamental one and vice versa. Clinging to habits as every human being does, I applied the aids in the same manner and was surprised by the results. While the first horse's nervousness grew into excitement, the same degree of aids did not get the other going. As it is vital for correct and successful work to know one's partner intimately I adopted the habit, later, of eliminating difficult exercises when first riding a new horse. We are indulging our human vanity if we produce difficult airs and figures with an unknown horse. So I have also taught my pupils to take time to get to know their partners and also to give the horse time to grow accustomed to a new rider. I learned how to study the horse's movements, his suppleness and sensitiveness to the aids. I took time to understand his temperament, his character, and his capacity to learn. The horse should have the opportunity to grow accustomed to the difference in weight of a new rider, which might even be distributed in a different way, and also to the different nuances in the appli-cation of the aids so that they are understood completely. Horse and rider *must* first of all understand each other in the language of the aids before they can find understanding in the balance, rhythm, and tempo that are necessary for the harmony they should strive to achieve.

Rarely, and never in later years, did I allow the spectators to infringe upon this necessary period of getting to know each other, even if the unlookers were waiting eagerly to see how the horse—sometimes it was even their own—would go under the new rider. Nothing can prevent me now from riding an indifferent horse briskly forward in order to awaken him by changes of speed and make him take pleasure in his own movement. An excitable horse I calm by steady and almost sleepy work and coax him into finding his mental balance, which is as important to animals as it is to humans. By this careful investigation rather than with some spectacular exercises I am able to decide on the appropriate intensity of the aids, learn about the strong and weak points of the new partner, and can build up the training progressively. It enables me to reach my goal more successfully and more quickly than by rushing ahead. Having laid the foundation of confidence and friendship in this preparatory period, I have my horse "there" when I begin with the real work.

One should also consider the differing attitudes of different horses towards rewards and punishments. The tender little soul blissfully accepts the smallest caress, as was the case with Neapolitano Africa, who would have purred like a kitten had he not been a Lipizzaner stallion. The slightest rebuke, however, was a tragedy for him and he became nervous and anxious. The more materialistic horse obviously prefers sugar or other titbits to patting and stroking as if he would say: "Don't make all that fuss, go ahead and give me the sugar!" In most cases such a horse is much less impressed by a reprimand and easily digests a much stronger one. This knowledge of character is an important part in the education of a horse and a sound foundation for successful co-operation.

As I have mentioned, not every school horse is necessarily suitable for dressage competitions, but at the Cavalry School each dressage horse had to be used as a school horse outside the season of horse shows. In the second year of my appointment there I was lucky to have as my riding instructor Major Jaich, who was a successful dressage rider himself. He limited to a minimum the unpleasant changes of horses and riders and had great ability as a teacher. He was an excellent instructor who directed with tact and whose knowledge and method had sprung from practical experience. His best assistant was my school horse Greif. The two of them enriched and consolidated my equestrian knowledge to a great extent.

Greif was a big strong chestnut gelding with great intelligence and docility. Although his paces were not too brilliant, he ranked among the best school horses and was chosen to participate in the dressage competitions at the forthcoming horse shows in the spring of 1930. Thus a definite goal was given to my training and I accumulated valuable experiences in these lessons. Under the expert instruction of Major Jaich, Greif grew into an excellent teacher who took me through the dressage training up to the standard of a difficult class. On his back I learned lateral work in all paces, flying changes at every second stride, and pirouettes. The rider can learn these exercises only in this practical way and not from explanations of even the best instructor.

First of all I learned from this well-trained school horse that with riding the regularity of the movements has the same importance as the rhythm in music. To begin with I had to learn to feel this regularity and then to realize the difference whenever it changed and apply the correct means to regain this most beautiful feeling a horse can convey to his rider. Whenever his steps became irregular I could clearly feel it in the movement of his back and would then ride him briskly forward at a rising trot until he had regained his balance. When he made hasty steps I had to reduce his speed until tempo and rhythm were again regular. The most important thing was to take care not to disturb his balance with my seat. In this way I was able to maintain the same rhythm on the straight line as in lateral work. In lateral work the horse moves forward and sideways and his legs cross each other. It is a frequent fault in this movement that the horse either increases or decreases his speed. When I succeeded at last in maintaining the same rhythm whether increasing or decreasing the tempo and was able to bring about this difference by lengthening or shortening the horse's strides instead of making them faster or slower, I began to feel the full harmony of all movements. This difference of length in the horse's stride in the different speeds while the same rhythm is maintained gives brilliance to riding just as *fortissimo* and *pianissimo* give brilliance to music.

It was Greif who made me understand the flying change, that is, the flying change of lead in which the horse changes from, say, the canter right to the canter left without intermediate steps. The term right or left canter refers to the leading foreleg. For example, if the left foreleg is the one that reaches out, we speak about a canter left. Greif taught me that the rider should not attempt to indicate this change of lead to the horse by twisting his body or throwing it from one side to the other but by quietly changing the aids of leg and reins, on the condition—and this was the most important thing—that the horse moves in a lively collected canter. Thus Greif made me consider more seriously the basic gymnastic schooling of the horse, which is the foundation for more advanced training. If it is neglected, numerous difficulties will arise that will eventually hinder progress.

After a while I was able to induce Greif to execute a flying change without my aids being noticeable to the onlooker and to increase the difficulty of the exercise by repeating it after a given number of strides until Greif made a flying change after every other stride. If with all my other dressage horses later on I seemed to achieve flying changes without an apparent effort, I am indebted to Greif and the experience I gained in my work with him, which taught me never to neglect the basic schooling, i.e., the correct development of the paces.

Greif taught me also how easy it is to achieve pirouettes if the horse is in full balance. A well-balanced horse should maintain the regularity of his steps even in the smallest turns and in the pirouette should not change the rhythm of the canter but turn in regular bounds around the inside hind leg. If he loses his balance and consequently his rhythm, we have proof that the horse was not ready for this difficult exercise. The rider should concentrate again on cultivating the basic paces and ride briskly forward, executing changes of speed and small and large circles. He should practice extension and collection until the horse maintains the rhythm and the regularity of his stride even in small and smaller turns and voltes. Thanks to Greif again, there were never difficulties with my own dressage horses in the following years. After the conscientious preparation of the foundation, these difficult exercises seemed to drop into my lap like ripe fruit. And the success of my cooperation with Greif became apparent not only in my enriched experiences but also in the numerous trophies we won in various horse shows.

The second horse that I rode under the direction of Major Jaich was Jodo, a very good-looking chestnut gelding from the federal stud farm. He was the first horse that I had trained all by myself, beginning with the young remount and proceeding up to the standard of a school and dressage horse. Jodo was full of temperament and good will and he learned quickly and easily, but he had to be given enough time to understand what was required of him. Above all I had to be careful not to make him nervous. As a young rider I was full of zeal and ambition to achieve noticeable progress and so it happened repeatedly that I overlooked this point and made excessive demands on him. Fortunately I had Major Jaich at my side to interfere at the right moment and prevent me from making grave mistakes. I had to take Jodo into a walk, pat him and talk to him until he had calmed down. When he was quiet I was allowed to begin again very carefully with the exercises. The right advice at the right moment is of invaluable help but can be given only by an instructor who has learned by practical experience to adjust work appropriately to the degree of training.

However quickly I succeeded in calming Jodo when I conscientiously followed Major Jaich's advice, I had great difficulties in regulating his paces. At the trot he had a tendency to take hasty steps. In the beginning it was impossible to ride an extended trot, which is an increase in speed by taking longer steps and by no means faster ones. My instructor employed a method that led to success in this case but that was not suitable for every horse, as I found out later. He ordered me to push Jodo forward at the rising trot until he finally took longer steps and then to reward him by a period of rest at the walk. Gradually this method proved effective with Jodo and at the end of his training he was able to perform a very brilliant extended trot. But I did not obtain the same result with other horses, especially not with those with a high knee action, such as the Lipizzaners. When pushed forward energetically, they went faster but also were more and more hasty in their steps. They became nervous and excited and lost the regularity of their paces altogether. When talking about the Lipizzaners I will explain this phenomenon.

Having worked through the winter, Jodo and I entered several competitions and right from the beginning were first or at least among the first, which was rather remarkable inasmuch as these were my first dressage tests on a horse that, apart from my short episode with Napoleon five years ago, I had trained entirely on my own. During that year of 1930 I was successful in all the horse shows in dressage tests as well as in jumping competitions—until a fall laid me up for many months.

I had to take a young thoroughbred mare over a course for the first time and she was so excited about this new experience that she rushed like mad up to a fence that had a bar across the top. She did not jump high enough and the bar got caught between her front legs and we both rolled on the ground. The fall itself would have been nothing serious but when we both had scrambled back on our feet she kicked out with both hind legs—out of fear or anger, I never knew—and hit me in the back. I went down as though struck by a lightning, was unable to get up, and was carried out of the arena with a crack in my spine. It was a very painful injury and took a long time to heal, but there was also a positive side to it. When at last, after having been partly paralysed, I was able to ride again, I had to give up jumping altogether because I could not lean forward. So I concentrated on dressage riding with all my zeal and ambition, although in the beginning I had to be lifted into the saddle.

Three years later I rode school horses again when I was posted as a student to the Spanish Riding School. And there for two years I had the privilege of learning from the Lipizzaner stallions. The Spanish Riding School is the oldest riding academy in the world. Its existence may be traced back as far as 1565.

Formerly a property of the imperial court it was taken under the control of the Department of Agriculture after the fall of the Austro-Hungarian monarchy in 1918 and continued its work of cultivating the classical art of riding. Every year the best officer of the Cavalry School was sent to the Spanish Riding School for about six or twelve months of more advanced training.

In these Lipizzaners I encountered extremely intelligent and powerful teachers who registered the smallest fault in seat or guidance and were forever ready to take advantage of their students. This "dangerous" intelligence was compensated for by the immediate advice of the riding instructors. In the daily lessons each of the three head riders dealt with a single pupil at a time, who rode a stallion that the instructor himself had trained and ridden, and with whose character and strong and weak points he was thoroughly familiar. Consequently he was able to give the appropriate order the very moment it was needed. This is certainly the most ideal method of instruction for a rider.

Up to my appointment to the Spanish Riding School my lessons had taken place in groups—one might call them classes. The instructor had to teach eight to twelve riders at a session. There were several possibilities for organizing these lessons. The instructor could take all pupils at the same time, which more or less restricted the lesson to commanding the paces and exercises and allowed only very brief corrections of the single rider. In most such cases the lesson was hard more than a shouting of "Trot!" or "Walk!" and the possibility of learning was also very limited because each student had to pay attention to the other riders. The horse as a teacher hardly came into the picture even if he possessed the capacity. An alternative was that the instructor took on one pupil after another, correcting the worst faults of the rest who worked on their own in the meantime. If he was fair and just and wanted to give each rider the privilege of this private instruction, there were not more than five to seven minutes to give to each, a span of time far too short for even the best teacher. This was in theory. In actual practice most of the instructors concentrated on a few favourite students and did not pay too much attention to the rest.

What a difference there was in the detailed and thorough instruction at the Spanish Riding School! Each of the school stallions had a personality of his own, which was marked by the personality of his rider, who had formed his individual character. The basis of the training was the same for all of them and yet the personal touch was unmistakable. Every four weeks I had a new school horse and a new instructor and I had to adapt myself to this change. The slightest difference in the training also had a repercussion on the training of the other dressage horses which I rode in the afternoon in the Prater, a large natural park on the outskirts of Vienna. Usually they took a few days to adjust themselves to the different nuances of the aids.

Riding master Polak was a great pedagogical talent, as just in giving reprimands as in giving praise. He expressed his commands in precise form and knew how to encourage the rider and give him confidence. His horses, too, went in much the same way. They were light and steady in contact and followed the slightest command. Temperamentally they were as easy and cheerful as their trainer, who was a great music lover and played the violin excellently.

Head rider Zrust had great instinctive knowledge about his horses. He was very calm with his students and followed the rule that what cannot be obtained now will succeed without effort some other day. Instead of criticising he preferred to say something agreeable, and when a pupil could not cope at all with a stallion, he mounted him himself and by the influence of his seat and legs solved the hardest problems without difficulty. His horses, however, were not as easy to ride as those of Polak and were also more difficult in temperament. They demanded an extremely quiet seat and a well-balanced application of the aids of reins and legs. But when they went well they conveyed a wonderful feeling to the rider.

Head rider Lindenbauer was an industrious man and very serious about life in general and riding in particular. He was not satisfied with himself very often and therefore did not believe in expressing any approval. The student heard hardly anything but criticisms until he succeeded with his exercises, which usually took several lessons and sometimes made him feel quite discouraged. Lindenbauer's horses went in a similarly severe manner: they demanded a correct seat, strong aids of the legs, and a firm contact with the bit. They were more work to ride inasmuch as they gave nothing without being obliged to do so, which corresponded exactly to the outlook on life of their master.

It is to the credit of the three great head riders that they preserved the standard of classical riding at the Spanish Riding School even after the breakdown of the Austro-Hungarian Empire. They continued the tradition that had been handed down through generations and they did not merely talk about it but lived it. They proved it true that the character of the rider forms his horse both physically and mentally. Under their wonderful tuition the stallions themselves grew into great teachers who helped to spread the fame of the time-honoured Riding School. From all over—from Sweden, Hungary, Germany, Switzerland, Denmark, and even Mexico—officers came to the School to learn the classical art of riding.

My first instructor was riding master Polak, who in my eyes was the best rider and unsurpassed as a teacher. My first school horse was Pluto Kerka, who reminded me immediately and unmistakably that the reins were for the horse to be guided and not for the rider to hold on to. When my contact grew too strong he leaned on the rein with all his weight or he rushed off. He could not have demonstrated more clearly how important it is to have an independent seat. But when I was able to accomplish the giving and taking action of the reins, sitting upright and bracing my back, Pluto Kerka would move with enormous impulsion and give his rider the completely new feeling of controlled power. This wonderful feeling was lost the moment the legs did not remind Pluto Kerka that the horse will move in full balance only when the hind legs carry a sufficient proportion of the weight of both horse and rider. In this respect there was much to be learned from Pluto Kerka that, as I have mentioned before, was of great help also when hunting.

Speaking about the feeling that Pluto Kerka gave me, it was by no means as I described it right from the beginning. When I rode him for the first time he surprised me by his smooth but at the same time extremely powerful movements, which I had not yet experienced with any horse. Riding without stirrups, my seat, I admit, ran into trouble, especially because the stallion was rather small and my legs are very long. When I shifted my weight about trying to regain my seat, I irritated Pluto Kerka and immediately received the message in the change of his movements. When I tried to reestablish my balance, he struck off into the canter instead of continuing his regular trot, or worse, he moved in a passage-like hovering trot that disconcerted me even more. I almost had the impression that I was on a horse for the first time in my life. I felt completely at the mercy of this ardent Lipizzaner stallion and I would never have thought that this could happen to me after all those years of riding experience. The wise old truth that with riding there is never an end of learning did not help much in this situation.

Riding master Polak, however, knew how to comfort his pupil: "Don't worry, Captain. This has happened to every new rider here!" and began to correct my seat. I had to lower my heels and sit deeper and heavier into the saddle until my weight was distributed equally on both seat bones with my spine vertical to the center of the saddle. This is how he helped me to find my balance and with Pluto Kerka calming down at once I regained my mental balance, too. Now the stallion knew what I expected from him and was no longer disturbed by my uneasy seat.

The most important thing I learned in these first lessons at the Spanish Riding School was that it does not count so much "what" is done as "how" it is done. As in any other sport, in riding it does not matter what kind of exercise the horse is executing but in what manner he performs it. But soon it dawned upon me that the correct "how" is the most difficult thing on earth. On Pluto Kerka I had to learn all over again how to break into a trot or strike off into the canter. But this time with the correct aids of seat and legs, which means that the onlooker has the impression that the rider is thinking and that the horse is executing his thought after an imperceptible communication. How difficult it is to fulfill this simple demand was proved in those first lessons with my two new masters.

Polak severely controlled my seat in all transitions and Pluto Kerka did not strike off into a canter, for instance, before he had approved of my aids and found them correct. And so it happened that in spite of years of experience on horseback I was sometimes incapable of striking off into a canter! Either I allowed the stallion to become too fast at the trot which preceded the canter, or I applied the reins too firmly and he happily offered a passage. I admit that I often felt completely ignorant and like a beginner but then on some other occasion I heard Polak's "Very good!" and picked up courage again. Maybe I was not as incapable as I sometimes felt. Gradually Polak's words of praise came more and more frequently and my despair decreased in the same measure. I was proud and pleased when after a few weeks I was able to take Pluto Kerka correctly through the corners, to execute well-rounded voltes and other exercises, and to achieve smooth transitions of paces and speed.

Perhaps it sounds strange to speak about a round volte since a volte is a small circle of six yards diameter and every circle is supposed to be round. Although a circle is supposed to be round, a volte is not always that way, as is often proved in dressage tests. In a correct volte the horse is bent in his whole body according to the circle and the inside hind leg should step under the center of gravity and therefore be bent more than the other legs, which demands a greater effort. If I did not apply Pluto Kerka's outside rein sufficiently, he turned his head too much to the inside, and if in addition, my outside leg did not hold him on the track, his hind legs would not step into the hoof prints of the forelegs. Consequently his hindquarters swung to the outside and soon there was no longer a round volte but a many-sided figure. These voltes caused more headaches to us pupils than the later execution of the most difficult exercises, which we were to learn comparatively quickly on the foundation of this minutely detailed basic training.

When I was able to perform these simple exercises according to the demands of classical riding and to the satisfaction of my instructor, Polak gradually increased the degree of difficulty. Finally, as a reward at the end of the lesson I was allowed to ride a passage on Pluto Kerka. Passage is a solemn and impressive movement which may be compared to a trot in slow motion. In the beginning, Polak with his whip supported my leg aids, which are particularly important in this pace, for the passage is dependent on the lively activity of the horse's hindquarters. Later I had to rely solely on my own aids when I wanted to enjoy having my stallion float weightlessly above the ground. The Lipizzaner has a special talent for the passage. If he is correctly trained he cannot be equalled by any other horse in this brilliant and expressive pace. Maybe this is the reason why at the Spanish Riding School the passage is called the "Spanish step"!

Lipizzaners may be very cunning, too, if they find out how to make life easier for themselves. There was the stallion named Maestoso Borina, who reached the unheard-of age of thirty-three years and whom I kept in retirement in the stables when I had become Director of the School. Under his master, the head rider Zrust, he was able to show a very brilliant passage, but one day when he was being ridden by an elderly civilian student, I saw him perform a rather strange movement which with some imagination might have been taken for a passage. Lifting his front legs high and slowly as for a passage, he followed with his hind legs at a comfortable walk, swinging his back in such a way that his rider bobbed up and down in the saddle. When I pointed out this extraordinary sight to head rider Zrust he winked at me and smiled: "Just leave him alone! Why shouldn't he? The old gentleman is happy because he thinks he is riding a perfect passage—and the stallion does not tire himself out!"

Polak's favourite was Favory Montenegra, to whom I owe a great deal. He was a gorgeous stallion, very graceful and remarkably intelligent. Under his master he was capable of performing piaffe and passage with a perfection I was absolutely unable to achieve. Either my seat disturbed his balance, to which he reacted immediately with less elevated steps, or I applied the reins too strongly so that his hind legs were pushing more than carrying the weight and the movement was no longer floating. Often I was in despair of ever reaching perfection, but then for the fraction of a second I felt how the stallion became higher in front and as light as a feather before this extraordinary sensation was lost again. When I succeeded in controlling my seat and guiding the stallion with ever lighter contact, these moments were more and more frequent until Favory Montenegra effortlessly floated above the ground in a piaffe and passage of such brilliance that the spectators at the morning training broke into spontaneous applause although this was not at all "done" in those days. When Polak nodded "beautiful" in my direction I felt royally rewarded. Forever will I be grateful to these two great masters.

Most of my lessons with head rider Zrust were on Conversano Nobila. I was allowed to ride him even though he went under his master in the Sunday performance. As he gave me quite a bit of trouble I learned from him how to ride the more difficult horses. But when I succeeded in making him understand what I wanted, he gave me the wonderful feeling of a passage full of impulsion. Presently I found out that there was a difference between his passage and that of Pluto Kerka. Pluto Kerka bent his forelegs in the front knee and lifted his forearm until it was horizontal to the ground before putting it down in a beautifully round motion which gained little ground to the front. Conversano Nobila lifted his legs in the same way but stretched them out more before putting them down in a longer and more forward action. I was told that the first kind is called the "round" passage and the second kind the "long" one. Later I found out that horses with a high knee action have greater ability for the "round" passage but that in the extended trot their legs do not reach forward to a very great extent. Those that are capable of a brilliant extension in the trot tend to perform a "long" passage, which is what we see with most dressage horses since they are generally half- and Thoroughbreds and very seldom Lipizzaners.

This description should not, however, give the impression that I was riding the paces of the high school, among which we count the passage, right from the beginning of my lessons with head rider Zrust. On the contrary, it took a long time to obtain this privilege because at first I had great difficulties with Conversano Nobila. I was unable to collect him because he was inclined to go above the bit. Lifting his head and losing contact with the bit, he dropped his back and by this attitude made it impossible to execute any exercise correctly. Zrust had infinite patience with me and I was intent on following his example. I pushed Conversano Nobila carefully forward with both legs and tried to absorb the impulsion with my braced back and the reins well applied. He was supposed not to increase his speed but with a beautifully shaped neck become short in his whole body—collected is the technical term.

Finally I succeeded in achieving this form when riding on the large circle, and was able to begin work on the track in the whole arena, trying to maintain this collection when performing various exercises. If I lost it again I had to return to the large circle, where it is easier to obtain collection because of the increased bend of the horse's inside hind leg. Thus I realised the meaning of collection, which might be compared to the mental concentration of a human being. If the collection was assured, if Conversano Nobila accepted the bit in the correct attitude and position of head and neck and his hind legs stepped sufficiently under his body, then even the most difficult exercises succeeded without apparent effort. If I did not obtain the correct collection, horse and rider were covered with sweat without obtaining a satisfactory result. This

COLONEL ALOIS PODHAJSKY · **197**

proves how important it is to prepare the horse correctly and how much of the daily work should be devoted to this preparation. It consists of the correct execution of the simple exercises such as straightening, loosening, and relaxing the horse, physically and mentally, until he is concentrating completely on his rider. At this point the rider may collect his horse and then even the most difficult airs of the high school seem easy as play. Conversano Nobila was the first Lipizzaner I rode after being appointed Director of the Spanish Riding School in 1939, thus renewing an old friendship.

It was a special mark of distinction when head rider Zrust entrusted his favourite horse, Conversano Savona, to my care. In the performances he presented this beautiful stallion in the levade in the pillars and in hand and sometimes in the most superb manner under the rider. For many years Conversano Savona had been the best in levades. In the lesson he had to be led with very delicate aids and not disturbed by any awkwardness for he was full of temperament, which he preserved until his old age. If Conversano Savona worked especially well with me, I felt very happy and his master also beamed. As a reward I was allowed to perform a levade with this wonderful Lipizzaner.

In the levade the horse rises on his lowered hocks with his forelegs tucked under him and remains motionless for a few seconds in this position. Many equestrian monuments depict horse and rider in this attitude—for instance, that of Prince Eugene of Savoy which stands on the Heldenplatz in Vienna. In bygone days the airs above the ground, that is, exercises in which the horse lifts his forelegs or both fore- and hind legs off the ground, belonged to the training of every school horse and every rider. They may be seen on many old etchings and paintings. Today they are preserved in their living form only at the Spanish Riding School.

The correct levade is developed from a lively piaffe in which the hind legs will step more and more under the body until the weight is finally shifted onto the hindquarters and the forehand is lifted off the ground. I had a strange feeling when Conversano Savona did his first levade with me. He lowered his hindquarters as if he was going to sit down and lifted his forelegs until his body formed an angle of forty-five degrees to the ground. I sat on an oblique basis and had to maintain unaltered the position of my body vertical to the ground. If I leaned forward ever so little Conversano Savona ended his levade. The same happened if I took my body behind the vertical line. To me he seemed like a juggler who will try to step under the center of gravity of the object he is balancing. It was yet another proof of the eminent importance of balance in any kind of equitation.

When head rider Zrust died in 1940 I took Conversano Savona under my special protection and tried to make his retirement the pleasant one he certainly deserved. In hand he showed the levade for many more years and gave pleasure to thousands of spectators from all over the world. When he died this great stallion from whom I had learned so much was twenty-nine years of age, which was the best proof of the correct training by his master. For like any other gymnastics, riding should strengthen the horse and prolong his life.

With head rider Lindenbauer it was chiefly Pluto Austria that I had to ride in the lessons. This stallion demanded that the aids be given in a particularly strong manner. Besides he had an inclination to go above the rein. He carried his head high and paid more attention to what was going on around him than he did to his rider. Because he raised his head and neck too high he dropped his back and consequently could not step sufficiently under his body with his hind legs. If this was the case his movements became very uncomfortable, so rough and difficult to sit that I bumped clumsily on his back. The more heavily his rider hit the saddle the higher he raised his head and neck and the more he dropped his back. It was by no means a pleasure to ride him, especially not with the criticisms of the instructor as a musical background. Once dismounting after such a lesson without any tangible result and having saluted head rider Lindenbauer according to the tradition of the School, I sighed in complete dejection. "I think I better give up riding altogether," I said. "I am never going to learn it!"

Lindenbauer was all the more vexed by this remark. "Nonsense, Captain, you should have more confidence in yourself!"

This put the lid on my discouragement and I replied: "Even if I had had confidence in myself this lesson today would have shattered it completely. But it's my nature that I am hardly ever content with myself!" Smiling at last, Lindenbauer shook my hand and said that he could understand me so well because he, too, was always so strict with himself.

At long last I succeeded in riding Pluto Austria energetically forward and by repeated short actions of the reins made him accept the bit with a lowered head and a long neck until he arched his back and his hind legs were able to step sufficiently under the body. This made the correct collection possible and I could sit comfortably and with a good feeling at last.

There was another school horse who gave me some trouble. His name was Maestoso Africa and not Maestoso Austria. The reason I mention this is because a book was published with the title *Maestoso Austria* when I was Director of the School and many visitors came to see this famous stallion. They were very disappointed when all I could show them was either Maestoso Africa or Pluto Austria. A stallion with the name of Maestoso Austria has never existed at the Spanish Riding School.

Maestoso Africa was a problem for me to ride because he was very small and I had great trouble placing my long legs and putting my knees in the correct spot. Since the aids of my legs could not be fully employed I was reduced to giving the aids mainly with the weight of my body. This was quite difficult in the beginning but helped to establish an independent seat. After a while Maestoso Africa and I got well on together and I was very pleased when head rider Zrust asked me one day teasingly whether I would not want to be transferred to the Spanish Riding School and employed as a rider since I rode Maestoso Africa better and especially in a more brilliant passage than his own rider. Although said as a joke this remark was a sign of esteem which any in-structor should express to his pupil at the right moment. When I was an instruc-tor myself I followed this example whenever appropriate praise was justified.

During the two years in which I was stationed at the Spanish Riding School as a student I had the opportunity of studying the characters of both horses and riders and, in the twenty-six years during which I was responsible for the School as director, I enlarged my knowledge considerably. Just as human professors develop into real characters in the course of their long lives, so did the four-legged teachers who all year round had to submit in obedience to their trainers and also to endure the awkwardness and clumsiness of the stu-dents. It was certainly no pleasure to have to begin all over again with each new pupil, forever feeling the wrong kinds of aids and suffering an incorrect seat that irritated the balance. But because they were personalities they found out how to take it easy or to play tricks on their riders, as did Generale Malaga, a school stallion who had been trained by head rider Zrust.

Generale Malaga's specialty was pirouettes. With great skill and perfec-tion he performed this exercise, which is the smallest turn at the canter. Once there was a dressage rider, a lieutenant colonel who had encountered difficul-ties when he wanted to teach these pirouettes to his dressage horse. He came to head rider Zrust for a few lessons in order to learn the correct feeling of this exercise. He was a very good-looking officer and quite arrogant. He brought his wife to the School so that she would be able to see how well he would ex-ecute the pirouettes right at the first attempt. He mounted Generale Malaga and began to limber him up, disregarding Zrust's corrective remark that he should not take his upper body so much forward. He replied simply that he was used to riding like this and that the position of the upper part was a matter of taste and varied according to the individual. Zrust shook his head and pointed out that the stallion was accustomed to the rider sitting in the manner traditional with the classical art of riding, and that he was unable to feel the aids of the seat of the rider leaned forward. The lieutenant colonel shrugged and retorted: "He will have to get accustomed to it. After all, I am the boss!" Zrust lifted his shoulders as was his habit and said that Generale Malaga was sufficiently warmed up and the officer might begin the pirouettes now.

Full of enthusiasm the lieutenant colonel followed the suggestion. He paid hardly any attention to the commands of Zrust and rode as near as possible to where his wife sat so that she would be able to admire his beautiful pirouette at close range. Generale Malaga, however, obviously thought that it was too much to insist on pirouettes without exercising the appropriate influence with the correct seat. In the middle of the turn he performed a tremendous leap and the rider sailed through the air. Zrust winked an eye towards me: "A hair's breadth and Mandi [this was what he called the stallion] would have landed him in his wife's lap. Why didn't he believe me when I told him that he should sit more upright?"

By the way, the stallions were not at all impressed by any kind of uniform. They unseated the lieutenant colonel in mufti just as readily as the major in uniform even if he came from across the ocean. The Mexican Major Rodriguez was stationed at the Spanish Riding School for two years and later was for many years the teacher of the famous and successful Mexican jumping rider General Mariles. He, too, was deposited in the sand, by Maestoso Sardinia, after a short altercation, but got on his legs with the agility of a cat, bent down, and said to his instructor with a smile that he had wanted to pick up his whip which he had dropped. Thus he saved his face and avoided paying the usual fine of ten pounds of sugar. The instructor did not dare to contradict the foreign officer.

We have already talked about the cunning Maestoso Borina. He did not limit his tricks to the arena but expressed his personality at every occasion. When he was advanced in age he was included among the happy few who appeared in the floodlights of the Vienna State Opera. In the Opera *The Girl of the Golden West,* to the melodies of Puccini, he had to carry the famous singer Maria Jeritza onto the stage. She was an accomplished rider, and he made an excellent appearance as he entered with graceful steps and stood like a monument while the artist sang her aria. It was a most impressive scene, and Maestoso Borina seemed thoroughly to enjoy the special applause he received. Soon he knew his part so well that he was not to be held backstage and pushed ahead when the music for his scene began. One day there was a rolled-up carpet in his way. Madame Jeritza, very excited, demanded that this obstacle be removed, and in that moment the music set in. There was no holding Maestoso Borina. With determination he cleared the obstacle, much to the dismay of the lady on his back, and precisely on time, he appeared before the public, which greeted him with applause while his rider tried to recover breath for her song.

Having grown old and wise, Neapolitano Montenuova ranked among those conscientious creatures who take their work very seriously and know exactly what they want. This stallion had been trained by head rider Linden-bauer, who tenderly called him Peppi, which in Vienna is short for Joseph. He had enhanced the school performances by his great abilities and the beauty of his movements for more than twenty years. In his old days—he reached the age of thirty-one years—his task was to examine the candidates for careers as rid-ers at the Spanish Riding School who, until 1944, came from the Army. While willingly following the commands of good riders and executing all exercises with his habitual submission, he found out the weak ones with incredible in-stinct and embarrassed many a rider who took himself for a great artist.

There was another of these characters who helped him as a co-judge. Pluto Siglavy had formerly performed caprioles and his trainer Polak had called him Schatzl, which means "little treasure." Having reached the age of twenty-two years, he no longer appeared in the performances but continued to serve as a school horse. He was more severe than Neapolitano Montenuova and when he encountered a clumsy rider he wasted little patience on him. With a tremendous capriole he set an end to this unpleasant experience and landed the all-too-hopeful candidate in the sand.

On one occasion I was confronted with a difficult situation. I had to choose one candidate from two young riders of approximately equal qualifica-tions. Together Neapolitano Montenuova and Pluto Siglavy were brought into the arena. Both rides mounted at the same time and rode in accordance with my commands, which gave me the opportunity to compare their abilities. Again they seemed quite equal and the decision was really hard to make. All of a sudden Pluto Siglavy came to my rescue and spilled his rider. I was glad to have support for my decision, but in order to be absolutely just, I had the riders change horses. What followed now was totally unexpected. Maybe Pluto Siglavy was annoyed by this additional work and, remembering the pleasure and relief of a capriole, after a few minutes landed the second candidate in the sand, too. Thus he evaded his responsibility and left the difficult decision entirely to me.

Oh, those school stallions—there is no end to stories and anecdotes about them. I have certainly learned to respect their personalities and to ac-knowledge them as teachers. On the other hand they become teachers only when the rider endeavours to understand their reactions and their behaviour. Since they cannot speak they are limited to signals. Perhaps many a rider may even be called lucky that they are unable to speak because they would often have occasion to put in complaints about incomprehension, ignorance, impatience, injustice, and ingratitude. Instead they serve man in silent and irrevocable loyalty.

From Sailboats to Snaffles in One Easy Marriage

From *Horsefolk Are Different*

BY COOKY McCLUNG

C ooky McClung has been called, and with good reason, "the Erma Bombeck of the horsy set." Her columns in *The Chronicle of the Horse* are one of the first things that subscribers turn to. And as anyone who knows Cooky is well aware, she's just as entertaining in person as she is in print.

Before he met her, the man spent his leisure time sailing. On weekends or long evenings he'd simply hop in the boat, cast off and up the mainsail, tacking to and fro among the whitecaps. Before he met her his life had order and regimentation and schedules he could stick with. He had a house with a yard and a toolshed.

But she had horses. He met her and fell in love and married her, and part of the wedding vows were "love me, love my horses." It was part and parcel of the whole relationship.

The order and regimen in his life floated across the horizon with most of his friends sailing off to leave him while he spent his weekends going to horse shows. Her schedules became his schedules, if you could call them that, which he never did because they varied from week to week and even day to day. The only constant in this new world of variables was that the horses were always fed on time.

He pondered the fact that, unlike the horses that were now a part of his life, his boat only ate when he used it. It did, of course, need gasoline in the tank to get him home should the wind happen to die down to nothing. His new bride pointed out, ever so subtly of course, that horses did not need to rely on anything so fickle as a puff of wind to move along.

Because the house with the yard and toolshed was in no way sufficient to keep several big, strong horses, the couple sold the man's house and went in search of a farm. To be fair, she looked very hard for a farm somewhat near a body of water where her spouse could still enjoy his beloved boat.

They compromised finally, and found a lovely house with a large pasture, two fine paddocks and a barn just 200 feet from their dwelling. They moved the boat to a cove 26 miles and two toll bridges away. If the man noticed a slight inequity in the fact that she could merely throw on a jacket over her pajamas and hop down to feed the horses, while he had to shave and pack a lunch to visit his boat, he was courteous enough not to mention it.

Although he was a fair enough handyman, tinkering about with his boat to keep the cogs and wheels and pulleys working, he had never had much experience keeping a farm in order. The boat had a large anchor that plunked into the water and a heavy rope on the bow that secured it to the dock where the boat obediently stayed until he wanted to use it. The man learned rather quickly that horses needed more elaborate forms of restraint and even if tied they often became disobedient.

The stable itself was in pretty good repair, and the man found little to do other than to fix the odd latch, fill in some holes in the stall floors and clear out a few months' accumulation of cobwebs and dirt. Neighbors visited often, and the man grew more familiar with horse terminology. When early on, one suggested he put a loafing shed in the big pasture, the man said, "That sounds nice; what's a loafing shed?"

The neighbors showed him what a loafing shed was, and that they could be built in different sizes, depending on how many horses wanted to stand under it (without fighting for space) in a thunderstorm. The man had never worried too much about his boat being out in a thunderstorm, even if it included lightning. Lightning was a consideration with horses wearing iron shoes, and did not bounce off them as harmlessly as it might a boat's mast.

And of course he had to install water troughs in the pasture and the paddocks, with no-freeze lines running to them. In the winter, when water froze, the boat was lifted out of its habitat and put into storage until the spring thaw. Horses, the man's bride pointed out again, were quite usable all year 'round. Even if one put them in storage, however, they still needed to eat.

The man also discovered that, while boats had a great number of accoutrements, horses had more. Naturally, the horses had come with quite an extensive wardrobe of tack and sheets and blankets and saddle pads and bandages and galloping boots. But it seemed something was always wearing out or being outgrown, something always needed breaking in, sewing up or soaping down. Once, when the man's wife was away for an afternoon, he decided to surprise her by washing four dirty turn-out blankets in their new washing machine. The Maytag repairman had something to do the next day.

And then, of course, there was the actual riding part. The man soon realized that if he wanted to spend more time with his new wife, he'd better learn how to actually get on and steer a horse. He envisioned cantering over the lovely countryside together, romantically picturing the television ad of horses moving gracefully along in slow motion as the couple smiled lovingly at each other. Reality was somewhat different.

While there was more to do to get a boat underway, once abroad with all the sails in place, one had only to stretch out on the deck and more or less guide the sail to determine the boat's direction. Because he was an intelligent man, it took him only a few seconds to discover that, even in a ring where he started to ride, if he just sat limply on a horse and barely held the reins, the direction the horse would choose would very likely not be the one of the man's choice. The horse would choose to simply drop his head and eat grass, thus allowing the man to slide unceremoniously down his neck, or would head for the barn and wait for dinner.

One had to be more in command, so to speak, upon a horse than on a boat deck. There was no first mate to give orders to if the horse happened to drift in the wrong direction. Also, the man pointed out after having done it several times, if he fell off a horse it hurt a lot more hitting the ground than if he fell off the boat and hit the water. Also, nine times out of 10, the horse would not wait for him to get back aboard. Neither, insisted his bride, would a boat, only a horse didn't go all the way to England if turned loose.

Because the man loved his wife dearly, he persevered. He traded his docksiders in for field boots, his cutoffs for breeches and his sweatshirt for a well-tailored hacking jacket. And he practiced every day, after work on long spring and summer evenings and every weekend, riding around the ring until he mastered posting to the trot and sitting to the canter, and gained enough experience to go across country.

They had searched and searched to find the man a horse with a personality like his boat's, a horse that did pretty much what you told it to do. His wife's horses, while tractable enough with an experienced rider, took advantage of a novice, and the man often longed for an anchor to "throw overboard" when they got going a little too fast.

Actually, the turning point in the man's formerly tidy, well-balanced life came when he got his very own horse. Even his den metamorphosed from a place with framed pictures of whaling vessels and artifacts of nautical persuasion, to one with blue and red ribbons and pedigrees of fine Thoroughbred lineage on the wall and bridles hanging over the back of his easy chair.

Not unlike a new parent, he took an avid interest in his own horse, fussing and pampering. While he had once secretly thought that, unlike sailing, riding was a pastime invented so that people could avoid work, now it became his avocation. He found himself making trips to the tack shop to buy articles he had formerly been unable to spell, and at dinner parties he began to take an active aprt in horsy discussions.

He even considered canceling his vacation plans. No one would take care of his horse the way he could. He was not concerned any more about his house. The house could burn to the ground. But he worried terribly that the horse would not be fed properly or that it might hurt itself and whoever was left in charge might not notice.

Some evenings his wife would find him just sitting in the pasture among the daisies like Ferdinand among his flowers, watching his very own horse as it strolled about chomping grass. The man entered small, local horse show classes, bringing home ribbons in such things as adult equitation and low hunter to add to the den wall collection. The following fall he was introduced to foxhunting, and thus began the demise of the man's boating interest.

His wife suggested that the man could still sail in the summertime and hunt in the fall and winter and go to some shows in the spring. But, of course, the horse might lose condition, and there was so much to do.

The man could be found forever revarnishing the stall doors, mowing the pasture, cleaning tack and displaying it on the new racks he'd built, or even mucking out. Mucking out, the man insisted, was good exercise and gave one time to contemplate the good things in life.

Finally they took one last trip to the cove to visit the boat, sitting forlornly in the water with cobwebs on the mast. "I suppose," said the man thoughtfully, "that it's time to sell the boat to someone who will really enjoy it." Watching it bob about on the mooring, he added, "I loved that boat a lot, but in all the years I had it, it never loved me back."

The Diverting History of John Gilpin

BY WILLIAM COWPER

illiam Cowper (1731–1800) was an eighteenth century pre-Romantic poet and essayist who is best known for religious writing. "The Diverting History of John Gilpin" is a rollicking account of what happened when the subject's horse overshot the destination not once but twice (it reminds me of the line about not wanting a horse that goes in a snaffle but one that *stops* in a snaffle).

John Gilpin was a citizen
  Of credit and renown,
A train-band Captain eke was he
  Of famous London town.

John Gilpin's spouse said to her dear,
  "Though wedded we have been
These twice ten tedious years, yet we
  No holiday have seen.

To-morrow is our wedding day,
  And we will then repair
Unto the Bell at Edmonton,
  All in a chaise and pair.

My sister and my sister's child,
  Myself and children three,
Will fill the chaise, so you must ride
  On horseback after we."

He soon replied,—"I do admire
    Of womankind but one,
And you are she, my dearest dear,
    Therefore it shall be done.

I am a linen-draper bold,
    As all the world doth know,
And my good friend the Calender
    Will lend his horse to go."

Quoth Mrs. Gilpin,—"That's well said,
    And for that wine is dear,
We will be furnish'd with our own,
    Which is both bright and clear."

John Gilpin kiss'd his loving wife;
    O'erjoyed was he to find
That though on pleasure she was bent,
    She had a frugal mind.

The morning came, the chaise was brought,
    But yet was not allow'd
To drive up to the door, lest all
    Should say that she was proud.

So three doors off the chaise was stay'd,
    Where they did all get in;
Six precious souls, and all agog
    To dash through thick and thin.

Smack went the whip, round went the wheels,
    Were never folk so glad,
The stones did rattle underneath
    As if Cheapside were mad.

John Gilpin at his horse's side,
    Seized fast the flowing mane,
And up he got, in haste to ride,
    But soon came down again;

For saddle-tree scarce reach'd had he,
　　His journey to begin,
When, turning round his head, he saw
　　Three customers come in.

So down he came; for loss of time,
　　Although it grieved him sore,
Yet loss of pence, full well he knew,
　　Would trouble him much more.

'T was long before the customers
　　Were suited to their mind,
When Betty screaming, came downstairs,
　　"The wine is left behind!"

"Good lack!" quoth he, "yet bring it me,
　　My leathern belt likewise,
In which I bear my trusty sword
　　When I do exercise."

Now mistress Gilpin, careful soul!
　　Had two stone bottles found,
To hold the liquor that she loved,
　　And keep it safe and sound.

Each bottle had a curling ear,
　　Through which the belt he drew,
And hung a bottle on each side,
　　To make his balance true.

Then over all, that he might be
　　Equipp'd from top to toe,
His long red cloak, well brush'd and neat,
　　He manfully did throw.

Now see him mounted once again
　　Upon his nimble steed,
Full slowly pacing o'er the stones
　　With caution and good heed.

But, finding soon a smoother road
   Beneath his well-shod feet,
The snorting beast began to trot,
   Which gall'd him in his seat,

So "Fair and softly," John he cried,
   But John he cried in vain;
That trot became a gallop soon,
   In spite of curb and rein.

So stooping down, as needs he must
   Who cannot sit upright,
He grasp'd the mane with both his hands,
   And eke with all his might.

His horse, who never in that sort
   Had handled been before,
What thing upon his back had got
   Did wonder more and more.

Away went Gilpin, neck or nought,
   Away went hat and wig!
He little dreamt when he set out
   Of running such a rig!

The wind did blow, the cloak did fly,
   Like streamer long and gay,
Till, loop and button failing both,
   At last it flew away.

Then might all people well discern
   The bottles he had slung;
A bottle swinging at each side,
   As hath been said or sung.

The dogs did bark, the children scream'd,
   Up flew the windows all,
And ev'ry soul cried out, "Well done!"
   As loud as he could bawl.

Away went Gilpin—who but he?
　His fame soon spread around—
"He carries weight!" "He rides a race!"
　"'T is for a thousand pound!"

And still, as fast as he drew near,
　'T was wonderful to view,
How in a trice the turnpike-men
　Their gates wide open threw.

And now, as he went bowing down
　His reeking head full low,
The bottles twain behind his back
　Were shattered at a blow.

Down ran the wine into the road,
　Most piteous to be seen,
Which made his horse's flanks to smoke
　As they had basted been.

But still he seem'd to carry weight,
　With leathern girdle braced,
For all might see the bottle-necks
　Still dangling at his waist.

Thus all through merry Islington
　These gambols he did play,
Until he came unto the Wash
　Of Edmonton so gay.

And there he threw the Wash about
　On both sides of the way,
Just like unto a trundling mop,
　Or a wild-goose at play.

At Edmonton his loving wife
　From the balcony spied
Her tender husband, wond'ring much
　To see how he did ride.

"Stop, stop, John Gilpin!—Here's the house!"
　　They all at once did cry;
"The dinner waits and we are tired:"
　　Said Gilpin—"So am I!"

But yet his horse was not a whit
　　Inclined to tarry there;
For why?—his owner had a house
　　Full ten miles off, at Ware,

So like an arrow swift he flew,
　　Shot by an archer strong;
So did he fly—which brings me to
　　The middle of my song.

Away went Gilpin, out of breath,
　　And sore against his will,
Till at his friend the Calender's
　　His horse at last stood still.

The Calender, amazed to see
　　His neighbour in such trim,
Laid down his pipe, flew to the gate,
　　And thus accosted him:—

"What news? what news? your tidings tell,
　　Tell me you must and shall—
Say why bare-headed you are come,
　　Or why you come at all?"

Now Gilpin had a pleasant wit,
　　And loved a timely joke,
And thus unto the Calender
　　In merry guise he spoke:—

"I came because your horse would come;
　　And if I well forebode,
My hat and wig will soon be here,
　　They are upon the road."

The Calender, right glad to find
   His friend in merry pin,
Return'd him not a single word,
   But to the house went in;

Whence straight he came with hat and wig,
   A wig that flow'd behind,
A hat not much the worse for wear,
   Each comely in its kind.

He held them up, and in his turn
   Thus show'd his ready wit:—
"My head is twice as big as yours,
   They therefore needs must fit.

But let me scrape the dirt away
   That hangs upon your face;
And stop and eat, for well you may
   Be in a hungry case."

Said John—"It is my wedding-day,
   And all the world would stare,
If wife should dine at Edmonton,
   And I should dine at Ware."

So, turning to his horse, he said—
   "I am in haste to dine;
'T was for your pleasure you came here,
   You shall go back for mine."

Ah, luckless speech and bootless boast!
   For which he paid full dear;
For, while he spake, a braying ass
   Did sing most loud and clear;

Whereat his horse did snort, as he
   Had heard a lion roar,
And gallop'd off with all his might,
   As he had done before.

Away went Gilpin, and away
    Went Gilpin's hat and wig!
He lost them sooner than at first,
    For why?—they were too big!

Now Mistress Gilpin, when she saw
    Her husband posting down
Into the country far away,
    She pull'd out half-a-crown;

And thus unto the youth she said
    That drove them to the Bell—
"This shall be yours when you bring back
    My husband safe and well."

The youth did ride, and soon did meet
    John coming back amain;
Whom in a trice he tried to stop,
    By catching at his rein;

But not performing what he meant,
    And gladly would have done,
The frighted steed he frighted more,
    And made him faster run.

Away went Gilpin, and away
    Went post-boy at his heels!—
The post-boy's horse right glad to miss
    The lumb'ring of the wheels.

Six gentlemen upon the road,
    Thus seeing Gilpin fly,
With post-boy scramp'ring in the rear,
    They raised the hue and cry:—

"Stop thief! stop thief—a highwayman!"
    Not one of them was mute;
And all and each that pass'd that way
    Did join in the pursuit.

And now the turnpike gates again
   Flew open in short space;
The toll-men thinking, as before,
   That Gilpin rode a race.

And so he did, and won it too,
   For he got first to town;
Nor stopp'd till where he had got up
   He did again get down.

Now let us sing, Long live the king,
   And Gilpin, long live he;
And when he next doth ride abroad,
   May I be there to see!

Tip on a Lost Race

BY CAREY WINFREY

C arey Winfrey, at present an editor at *People Magazine,* is a product of
Columbia College, the Marines, Columbia Graduate School of
Journalism, and the racetrack. As this selection from his memoir
Starts and Finishes: Coming of Age in the Fifties indicates, the last of
these institutions may have been of the greatest educative value.

His father, Bill Winfrey, was voted into the Racing Hall of Fame in 1972.

It was only by coincidence that my father arrived the week before I
did. He had come East for the yearling auctions to advise a wealthy Mexican in
the art of buying horses. The previous year the Mexican paid some $100,000
for a nineteen-year-old stallion and, horse longevity being roughly one-fourth
of a man's, there had been suggestions that he seek the advice of a horseman
before continuing his speculations in equine bloodstock. That's what my father
was doing in Saratoga.

I had seen him last in California. I drove up to the stable one morning
early. When I got out of the car, the first thing my father said to me was,
"You're certainly wearing your hair long."

"I guess so. The effete East, you know."

"Well, if it gets any longer," my father said, "you can stay in the East."
Then he apologized. "You're grown now," he said. "You can do what you like."
But he looked at the ground a lot the rest of the weekend I was there.

My father had already returned to California by the time I got to
Saratoga. But it was almost as if he were still there. Everywhere I went, people
told me that they'd seen him and how well he looked.

Six years ago my father set an all-time money-winning record as a trainer of thoroughbred horses. Led by two two-year-old champions (Bold Lad and Queen Empress), his stable won nearly a million and a half dollars in purse money (of which my father, as trainer, got roughly 10 per cent). Astounding to many, the next year he walked away from that same stable—easily the best in the country—citing personal reasons for his resignation. The wire services carried a blurb about Bill Winfrey "retiring" from racing at the age of fifty. He didn't retire though, and even today there is lingering speculation around the racetrack as to why he left. The only reason my father ever gave was that the job took too much time away from his family. I certainly never had any trouble believing that that was the real reason. Still, there were a lot of rumors that my father had not gotten along all that well with one of the stable's owners, Ogden Phipps, a thoroughbred breeder, member of the Jockey Club, racing official, and one of the half-dozen or so most powerful men in American racing.

I am nine or ten years old and deep asleep in the still hour before dawn. In a little while my father will come and sit on the edge of my bed, rubbing my back slow and warm to wake me. But now I am dreaming: I am watching Les or John or one of the other grooms braid the tail of a gleaming chestnut colt, beautifying him for a race. I am sitting cross-legged at the door of the stall, listening to the soft, whispering psssssssss, psssssssss music the groom makes, exhaling, to keep the horse hairs from getting in his mouth, when my father appears, upset. "The jock can't ride," he announces to no one in particular. "We'll have to scratch."

Now the dream gets a little hazy. But somehow, miraculously, there I am, splendidly annointed in racing silks, the whip in my right hand, the stirrups pulled so high my knees touch my hands. Now the dream is clear again. We are led into the starting gate. I hear my heart tharumping in my chest. "No chance, Mr. Cassidy," I yell to the starter. Then my horse is still. The bell rings, the doors fly open, and with an incredible lurch that all but throws me from the saddle, we are off. I hit the colt three times with my whip, each time in stride—bam, pause, bam, pause, bam—just to get him going. We settle back for the stretch drive and I lean back holding him in, saving his speed, rating him, riding easy. When we round the last turn and head for home, I begin to hear the roar in the grandstand. I am whipping again, now, as we pass horses on the outside, the colt and I moving as one. Now there is but one horse in front of me and, as I creep up on him it is all I can do to keep asleep for my inevitable, but still incredible . . . Victory . . . by a nose.

Maybe a jockey was the only thing I ever really wanted to be. The thought occurs to me now, walking my father's and grandfather's paths here at Saratoga. Breathing this air that is a perfume of linament, pine, oats, straw, and, yes, manure, I am once again "Bill's boy," my father's son, dependent on his praise for my solace, ready at his bidding to remount a frisky palomino that has just run off and thrown me.

We would get up those mornings about 5:30, my father and I, splashing cold water on our faces to wake us, moving quietly through the house so as not to disturb my mother. The streetlights would be haloed in the morning dew as we drove through near-deserted streets, the radio blaring Frankie Laine and "Mule Traaaaaaaiiiin . . . clippety cloppin' over hill and dale . . ." We would sing to the radio, in tune only with each other. I would lean against my father's warmth and never suspect there was any other thing to be but happy.

We'd arrive at first light, and the first set of horses, half a dozen or so, would already be saddled. The exercise boys, seeing us arrive, would put down their coffees and get ready to get aboard their horses. I would walk down the long shed past two dozen horses in their stalls. It was a ritual my father insisted on—saying good morning to the grooms and exercise boys who worked for him. "Good morning, 'Apples,' " "Good morning, Harold."

Once the riders had mounted, the exercise boys would lead the horses to the training track, while I would follow my father on foot to the clocking stand, stopping with him along the way as he exchanged cheery small talk ("You know my boy Carey") with the other trainers. The fact that I never managed to decipher it never prevented my enjoying the cryptic language of the clockers: "Twenty-two and two for the bay colt. What'ju get him in, Jack?" By the time we'd get back to the stable, the grooms would have unsaddled the horses and would have started washing them. The exercise boys, each holding the shank of their mounts, would relive the workout, speaking the present-tense vernacular of race-trackese: "Well, we break real good at the quarter pole, but then this filly she see a bird or something and she break stride . . ." The horses, sweating and frisky now, would kick out with their hind feet as the grooms ("Hey now poppa, what'sa matter with you") lavished steaming buckets of hot water on their sweating bodies, applying it in great dripping sponges before whisking them dry with long aluminum scrapers. Often, after the horses' baths, my father would let me take the shank of a quieter colt or filly and I'd join the seemingly endless oval parade around the cooling-out ring.

But the best part of the morning was when it came time to ride the pony. For as long as I could remember, my father's pony was named Bill. I don't know how many Pony Bills there were in all in the years I spent weekends and summers at the track, but I do know that I fell off just about every one of them. Even if I was hurt, as happened a couple of times, my father would always make me get right back on and ride some more.

I never suspected that such rides would mark the end of my memory's view of childhood. I didn't know that my parents would soon be divorced, or that I would be sent, in the fifth grade, to a military school in Maryland—out of range, the thinking ran, of any of the attendant acrimony. Nor could I know that I would come to look upon such mornings at the racetrack as my strongest ties to earth and place, my strongest link to the kind of heritage I would read about in the library of that school.

A dream much like mine had actually come true for my father. Twice, in fact. As a boy of nine, he won his first horse race, riding a circus pony named Sparkle, not too much bigger than he was, at the old Jamaica track on Long Island. I don't know how many other horses there were in the race, but I have been told they were under considerable restraint. In the picture taken in the winner's circle, my father's nine-year-old face is very serious, but the men standing around in black suits and hats behind him are all smiles.

When he was seventeen, he won his second race, this time in real competition. "Congratulations," says the telegram in my grandmother's scrapbook. "Bill won his first race today." It was signed by my grandfather, "Carey." Next to it, a yellowed clipping is more detailed: "Willie Winfrey rode his first winner here this afternoon. Son of G. Carey Winfrey, well-known owner and trainer, Willie has been trying to crash the winner's circle since early in the last Florida campaign. . . . Eight answered the call, but little Willie showed them the way home. He brought the B. B. Stable's two-year-old from behind in a rattling stretch drive to take command in the closing strides. The stable gang gave the little boy a great big hand."

The applause notwithstanding, my father has always said that the greatest mistake he made in life was quitting school in the ninth grade to become a jockey.

My father's riding career lasted less than a year. Having put on too much weight to continue as a jockey, he became, at eighteen, the country's youngest licensed horse trainer, taking a string of my grandfather's stable up to Canada. By the time I was born (1941, the year Whirlaway won the Triple Crown), my father had a small reputation and was developing better and better horses for a series of owners. When, in the late 1940s, Alfred G. Vanderbilt asked him to take charge of his once-commanding stable, my father willingly accepted and the next year found himself with three stakes winners (Bed O Roses, Next Move, and Loser Weeper); he had become one of the most talked-about young trainers in the country. But his greatest success was yet to come. As I cried myself to homesick sleep in a dormitory near Baltimore in 1951, at Vanderbilt's Sagamore farm a few miles away a spirited gray yearling was growing stronger and more powerful. My father said he could have trained himself. Television's first equine celebrity, Native Dancer would win twenty-one of his twenty-two races, make the cover of *Time* magazine, inspire fan mail from matrons who didn't know a furlong from a furlough, and turn an already swell-headed kid into a vicarious braggart who went around telling people he was "Bill Winfrey's boy."

The Ponies Are Talking

BY HOLLY MENINO

A former Olympic dressage rider on the United States Equestrian
Team, Lendon Gray is now a leading instructor and commentator.
In this selection from *Forward Motion* by Holly Menino, we see the
efforts of a dedicated and intelligent instructor in providing the
framework for the education of a horse and rider (and in the process we learn
a few valuable things about training).

"They have no syntax," the Stoics reasoned about animals, "therefore
we may eat them." My friend Roger is less self-serving but shares this belief
about animals and language. On a weekend trip to Saratoga, he went to the
track but did not bet. "I'll step up to the window just as soon as the ponies start
talking."

Lendon Gray knows the ponies are talking, and she knows how to talk
pony. The two-time Olympic dressage rider and the people who train under
her spend their days—or, at the very least, their weekday mornings—working
out the syntax of classical horsemanship. This is the same horsemanship that
Keith Taylor trains for in the first phase of combined training, and its movements are also the basis of a show jumper's skill. But at Lendon's Gleneden
Farm, dressage is practiced intensively as a discipline unto itself.

Lendon has a big, clear voice. It is pleasant and it is very loud. She may
be riding a turn at one end of the huge indoor arena and giving instructions to
a pupil riding along the other end, and when her voice reaches the student on
the horse, I'm sure it is still loud. It seems remarkable to me that Lendon can
speak at the same time she is riding, let alone analyze someone else's riding and
call out instructions to improve it. She is putting out a good deal of physical
effort, and this is something many riders I've talked with feel is generally

unrecognized—"Yeah, all you gotta do is sit up there, right?" was the way one of Keith's event rider friends typified the general run of ignorance among sports fans. But Lendon is able to ride, watch her students, and articulate what they should do. It is impossible to ignore, but her voice always suspects that it is being ignored. "You have asked the question," Lendon declares, "and now you must have an answer. You *must* get an answer."

Fifi Clark, like most of Lendon's clients, is female. She is tall and in her fifties, silver and gold patrician. She is fit and determined and riding a hefty bay mare. It is ten o'clock in the morning, when traffic in the Gleneden arena near Bedford, New York, is at its peak. Just north of New York City only a few miles from the Connecticut border, Bedford, the village and the outlying homes, scatters judiciously among private grassy hills, old trees, and stone walls. You can't see many of the houses from the road. Similarly, the house and barns on the farm where Gleneden is housed are set back from the road at a protective distance. Lendon's operation shares the estate with a thoroughbred breeding facility. The indoor school is the largest of a group of yellow buildings set in the middle of shady, fenced paddocks and protected from travelers on the county road by a lane with a security gate and the big maple trees that border the road. The cars parked in the stable courtyard are Mercedeses, BMWs, and Volvos. Lendon has left her much-used Subaru just beyond the wide door to the indoor arena and made a quick circuit through her office in the front of that building before heading out to the mounting block, where one of the Latino grooms waits with a small gray horse. Five other women have brought their horses into the building. There is a lot of discussion going on, many attempts to talk pony.

In its strict meaning, "dressage" is simply the training of the horse. In use, though, dressage has become the art and intensely competitive sport of training in the classical movements. Like figure skating, dressage emphasizes the power and beauty of motion, and competitors in the sport are judged on accuracy and the élan with which they perform prescribed movements. The movements the horse and rider are asked to perform depend on the horse's stage of development. At the lower levels, the tests demonstrate simple movements with long intervals of modulation between different gaits and maneuvers. The higher the test level, the more difficult the coordination asked of the horse and the more rapid the transitions between movements.

Lendon Gray is one of the most successful practitioners of dressage in the United States. She has won more national titles than any other trainer in the country, and she has become known for her ability to make brilliant, expressive horses out of unlikely candidates. She has a round valentine face and a small, sweetly shaped mouth. She is forty-six, not large, but she carries herself with the same great authority carried by her voice. Sitting a horse, she looks taller. She is straight and supple, centered, and there is relaxed symmetry in her activities. When she enters the grand prix arena in formal attire, her concentration is fierce, a force that shuts out show grounds, audience, judges, everything except the white boundary of the arena, the letters that mark the points of transition, and the responses of the horse under her. This concentration is evident in her riding at home. Somehow, although she is answering my questions and supervising the other women riding in the arena, her focus never drifts from her horse, Last Scene. A small gray horse with black legs, he has delicate, refined ears and the round dark eyes you see in illustrations of ponies in children's books. He is the horse Lendon has most recently introduced to the movements of the grand prix test, the ultimate competitive goal of a dressage horse.

Big windows above the long sides of the arena allow daylight to fall on the riders' heads and the soft brown footing. Hoofs grind the tanbark into fine shreds and mix it with the animals' manure. Most of the women here are clients. They pay Lendon to stable their horses under her management and ride under her tutelage. As is typical of dressage riders, most of these students develop an intimate knowledge of their own particular horse. While they do not actually handle routine stable work, they devote many hours beyond their time in the saddle to their horses. They become keen observers of horse motion, always on the alert for some encroachment on their horses' soundness, and they put a good deal of thought into the details of the horses' well-being, feeding and fitness, turnout and blanketing. One longtime observer of horse sports remarked to me that a dressage rider could look at the horse standing in his stall and instantly detect a new fly bite on the animal.

Although some of Lendon's students compete in dressage, a number of them ride with her for the sole purpose of initiation into the art. They are the legatees of a school of horsemanship that dates from Renaissance Italy but was first put forth humanely as a "scientific" system in 1623 by Antoine de Pluvinel, who ran a finishing school for young noblemen and was the riding instructor of Louis XIII. His *Manège du Roy,* a philosophical dialogue about the horse and its proper education, guided many other riding masters across the Continent who were entrusted with the education of aristocrats. In the manège, the riding school, the activities of the horse were routinized as gaits and movements. He was taught to travel straight forward by "treading the ring," trotting or galloping along narrow paths, and to be "just" in his turns by repetition of various exercises.

In Lendon's arena also, each woman rides a deliberate pattern. Each horse keeps his own cadence, and the arena reverberates with muffled polyrhythms cut through by the voice of Lendon Gray. She works like a ballet master with dancers as they work on their exercises at the bar—exhorting them, calling our sharp corrections, tapping a leg here, reaching up to reposition a hand. Keith Taylor has progressed through many of these lessons with Play Me Right and through the less complex tasks with Faktor. Play Me Right, for instance, can canter sideways and forward at the same time, the legs on either side of his body reaching past the legs on the opposite in the lithe X—no small feat of coordination—and Faktor does well in the turns and bends and adjustments in speed that are expected of a horse in the more elementary dressage tests. By way of becoming competitive in combined training, Keith has had to become a rider who could compete in dressage at the middle levels of the sport. The skills Play Me Right develops for the dressage phase are essential to the balance, thrust, and precise footwork the horse will call upon in the cross-country and stadium jumping phases.

What is different about the movements Last Scene performs with Lendon is the degree to which his balance is shifted back into his hindquarters. He is building tremendous isometric strength in his back end, and this allows him to be so light off his front end that Lendon can control an impressive range of motion with imperceptible movement of her seat and hands. When she gathers Last Scene back into himself like this, he is "collected," and collection is the legacy and mode of the manège. Beginning with the likes of Pluvinel and his British counterpart, the Duke of Newcastle, Renaissance trainers began to incorporate this rebalancing of the horse into a system of training that evolved in parallel with the very different techniques for educating horses and riders for military operations in which the rider leaned or perched forward on the horse. These military methods appear to have their origins among the nomadic warriors of Eastern Europe, for whom speed was a far greater consideration than poise or precision. Tension between the techniques of the manège and the traditions of the cavalry and hunt field has been ongoing. It has produced lively theoretical debates and a good deal of cross-fertilization among diverse schools of equitation, and it continues to act as a dynamic link among contemporary teachers and masters.

Dressage, the art for art's sake school of horsemanship, does not involve the speed or danger of other horse sports, but many top riders have left fast times and big fences for the intellectual stimulation of manège and the rigor of its search for purity of movement. Among Lendon's students, there are artists, cooks, lawyers, financiers, and an actor. They are, on the whole, people who understand the rewards of submitting to a discipline. As practiced at Gleneden, dressage is an ongoing process of development in which competition is an optional test of progress. It is a continuum of momentary performances as transitory as passages of music, and each of these performances is the result of the rider's intimate communication with the horse.

The big stolid bay mare carrying Fifi Clark is thundering along pleasantly. Everything about this mare is large, weighty. She is heavy equipment going to work. But there is something about the way the horse is responding that Lendon does not like, and it sends her voice up a few more decibels. "She is *ignoring* you. *Demand* an answer."

The silence Lendon hears is the curve of the mare's body as it trots a circle. She will not accept it. Although she continues to engage in dialogue with her own small gray horse, she keeps after Fifi until something shifts briefly. The change is momentary, but it is the answer Lendon was listening for.

"Good, Fifi—*super!*"

The language Lendon's students struggle with is unuttered. Its grammar is split-second sequencing of physical cues—the insistence of the legs, the tightening of fingers, the pressure of rein on bit and bit on mouth, the straightening of the rider's back, the sinking of her loins. This is the nature of riding because it is the nature of the horse. Horses do make sounds, and we have the words "neigh" and "whinny" to label them. But horse noise is usually an uncontemplated call, and what prompts it is some kind of need, such as hunger or, because horses are intensely social and their society depends on physical proximity, separation from other horses. But even when the horse is communicating with others in his herd, noise is cruder expression than what the horse achieves with his body. Dominance and fear, love and elation, are explained by one horse to others in terms of motion and place—where a horse puts her body, how he carries his tail, the curve of her neck, the angle of his ears.

Movement is the basis of our communication with horses, from trivial conversation to artistic endeavor. It conveys the subtlety of horse thought and horse intention. Lendon doesn't talk about *language*. She doesn't tell her students they are learning a language or insist they conjugate the verbs correctly as she did when she was tutoring Latin and Greek at Sweet Briar College. She assumes the language is there, and she assumes that her students are just looking for the right vocabulary. Later, when I began to visit Anne Kursinski, I found that she makes the existence of this language explicit in her teaching and writing about show jumping. Once a dressage rider herself, Anne still talks pony, and in her book on technique and training, she advises all who would ride to be aware that that is what they are doing, using language. When you sit behind the horse's shoulder and wrap your legs around his sides, you are in the conversation pit, the physical center of the animal. The sides of some horses vibrate, making a connection of your nerves with theirs. The sides or others seem dead, not like living matter but like a mattress. Either way, every impulse of the horse will pass through you, every word the horse says—if you can only hear.

Lendon listens to all kinds of horses. She is a democrat. In the dressage world, where big horses with extravagant movement have created the standard, this makes her an iconoclast. She rides some of these big horses, but just as often she rides diminutive Arabs, quarter horses, Morgans, ponies of various descriptions. She rides horses that have been schooled for the jumping arena, ex-racehorses, cutting horses, and once she brought out a horse that had been trained for the sole purpose of dog and pony shows. She believes in the process of dressage, that it will make even the most homely unaccomplished animal more beautiful and capable. In her hands, this is what happens. One of her clients has a small gray Arabian. On a summer weekend Lendon showed the horse in lower-level dressage and won the division. Two weeks later, she reported with great pride, the horse's owner, an endurance rider, won a hundred-mile competitive trail ride with him.

Under Lendon even the most ordinary animal works toward the highest levels, and she is openly sympathetic to the particular difficulties each horse must overcome. For riders, though, her patience is short. It can be stretched only by a student's absolute concentration on the work of getting the lingo down. She is kind and critical by turns as her riders adjust their posture or give up some tension Lendon identifies in a hand or an elbow. She snaps if a corner is ridden lazily in a shallow arc. She suggests, she demands, she implores so that riders working under her can do what she does on the little gray: sit their horses and understand the physical reverberations.

Lendon's gaze falls on another student, another faulty movement. This rider is a young, slight woman on a small stallion. It is a pretty bright bay and delicate enough that I had to look twice to determine its sex. The rider, who is named Karen, is sitting pretty enough, but evidently she is only passively engaged. A few minutes earlier, Karen withdrew a glove plaintively to demonstrate a callus the rein was leaving on the side of her finger. On the finger was a diamond the size of a throat lozenge. Lendon was not interested in the diamond or the callus. She was interested in how the little stallion was going and now she wants more from this rider. She criticizes the way the rider moves the horse through a corner. In a louder voice she demands a better turn. Then, forbidding another turn like the other, she places her own horse in the corner to force the line that will be ridden.

"Karen! How *can* you keep riding this way? I asked you for a *fast* trot. Do you think that's *fast*? Karen! Is he even *trotting?*"

Sweat begins to run down from the corners of Karen's eyes. Her makeup drips to the front of her T-shirt. This is not enough to bring any mercy, because Karen is making no effort to change.

"What are you thinking? I mean, *are* you thinking? Karen . . . *stop* the horse. Get off."

None of the other riders in the arena takes any notice of this. They are initiates, practicing toward the same perfection Lendon has shown them, and each of them has been caught in her sights at one time or another. They know her frustration is nothing personal. It is a question of correct movement. Lendon steps up on the little stallion and puts the question forcefully with her legs against his sides. The stallion lurches forward briefly, then recovers and gives Lendon her answer: intentional motion. He digs in and surges rhythmically along the wall of the arena.

"*This,* Karen, is *fast.*" She is talking about speed the way the jazz drummer Tony Williams talks about playing fast, rhythm that responds to a heightened accounting for the passage of time.

"See what I mean?" She dismounts and hands the reins back to her student, who avoids her gaze. "It's very clear, isn't it?"

She gets back aboard Last Scene and rides over to the observation seats and grins at me. "I couldn't let you go home without seeing me really get started." The next time I see Karen she herself will be riding Lendon's Last Scene. I think this is far too generous of Lendon, since Karen is too reticent to ride the horse as he needs to be ridden. But Lendon says it's not really so generous. Last Scene has a lot to tell Karen.

Early the first morning I visit Lendon, before the commuter traffic peaks and Lendon's clients can break free from the demands of their suburban households, the arena in Bedford is very quiet. I can hear a car go by way out on the road. I can hear the pigeons that preside from the steel rafters. Even in her absence, Lendon's voice is a presence. Her head working student, Liz Britten, is riding, and, watching her, I see the implications of Lendon's efforts with horses and students.

Like other working students, Liz is an apprentice who assumes responsibility for chores in the stable in return for Lendon's mentorship. She is very tall, a couple inches over six feet. Her dark hair is drawn away from her face in a classic chignon. She is a beautiful girl with wide-spaced eyes and lifting brows. Liz is much younger than Lendon, and patience dominates her manner—which is a good thing, since she spends a large portion of every day riding young horses, talking pony, repeating herself endlessly. But before her other riding begins, she rides Medallion, a horse Lendon has trained to the grand prix movements. There is some very fancy talk going on, an artful conversation concerning one of the most difficult movements a horse can perform, the *piaffe*. Except for the cadenced blows of the brown gelding's hoofs, the arena is silent. Liz attends to the horse, a meditative incline to her head, and Medallion attends to Liz with extreme effort. He is teaching her something.

Medallion has performed *piaffe* countless times. He knows how it goes, he knows the steps. But lifting each leg in correct sequence and cadence requires particular balance and intense coordination, and in order to accomplish these movements, Medallion needs to hear the words. They come from Liz's seat and hands, and they remind Medallion of the *piaffe*—ah, *that* move! As soon as he recognizes Liz's intention, he creates the movement. The horse draws himself together, as if he may squat down, but what he does is to remain in place, performing a slow and extravagant trot. It is heart-stopping in its intensity and exhilarating in its power.

Piaffe has been taught since the early Renaissance, but Liz could not know the movement until she had ridden it on a horse that had been schooled in *piaffe*. Medallion has the *concept* of *piaffe*. It is a horse concept, and having learned it from Lendon, he now understands the movement well enough to lead Liz to the physical instructions for it.

Medallion is now absolutely fluent in *piaffe* and the other movements that comprise the grand prix test. Lendon has spent years of physically and mentally demanding work to ratchet up the level of her communication with the horse, and most of what comes out of this work is self-awareness. Medallion is aware of his movement and his ability to assert control over it. When the horse completes a movement and can surge off into the next without correction, he assumes great authority, and when his work is over for the day, he saunters about the arena on a loose rein, his ears forward and his eyes wide. He senses his worth, and he makes it clear that the work is important to him. When it is interrupted, he feels a loss. Earlier that year, Liz had surgery on her leg. She was not able to ride but she continued in her work around the stable. Medallion began to express unhappiness. When anyone would pass his stall, he presented his face in the Dutch door and laid his ears back sourly. This brought no results, so he began hanging over the door to make sure no one would miss his glowering. Then one morning as Liz hobbled down through the shed row, he leaned far out into the aisle, caught her sleeve in his teeth, and pulled her to him. At some level he understands that he and Liz are undertaking something together. He wants to make the moves because movement is the way the horse defines himself. Prowess is his meaning.

It doesn't take much to pervert this meaning. The horse is a big, powerful, and very sensitive animal, and the use of force or even just clumsy expression can violate the horse's understanding. It's just a short trip over the boundary pointed out in a common saying quoted by Danish trainer Bengt Ljundquist: "Where art ends, violence begins," and at virtually every dressage competition where I've seen brilliant riders, I've also seen riders who cause their horses pain and confusion. They lack the physical equipment—they are too tense, they are too fat, or they ride too little—to speak the lingo. They lack the education. They jounce. Their hands jerk involuntarily at the horse's mouth. Their bodies pound the horse's back. Their legs flap at the horse's sides, their spurs digging randomly. They lack syntax. They can't talk pony.

On a cold March day I visited a stable in Connecticut where the footing outdoors was treacherous and forced the riders to crowd into the indoor arena. A woman brought a stiff black horse to the mounting block. The lady was well educated, pleasant, and in fact had a job teaching somewhere. She had just been to a dressage clinic, and the old horse was in for it. He knew it. The white of his eye showed as she climbed aboard. She put her spurs to him and worked on one rein. When he made a tentative effort, she repeated the abuse. In a minute or two the horse was hopping frantically. Even in the frigid arena, sweat broke out on his neck. She worked at him. He threatened to go up. She turned him in a dizzying little circle, a technique she had probably been shown to deal with rearing, but rearing caused by something other than herself. After fifteen minutes the old horse was in a lather and unable to trot forward, walk forward, or move naturally in any direction. The lady dismounted in frustration. "I just don't know what his problem is today." She did not know which questions to ask. She lacked syntax. She lacked even a basic vocabulary. Her old black horse was doomed to meaninglessness.

If you picture this horse and then turn to Last Scene, you will understand why dressage is a tradition of masters and students. It saves horses from bewilderment and makes brilliance possible. Lendon is part of the tradition of mastery. "I didn't choose this, you know," she has told me about riding. "I needed a job." This pragmatic explanation works, but she is too Yankee to explain also that the only reason it works is that, like Keith Taylor, she has the touch.

She grew up in Old Town, Maine, one of four children. Her father built the canoes for which the town is known, and she tells me he was also one of the first people in the country to experiment with water skis. Her mother came from a well-to-do family and brought to Old Town the first pleasure horse the local people had seen. The only people who rode there were kids who piled onto ponies, and they called Mrs. Gray's horse the "piggyback horse." The couple kept horses for the children, and Lendon and her older sister took intense and competitive interest in riding.

When Lendon went to prep school, she found she could make money by teaching people to ride. Later at Sweet Briar, she rode under Paul Cronin, who was interested in "educated" riding and had begun to systematize an approach to training hunters and jumpers based on the so-called forward seat that was becoming popular in this country. It would be several years before Lendon was introduced to the idea of collecting power and balance in the horse's hindquarters. She majored in classics, and after she graduated, she stayed on at Sweet Briar, teaching riding under Cronin and tutoring girls in Latin and Greek. During this period she became interested in event riding, and this led her to Margaret Whitehurst.

An independent and unusual person in her own right, Peggy Whitehurst had been a talented amateur rider with friends who rode on the early U.S. Olympic teams after World War II. She went on to become a commercial pilot for Pan American—evidently gender barriers had not yet been erected in the airline industry—and then married a physicist and settled on a farm in Tuscaloosa, Alabama. Using a couple of thoroughbred stallions and mares of various breeds, she began to develop a strong strain of homebreds, and by judicious pairing of these animals with top trainers, has produced horses that made the U.S. Equestrian Team lists for show jumping as well as dressage. But when Lendon came to the Whitehurst farm, her assignment was to develop the horses for combined training.

At that time, there was only nascent interest in dressage as a discipline unto itself, but when one of the Whitehurst horses, a mare named Crown Juel, began to make it clear that her talents lay outside running and jumping, Peggy said, "Why don't you try her in dressage?"

Lendon had never seen a horse perform a grand prix test and still hadn't when she took on a horse named Beppo to try for a berth on the U.S. team that would go to the 1978 World Championships. She shipped the horse to Maine for a few lessons with Michael Poulin, who coached her well enough that she was able to travel with the team to Europe as an alternate. Peggy Whitehurst continued to be a strong presence and support. Lendon took Beppo to the 1980 Alternate Games and around the same time began working with Peggy's Seldom Seen, the first horse Lendon herself trained to the grand prix level and the first of Lendon's "ponies," the small horses she has pitted successfully against the much larger, heavier types associated with dressage.

If you look at photographs of Lendon on horses during this period, you see that remarkably little has changed in the round, generous face, the small chin, the owl rims of her glasses, or the absolute correctness of her position. But details of angle and attitude show her eagerness as well as some uncertainty. How could she have known what she was in for?

At the time, Americans were even less competitive in world-class dressage than they are now. The European riders were backed by centuries of training and theory, bloodlines and study. Dressage as both an art and a competitive sport had been developed extensively—so much so that there were even styles of riding associated with particular countries. American riders had only one Olympic medal to their credit, a bronze won in 1932 by a military officer named Hiram Tuttle. Not many people in the dressage community knew enough to advise Lendon. Michael Poulin, who is known for being brilliant and quixotic, had respect for the classical principles and an intuitive understanding of what motivates a horse. He was based only an hour or so from Old Town, where she had grown up, so she didn't really have to leave home to ally herself. It was physically grueling—she was a working student and rose at three in the morning to be at Poulin's for a lesson at six before she started work—but it was productive. He gave her a lot, and even though she eventually paid off the actual bills, "I never did pay for what he gave me."

Peggy understood the obstacles that faced American riders, and although she was not able to foot the whole bill herself, she helped raise money to send Lendon to Europe to test Seldom Seen in the big time. According to Lendon, the Europeans were completely unaccustomed to seeing a little horse work in the same arena as their own breeds they had developed for the sport. But she says the European judges were more open to Seldom Seen's potential than the judges at home.

Stationed beside one of the first arenas Lendon rode into, a judge—one of three analyzing the ride—watched Seldom Seen's entrance wearily. "He probably thought, 'Oh, these damned Americans—what next?' " He lit up a cigarette and slouched down in his chair to endure the ride. As Seldom Seen was working through the first extended trot, the judge's eyes lifted. He straightened a little more when she rode into the half-passes, and by the time the little horse struck off into *passage*—which is essentially *piaffe* carried into forward movement—the cigarette was out. The skeptic was upright, dictating responsibly to his scribe.

Lendon and Seldom Seen did not take Europe by storm. She was there to watch and learn, to absorb as much of the techniques and theory that could work for the horse and her. She and Seldom Seen acquitted themselves well enough and they returned home to challenge the competition. There was a willfulness in all this, a young American on a pint-sized horse running through donated funds to ride with the elite in Europe. It was a will to know and to master. In dressage, as in art and music and literature—any endeavor where mastery is embodied and transmitted through personality—teacher-student relationships are complex.

Lendon left Poulin's operation in 1987. She was competing successfully with him, but at the same time she realized how dependent she had become on him, that she really missed having him tell her what to do in competition and even in day-to-day training. She says she is determined not to foster that kind of dependency in her own students. She wants them to exercise some initiative and try to work things out with their horses for themselves, as she does with Last Scene.

The little gray is aptly named. He is, in fact, the last of Peggy White-hurst's competition horses. When I saw him for the first time, he had been in training with Lendon for seven years, and although he was highly educated, he was just beginning to compete in the movements that Medallion knows so well. If he could sustain the physical and mental demands of high-level train-ing, he would develop even further until he too achieved mastery. Along the way, he would compete, and in spite of the hours she has invested in this horse, Lendon's ambitions for Last Scene are tempered by pragmatism. She points out that when it comes to competition, size can be a limitation. A small horse like Last Scene will have to do more—he will have to be more brilliant, and he will have to move with greater amplitude—in order to achieve the same marks as one of the big horses typical of the sport. Lendon met those challenges suc-cessfully with Seldom Seen, and it is altogether possible that Last Scene will also be able to make size irrelevant. But Lendon does not let her uncertainty about the horse's prospects in competition distract her from working toward Last Scene's eventual development. This will be a moment-by-moment pro-cess, and even as she mounts up, she is making each moment count.

When Lendon swings up on Last Scene and asks him to move off, two things are transformed, the horse and Lendon Gray. Last Scene grows rounder, like a horse in a Renaissance print, more powerful and precise in motion. He gains authority, and as I watch him change, I wonder if Last Scene's experience is something like what happened to me on a dance floor in California. There was a good orchestra, more than forty strings, playing Viennese waltzes. My partner, whom I had met moments before, was an expert on Schubert who had recently returned from a year in Vienna. I knew the box step. He could waltz. He was a strong dancer, and even in the first bars of music, I was waltzing, flying through intricate embellishments of the basic movements as if I knew what I was doing. But I couldn't have begun to replicate the steps after he released me. I don't remember his name or his face, but I remember with precision how his arms felt. His hold gave me authority, and I suspect this is what Lendon gives Last Scene.

Seated on the horse, she is elegant. She has long-legged grace, quiet poise, and when the horse is making his biggest moves, her body barely moves against him. She is carried effortlessly. When Lendon dismounts, she is an ordinary person again. She is no longer statuesque, just a woman of medium height and medium weight. She walks as if she's pushing something—a grocery cart or a stroller—and her hair bobs with every stride. When she looks away from the horses, she talks girl talk. "I *love* the sweater," she tells a client, a jewelry designer, and comments to me about her artistic verve: "Everything she does is that way. She *designed* this watch." She is often impressed by her students' accomplishments in business and art and with the horses, and her students seem to sense her appreciation of them. When they step down from their horses, they appear to leave behind any worries or resentments about the day's work. There is laughter and talk about parties and shows and shopping. The next morning, pony talk will transform them again.

When things work—when the conversation really flows and Last Scene carries Lendon through a pirouette at the canter—whose art is it anyway? *They have no syntax, therefore we may push them around?* Lendon may call the tune, but is she some kind of tough guy waggling a revolver at the feet of a victim—"Now *dance*"? The themes of this literature belong to the horse. They are natural ways of going—trotting, running, acting sexy—made self-conscious. Artifice and the motive to apply it are Lendon's contribution, but no rider could have dreamed up the movement if horses had not first shared their potential to create the movements and to take pleasure from them.

A good rider teaches this potential to her horse. A bad rider invites destruction of what comes naturally and could have been heightened by the horse's intentional participation. An indifferent rider creates a hack. A hack is oblivious to art. A hack ignores self-potential for art. What distinguishes Dorothy Parker from Eudora Welty is the difference between a hack and a horse. In much of her work, Parker, amusing as she was, took small things and made nothing of them. Welty saw the potential of small things and made magic of them.

The Riddler, my own sturdy horse with the quizzical blaze, is a hack. It isn't his fault. He is a good enough horse with a good enough heart, but he is ignorant. He talks only pidgin pony, and this is the fault of a series of indifferent riders, the last of them me. My ignorance compounds his. Out on the trail, we move together well. But on these outings we don't talk much. Things are fine until, like the woman trying to ride the old black horse, what I have in mind is beautiful. I ask him to move forward and sideways at the same time, but Riddler's answer is to lift his head and quicken his strides. I ask again. The jaw stiffens, the legs move faster. I squeeze harder with my legs. It is only when he begins to struggle with his head that I finally get the message and relax my grip on the reins. The horse lowers his head and goes ahead, traveling just slightly sideways.

The Riddler may be more prone to misunderstanding than a young horse in a good school. He is older, with memories of humans that cause intense anxiety, and when he is visited by one of these memories, he stops in his tracks and shakes and sweats. Since he doesn't talk good pony, he has only limited forms for expressing these memories and creating happy ones. But a rider like Lendon Gray could expand his expressive range and his trust.

I wish I could—and so do thousands of other people in this country, or at least the thirty thousand members of the U.S. Dressage Federation. It's a pastoral yearning, like the ones that send people out of the city to places populated by other creatures of different minds. People want to howl with the wolf. They want to fly with the condor, swim with the dolphin. They want to ride the horse. But with horses our relationships have become a culture by now, so you can't just buy your ticket and hire a guide. You have to learn the lingo.

Perhaps it is the limitations of so many riders that have brought psychics into vogue with horse owners. For a fee, they will speak the horse's mind to its human. Lendon reported with wonder and wry humor the experience of one of her clients. His game old horse was showing considerable stiffness at the beginning of each ride, but he would go on with his work until the gimpiness disappeared. His owner dialed a psychic in California, and the medium gave a rather lengthy report of what was on the horse's mind. This included two pertinent statements: "I like being part of things even though my feet hurt. I need salt." Almost any aging horse still in work could have made the first statement, but the complaint about the salt applied specifically. When the owner checked the horse's stall, he found that out of thirty-some salt holders in the stable, only his horse's was empty. The experience rattled Lendon enough to make her reluctant to consult a psychic. "I might be horrified by what some of these horses would say about me."

What the horse says *to* her, however, is urgently important. Pony talk may be the language of patience, but it is also the source of Lendon Gray's impatience. She is aware of an imperative need to get the lingo down quickly. A move made wrong is a scale with a wrong note that once played will take hundreds of other performances to make the phrase right and beautiful. She remains keenly aware of the risk of failing with a particular horse, of failing to ride, and this is what makes her raise her voice at a student. "Now. Do it *now. Please. . . ."* The fact that a student is well known or dauntingly wealthy or powerful will not make Lendon back down or even tone down. "I'm getting old . . . *now!"* Dressage is long. Life just may be enough time.

Personals

BY MELISSA PIERSON

To say that Melissa Holbrook Pierson's *Dark Horses and Black Beauties* draws from sociology, psychology and cultural anthropology would make the book seem far more academic than it is. It's not at all, as shown by this chapter, chosen for its depiction of the dynamics not only between people and horses but among the denizens of a working stable.

Yesterday I moved a ton of manure. Actually, it was the horses who moved it; I merely pitched it into a wheelbarrow and rumbled it over the rocky dirt and up to the top of the pile of more manure, then upended it and began again—a true Sisyphean task, because the cart always rolls back down, and you always have to go up once more. It gave me new appreciation for the digestive systems of these animals, with their constant need for grass or grass substitutes to be moving through the colon.

I have become one of the small army of part-time workers at Dominique's barn offsetting the cost of lessons by doing the endless things that need doing. And, indeed, she runs her establishment with martial precision, though there is never the sense that these are the kind of orders one chafes under, the kind meant to bat you into line. You just do them, because you are getting something better than money in return: the opportunity to take her orders in the ring.

We are, in fact, a small army composed of slave masters who are in turn enslaved by our slaves. We are the ones who assiduously pick up their excrement behind them, the ones who put our hands under their penile sheaths on a regular basis to make sure they're clean. We bathe, curry, brush, mane-pull, tail-detangle, hoof-pick, daub with salve, apply spray, and take off and put on blankets, fly sheets, leg wraps, bell boots. They stand there and loudly demand their food.

Yet, go into a stall; close the door. Wait a moment. Something will occur to you, something that seems to shift in the air between the two of you. It is the weight of power, the weightlessness of vulnerability, exchanging ions. The horse is there looking at you with eyes the color of chocolate pudding. He cannot escape you, or whatever it is you mean to do with him.

This particular army is rather haphazard in organization, yet every-thing gets done: I have never been in a stable so clean. *Standards*—the highest of them. Aisles swept, stalls picked out several times a day, water buckets scrubbed and refilled. Brushes cleaned, tack soaped. No aesthetic overlay, how-ever: no flowers by the driveway or sign to announce the place's name, a couch barely fit for the Salvation Army in the viewing room, and, more often than not, no paper towels in the bathroom. But the working bolts, in their well-oiled condition, are their own visual pleasure. The horses, the order, the order.

The first of the two sergeants in the line of command is Amelia, barn manager. A flow of wavy light brown hair, pleasant steady demeanor, quiet. She has, Dominique says, one of the great posts—elegant, natural. This is no doubt aided by her body, which is trim and athletic and without any folderol at all. She does everything as Dominique decrees, often as she pauses in the middle of the arena while seated atop her horse: "Amelia, please give Deedee an extra flake of hay, then bring in Jesse from outside. When you're finished with that, get Dandy ready for the lesson. You can use the Wintec. Oh, and since we don't have any clean pads, look through the pile to find the best—I think Wilant's will be okay; he didn't exactly sweat today." Stuart, the second sergeant, is a friendly ex-city refugee with buzz-cut red hair, a former teacher of guitar. He likes to have music on as he works, Lou Reed or occasionally *Classical Music's Great Waltzes.* On it goes: "Stuart, you can do the buckets on this side, and then a quick pick run on the other." Along with the stacking of hay and shoveling of sawdust, Stuart builds and fixes everything from new paddocks to tack boxes to a hayloft and additional stalls.

Then there is Catherine, Dominique's protégée. She's like any pretty teenager with porcelain skin and fine lemon-colored hair; her cheeks flush deep rose as she spends hours picking rocks out of the paddocks under a hot summer sun at Dominique's request, but it seems she doesn't sweat. She has one of those purely American, corn-fed, "large-boned" frames, completely in accord with that of her seventeen-hand horse, Fury, whom she rides in dres-sage competition. She wants to go as far as she can, she says, to Grand Prix if possible, "though most people don't know just how much work this is." She has the legs to be able to communicate with the big ("Yeah, a big teddy bear!") animal. Another frequenter of the barn comments with a laugh how butch she looks when riding with two whips: "Pop-pop-pop! Man, I love it!" Catherine and Dominique are more like school pals than teacher and student separated by more than twenty years; they crack up uncontrollably when one of them says, "People hear the name *Fury* and expect this great wild thing—ha ha ha!"

Besides Stuart and one other fellow who has come in for a lesson or two, everyone who works there or learns there is female. (Dominique jokes that she is going to rename the place Tits-in-Front Farm, since that is the posture correction she makes most constantly.) That is, until Dominique advertises in *The Chronicle of the Horse* for a full-time working student and gets Frank.

I talk with him as I stand in the tack room oiling Dominique's double bridle, so new it is stiff and the black dye comes off with the saddle soap. I ask him where he comes from; I am curious ever since two days ago, when I first saw him momentarily doff his ever-present cap to reveal his balding head and suddenly appear much older than I thought he was. His lanky body, perfect for the old-fashioned thigh-balloon breeches he favors, makes him look exactly like one of those young British cavalry officers of the twenties or thirties who used themselves to illustrate their own riding manuals. Now I realize: *Not just starting out—starting over.*

He has previously worked with standardbreds, raising and training harness racers. Now, he says, the stakes are getting too rich for his blood, with good yearlings going for fifty thousand dollars and Canadians and even Europeans getting involved more and more. He moved to another stable nearby, but some family intrigue or other—he was very vague—made him want to leave.

He says he is here now, beginning a new thing entirely, because he is motivated to become a better horseman. Because all of the good horsemen he knows are good people, too. There is a correlation at the deepest level, he says: compassion for the animal, desire to do right, the need for "clean living." I sense he is not referring to lots of carrot juice and regular visits to the gym; this is the old construct, and I smell religion lurking nearby, just as I feel sadness coming off him even when he means to reveal nothing.

I watch Dominique as I do my work, and I get good at not gawking too obviously. She reminds me of a dog trainer I knew, a trainer whom people accused of committing miracles. There is that look of tight focus, the tendency to teach by praise, and to come down on a fault "like a bolt of lightning," in the trainer's words, and just as quickly to release the pressure. When a couple of

horses in the box stalls that line the two aisles are participating in some foolish-
ness together—"They want attention," she says, "but I'm going to show them
that's not the way to get it"—her body suddenly compresses, losing a fifth of its
size. She moves so fast it's as if she's done a sci-fi teleportation, suddenly disap-
pearing from the arena only to reappear near the tack room, where she picks
up a dressage whip. In another flash she's in Wilant's stall. "Do you see this
whip? Do you see that wall? I am hitting that wall"—*whap, whap, whap*—"so
you know never, never to do that. And you, too"—now she's in the next stall—
"don't play around with"—*whap*—"that crap. I've had it." She closes the door
and walks away. The horses have not been frightened, exactly; they look like
students who have been caught out. A few minutes later she looks back at
Wilant, who now bears a different look, and she interprets it in cartoon-char-
acter words: " 'What'd *I* do? *I* didn't do nothin'!' " She laughs.

Then she is schooling a student's horse, and she talks incessantly. "*Good*
boy, *good* boy—whoops, not that—I said *not* that—you're not going to do
that—*good* boy—yes, yes." Of course, her body is doing the real talking. She is
keeping him "round," "soft," "moving out," "gathered up," keeping him from
swinging his hindquarters around as they circle, and especially from dropping
his head and shoulder down as they circle to the right. Later she explains, "His
head is, what—two hundred pounds? I'm not going to *carry* it for him." They
canter in tiny circles, and the pace never varies.

It enlivens my time, not to mention me, to have a special horse to love.
But it would be too heartbreaking, like choosing another woman's man, to settle on one of the boarders' horses; instead I choose, or am chosen by, Wilant,
one of the two school horses. He is a large Dutch warmblood with a black
mane and tail; a wash of dapples over his body is so light that it requires the sun
to become visible. One of his eyelids droops away from his eyeball at the bottom, as if it had gotten hooked on something once.

Actually, I have fallen for him slowly, during which time he gradually
became "my boy." There is something adolescent and unprotected about him.
Dominique says he came from a rider who did not know how to ride him—
she was not malicious, but her inabilities allowed twists and constrictions to
cramp him into unhappiness. It has taken Dominique time to free him again,
to show him how to flex and stretch and cure himself. He will never, though,
stop hanging his great pink tongue out the side of his mouth as he works, or
become angry enough for fits of head-tossing if a rider has heavy hands. While
I am on his back I try to will my weight away from him so as not to hurt him;
his head remains perfectly still with me because I attempt no contact at all—

a petty form of abuse, Dominique informs me, since it leaves a horse direction-
less. But she is amused by the deal we seem to have struck: I won't ask him to
work very hard, and he won't put up a fuss with me.

So it is a real surprise one weekend when Monica, the wealthy girl-
friend of the man who financed the barn and known by some as the Con-
tessa—she of the Cinderella's sister demeanor, perennially cross and critical—
while showing me how to polo wrap Wil's legs (condescendingly): "Now, if
you expect to do dressage, you have to learn to polo wrap"), stops and rests her
hand on his rump. Her eyes squeeze into a terse black line. "If you ride him
badly, I'll *kill* you."

Later Frank is working in Wil's stall as I slip in to give him a good-bye
carrot; I have become a walking cliché. "You know, I have to tell you," I say,
"I've sort of fallen for Wil."

"What is it about Wil?" he asks. "Everyone here's in love with him—
you, Dominique, Monica."

"It's that combination of 'Please be kind, please' with this big hunk of
manliness," I explain. "You know, the paradox of *Take care of me—I can take care
of myself?*"

"No," Frank says.

I watch unseen from across the barn as Amelia, untacking Lupe, plants
a little kiss on his withers minutes after he has bucked his way around the ring
with her onboard. He is a particularly difficult case, coming from the racetrack,
where the grooms liked to play a little "game" with him, turning him into a
cantankerous biter. But any horse's misbehavior or difficulty seems to make
Amelia soften all the more, and the louder they get, the calmer she gets. She is
constantly talking to and smoothing them, even when she is talking to someone else, unlike so many riders who seem barely to notice there's a breathing
thing on the other end of the lead they're hauling on. She is becoming my
model for how to be with horses, for nothing they do seems to inspire either
anger or fear in her. The next horse she rides, Chocolate, has decided no one
should mount him unaided from the ground, and when she tries he succeeds
in tipping her over onto her rear and then runs around the ring loose. She
springs up and runs toward him, waving her arms, to spook him away from the
open door. Then she asks for a leg up and mounts him. She speaks in low tones
to him, and he soon lowers his head in relaxation.

Frank doesn't last long; perhaps his desire for clean living is not being
met here, or perhaps he does not believe that horses are as Dominique says

they are, as she acts they are with every move in her repertoire. The next working student, and the ones after her, will be young women.

Likewise, Wilant does not remain alone in my affections, not after the arrival of Dutchess, a draft cross with the coloring of a cow and a head about the same size. I start loving her the moment Dominique comments that we look good together as we go around the ring—this is yet another shameful thing that speaks unkindly of my character—and I continue loving her as I build fantasies that maybe she, finally, after all these years, would be my first horse, responding to the propitious omen of my having bought a house located between those of two women who own horses. Only there is no one who will give me the twenty-five hundred dollars she will cost as well as the indeterminate amount more it would take to keep her.

She is strangely aloof, taking carrots but never presuming thereafter that they are her due. I have always been attracted to the thick exterior, and I set about trying to see if in her case it conceals a wounded softness within. I think we look for mirrors in our love. One night I dream that she has reared up to put her front legs around my shoulders in a hug, but when I wake I realize I must have conflated her with my black-and-white girl dog, who can actually do that without killing me in order to express her regard.

I sit on the floor of her stall, writing. I note that if the pen slips, it is because she is looking for, though not demanding, more carrots. Her head is down in my lap—a *big* head. Her lips are pink, wrinkled, and hairless, human skin, baby skin. I pay no attention to the music Stuart is playing—his taste describes everything mine is not, and sometimes Catherine and I exchange a glance when he leaves the barn and move as one to change the tape—but suddenly I become aware of the words Rod Stewart is singing at that moment: "You're in my heart, you're in my soul . . ." I laugh, because you couldn't put something like that in a movie; stupidly, ludicrously, obvious. Her ears are large and bovine, and her lips and tongue, though so large as well, are delicate enough to take a fingernail-size piece of the dried mango I am eating. She stands quietly over me right now, larger than life.

Good Horse Keeping

BY PAUL ZARZYSKI

P aul Zarzyski has been an amateur and then a professional rodeo bareback bronc rider for more than a dozen years and a writer of poetry and prose for twice that length of time. A celebrated "cowboy poet," he has toured the world reading his works, of which he has published several collections.

That this entertaining and insightful selection contains the extra added attraction of poetry makes it all the more irresistible.

Life is a catch pen full of rodeo broncs, and way I figure it, forty-six years into this buck-out, the mission is to decide, early on, *Did you come to hide or did you come to ride?* If the latter, it doesn't take too many seasons forked to this buckin' horse orb named Earth before we learn the crude rude truth of the old adage: *Never a pony couldn't be rode, never a cowboy couldn't be throwed.* And subordinating this proverb is yet another cowpoke dictum: *Get pitched off, climb right back on.* Rodeo, like Poetry, can get into your hemoglobin, into the deep helices of DNA, and once there, it becomes your metaphorical makeup for life.

In Spanish, *rodear* means "to surround"; in colloquial Mexican, it means "a cattle roundup." *A-horseback* is understood, and understood so emphatically, that only bull riders (I can *cow*-poke fun at them here because most can't read anyway) might disagree that rodeo *means* horses. Moreover, I think rodeo cowboys relate to horses in ways that very well could qualify them as the staunchest of animal rights advocates. But let's put the raucous Yosemite Sam WHOA! on opening that Pandora's Saddlebag right now and lope off instead toward a few poems that have graced my Lariati-Literati Life because I choose to believe, my Muse has some Annie Oakley, Mr. Ed, Saint Francis of Assisi, Midnight, and My Friend Flicka in her bloodlines.

In the days when rodeo fever popped the cork and geysered the mercury out of my genuine Hopalong Cassidy bucking bronco thermometer, all I thought about was horses, Horses, HORSES! My focus burned so intensely that I became unable to discern the word *house* in print, which made for some interesting magazines at the newsstand. You had your *Horse Beautiful,* your *Good Horse Keeping,* your *Horse and Garden.* Same syndrome occurred with the word radio: National Public Rodeo, Rodeo Free Europe, Rodeo City Music Hall, and that little kid's wagon called a Rodeo Flyer. In any case, I'd be driving all night between rodeos and listening to the rodeo—I mean radio—to stay awake, and I'd look up at that full moon, and its Rorschach test shadow always appeared to me as the image of a bronc rider sittin' pretty in his leather throne on a high-rollin' bucker. Years later, I wrote this "rodeo romance."

THE BUCKING HORSE MOON

A kiss for luck, then we'd let 'er buck—
I'd spur electric on adrenaline and lust.
    She'd figure-8 those barrels
on her Crimson Missile sorrel–
    we'd make the night air swirl with hair and dust.

At some sagebrushed wayside, 3 A.M.,
we'd water, grain, and ground-tie Missile.
    Zip our sleeping bags together,
make love in any weather,
    amid the cactus, rattlers, and thistle.

Seems the moon was always full for us—
it's high-diving shadow kicking hard.
    We'd play kid games on the big night sky,
she'd say "that bronco's Blue-Tail Fly,
    and ain't that ol' J. T. spurrin' off its stars?"

We knew sweet youth's no easy keeper.
It's spent like winnings, all too soon.
    So we'd revel every minute
in the music of our Buick
    running smooth, two rodeoin' lovers
cruising to another—

beneath Montana's blue roan
bucking horse moon.

   The Augusta show at 2, we'd place again,
then sneak off to our secret Dearborn River spot.
   We'd take some chips and beer and cheese,
skinny-dip, dry off in the breeze,
   build a fire, fry the trout we caught.

   Down moonlit gravel back to blacktop,
she'd laugh and kill those beams for fun.
   That old wagon road was ours to own—
30 shows since I'd been thrown
   and 87 barrels since she'd tipped one.

   We knew that youth won't keep for rainy days.
It burns and turns to ash too soon.
   So we'd revel every minute
in the music of our Buick
   running smooth, two rodeoin' lovers
cruising to another—
   beneath Montana's blue roan
bucking horse moon.

   Ahhh, "sweet youth"—and no, it's truly not an "easy keeper" (said of a horse who winters well, holding his weight on minimal feed). And though the equine species, from sixty-million-year-old eohippus (the prehistoric "dawn horse," no bigger than a cocker spaniel) to today's mustangs, has drunk out of a lot more watering holes than we Homo sapiens, they haven't discovered the fountain of youth, either. Depending on vocation, a horse is usually considered to have reached retirement age of anywhere from six to eight years (race-horses) to twelve to fourteen years (roping, reining, show horses) to eighteen to twenty-two years (ranch/stock horses). On the average, horses age approximately three years for every human year. By the time they're twenty or twenty-two, they're often referred to as "pensioners" and put out to pasture just like us two-legged folks. If there *were* an Adam and Eve, and if they *were* responsible (having bitten into that measly McIntosh) for the injustices and disparities of today's world, I especially hold against them the so-called fact of life wherein the most common four-legged members of our families—dogs, cats, horses, rabbits, etc.—enjoy only a fraction of our longevity. It ain't my fault; I don't even like apples that much, and usually wind up feeding them out of the fruit bowl to our twenty-three-year-old mare, Cody (her favorite treat, next to getting into the bird feeder). Therefore should I ever be designated Creator for a Day, one of my first duties will be to see to it that horses live as long as parrots or turtles.

Speaking of religion, of the miracle of life, of that glowing, glowering coal of youth that stays a-smolder and waiting, in most of us I hope, for a stiff wind to blow away the soot and ash and expose the fire, I watched Big George Foreman—who trained like a Clydesdale as he harnessed himself to a jeep and pulled it around his neighborhood—convincingly win a fight recently against a very strong thirty-two-year-old opponent. George is forty-eight. At the Red Lodge Rodeo years ago, I saw a black mare named High Prairie buck off the World Champion Saddle Bronc Rider and do a little soft shoe in the middle of him to add just a skosh of injury to the incredible insult. In the midst of a couple dozen cowboys straining to restrain their chuckles in back of the bucking chutes, I swear I heard old High Prairie nickering all the way back to the catchpen: ". . . never a cowboy couldn't be throwed, be throwed, be throwed." I *know* Sonny and Pat Linger, High Prairie's guardians, heard her because they made no effort at all to curb their knee-slappin' delight. By the way, that horse was thirty-three years old at the time. I wonder if Big George will still be climbing into the ring at ninety-nine?

I wish my saddle horse Buck (short for Buckskin, actually), could have lived into his George Years (Foreman, Burns) as High Prairie lived so vibrantly into hers. The morning I found him dead in the corral, I phoned the neighbor—hoping to borrow his tractor—and when, in relating my situation, I choked up and broke down, he responded, "It's just a horse." Understand that he's not a cruel man; unlike myself, who didn't begin hanging around horses day-to-day, until my twenties, he'd likely been aboard them since he was three or four; his family had owned dozens, bought and sold them, watched them come and go, live and die. Although I had come to know "intimately" hundreds of rodeo broncs, Buck was sort of my first, shall we say, partner. I don't know if my good friend and neighbor ever sat in front of the TV at midnight while eating a bowl of Wheaties, mid-January Montana windchill temps pushing eighty below zero, and thought to himself, "Wonder if my horse is craving a late-night snack, too," then bundled up in umpteen layers and plodded, like a moon-walking astronaut, to serve up a half canful of grain and a couple alfalfa flakes? Maybe he has. And maybe he's missed his lost horses as much as I've missed mine and grieved every bit as hard.

BUCK

The December my horse died, I did not
go to midnight mass
to celebrate with a single-sip of wine
Christ's birth. Instead, lit
between a nimbus moon and new snow,
I guzzled mescal and mimicked the caroling
coyotes down the crick
where weeks earlier I dragged Buck
behind the pickup—horizontal
hooves at an awkward trot
in the side mirror, an image
I'll take with me to hell. No backhoe,
no D-8 Cat to dig a grave with, I left
nim in deep bunchgrasss, saffron
Belly toward the south
like a warm porch light thrown
suddenly over those singing
No-el, No-el . . .

   "Riding the same ground
that past spring for horned cow skulls
to adorn our gates, I spotted four
bleached white as puffballs,
methodically stuffed them
into a *never-tear* trash bag,
balanced the booty
off one thigh and tried to hold
jog-trot Buck to a walk,
my forefinger hefting
the left rein to curb
his starboard glance.

One by one,
like spook-show aliens hatching
from human brisket, white shoots popped
through that hot black plastic
gleaming in moon sun that turned
my grasp to butterfat. And when I reached,
lifting to retwist my grip,
it was sputnik flying low, it was
Satan's own crustacean unleashed, it was the
prehistoric, eight-horned, horse-eating bug
that caught Buck's eye
the instant his lit fuse hit powder. Lord,
how that old fat pony, living
up to his name one last time,
flashed his navel at angels,
rattled and rolled my skulls like dice,
and left me on all fours
as he did on that Christmas—high-
lonesomed, hurt, and howling
not only holy word toward the bones.

I never again road east—toward Buck's bones. By now, I suppose someone could have picked up his skull and hung it on their gate or barn. I guess that thought bothers this former grave-robber a bit. Most ranches have established boneyards to which winter-killed stock is dragged for decades and decades. Renowned western writer Teresa Jordan offers a passage in *Riding the White Horse Home* about the critical moment in which a horseman works a colt toward the bones. The idea is to slowly and gently expose the young animal to everything and anything that might later, under sudden first-time encounters, instinctively cause him to spook. Whether they recognize it as such or not, horses do not like the look, or smell, of death. Ol' Buck illustrated this to me in no uncertain terms. I suppose most herbivores feel the same way.

The spring following Buck's departure, our mare, Cody, foaled on Memorial Day. I was in my rodeo-old forties—my riggin'-riding days pretty much history—and was struggling with resigning myself to a life between youth and death, complete with the reentry of the words *house* and *radio* into my old geezer language. I was missing then, and likely will forever miss, the challenge of, and the elation after, making a classy ride on a snappy bronc. I was also missing my rodeo *compadres*; the majority of them had, years back, begun to take on normal lives—marriages, mortgages, steady jobs, children— but the truth be known, I missed those bucking horses most, their personalities and temperaments far more akin to my own than that of fellow humans with whom I cross trails these days.

One of the premier horse gentlers in the West, Randy Rieman, who I have the honor of calling friend, is riding colts full-time for the Parker Ranch in Hawaii. He encounters very few horses that he can't coach toward feeling safe, at ease, and maybe even "fulfilled" with saddle and cowboy aboard. Randy told me recently, however, of one three-year-old, after days and days of groundwork, that bucked, under his first saddling, from 5 P.M. till sundown. A horse like that will probably wind up in a rodeo string and have a good long careeer of eight-second workdays, according to Randy. "My kind of guy," I thought, and kept the notion to myself, knowing how important it is to Randy to find—to watch and listen and feel for—whatever unique equine code and/or communication will convince each individual horse to place his trust in the funny-lookin' critter standing upright.

So Cody game birth to a healthy filly we named Rosebud— not Rodeo Rose or Widow Maker, Whiplash or Reller's Wreck, Snake Eyes, Aces-'n'-Eights, Sky Lab, Booger Red, Crash, Moonshine, or Midnight. And although it *was* Memorial Day, I felt no cemetery visitation obligation: Ol' Buck had not received a formal burial or headstone. Few horses do. One of the greatest rodeo champions of all time, however, not only has a marble, but one engraved with verse. I stood before his final resting place recently at The National Cowboy Hal of Fame in Oklahoma City and felt something power-ful in both the place and the words—

> Underneath this sod lies a great
>   bucking hoss
> There were lived a cowboy he
>   couldn't toss
> His bane was Midnight, his coat
>   black as coal
> If there's a horse heaven, please, God,
>   rest his soul.

—and what I felt somehow reflected off the poem I wrote that Memorial Day in praise to parturition, equine-style:

I AM NOT A COWBOY

because cowboys don't cry and I can't fight back
my 4-H'er greenborn rapture
while watching Cody foal—no white socks up front,
a blazed face breaking through the giant dew-
drop into the 10:15 A.M. sun,
two hind socks stretched side-by-side in the dirt
like reverse white-on-black exclamation marks, and
yup *it's a filly!* Because *real* cowboys frown
unless it's a *horse colt* with four black feet,
this poem, I suppose, should tone down
its jubilation. Sorry fellers, for losing it,
but this cute little filly finds her footing
fast as you can think that single big syllable
HEART. And she stays up, pivoting
off mom's legs, like a ring-wise prize
fighter using the corner posts and ropes,
to gather herself after taking
birth's hard shot. It's Memorial Day
but these tears are not for the fallen
because I'm out here cheering on new life,
no taps bugled sat in the breeze
through these balm-of-Gileads
as the suckling foal's curled upper lip
blossoms, her gums
the pink-red rosebud-persimmon
color I think of when I think of the living,
when I think, again, of HEART. Let's rhyme it,
for tradition's sake, with *smart.*
Let's make this poem *cowboy* and make up some
for the poet, who tries but just can't quite
swallow hard enough his joy
as four more quarter horse quarter note
hooves step their first

Rosebud-with-Cody
Sorrel stroll around our corral.
                        —*For Elizabeth*

Cody and Rosebud now make up one half of our quarter-horse quartet, which we consider the most interesting, in many ways, two thirds of our family of six. When we left the large ranch where Buck died and Rosebud was born, we had a hard time finding an affordable place with enough acreage on which to keep our four horse people. Folk close to our predicament admonished, "Why not sell them?" To which we sometimes replied, "For the same reasons, we suppose, you haven't opted as yet to sell Jimmy or Suzy." In my opinion there are few differences. Sure, it costs a little more to keep our horses in shoes and food, and their schooling doesn't come cheap, either—not to even mention vet bills and worming medicine. On the other hand, we didn't have to invest a single frustrating in day in potty training. There is, however, one extremely significant and difficult difference: unlike guardians of sons and daughters, we've had to come to accept, and even hope, that our horses will die before us. Only then can we ensure that their entire lives are lived with the most humane care a "people person" can offer a "horse person." On second thought, maybe God—Her Pegasus Paint Self—got it right after all?

Two Sisters

ELLIE PHAYER AS TOLD TO GERALDINE MELLON

I had the pleasure of knowing Ellie Phayer through two equestrian tourism junkets that she organized, one to Wales and the other to England's Dartmoor region. Her untimely death six years ago deprived the world of her energetic and caring spirit. This story here shows how beautifully horses can literally and metaphorically come to represent important segments of a human life.

I have a horse in Ireland. Truly, she's my horse. I've not bought her, but we all know she's my horse. Sister is a 16.3-hand dark bay. I don't know if she's the most beautiful horse in the world. I do know that never have I had such telepathy with a horse. When I'm mounted, boundaries dissolve. Horse and rider—sisters, if you will—share one body, one mind and yes, one soul.

Sister and I met one misty Irish morning on the Connemara coast, a day nearing the end of one of the legendary Willie Leahy's cross-country rides. The previous evening a fellow rider had challenged me to a race, come dawn. "A race it is in the morning then," agreed Willie. That night, without my knowing, Willie sent 90 kilometers to his stable for my special mount.

"You'll have Sister," he said next morning, and Sister stepped out of the horse box into my life. Surprised, delighted, I quickly saddled and mounted, eager for the prerace warm-up. Willie, in the meantime, set off inspecting a mile and a half of beach to make sure the "track" was safe.

From the beginning, Sister and I were of one mind. During the warm-up we connived, Sister and I. Sensing her power, I held her sharply in check. She immediately agreed with this strategy and obligingly relaxed, craftily hiding her true feelings and capabilities. Like two skilled poker players lurking behind a calm, almost lazy facade, we knew . . . we knew.

251

Warm-up over, Willie yet a distant pinpoint, we quietly watched the 20-odd riders stationing themselves along the course in gentle surf. Unexpectedly, my life began to flash before me. What a long way from the intellectual little Brooklyn girl, the girl whose musical talent led her to the brink of the concert stage. The young wife, mother and scholar turning to music of another sort, the lyrical magic of English and Irish literature. The young woman whose life lost its melody with the death of a beloved four-year-old daughter. Divorce. Teaching and single-parenting a son. Nervous years cured with self-doubt, grief, unnamed fear. And the son, nearly a man, gone to college.

Abruptly my thoughts returned to the race, and I gleefully anticipated flying with Sister, my Pegasus. Instantly catching the mood, she tensed, pricked ears in readiness. Not yet, Sister, not yet.

Retreating into the past, I recalled a certain horse ride, one of my first. The horse sped away at what I took for a dead gallop. Far from being frightened, I loved it and experienced total, absolute glee, the same emotion now dancing invisible pathways between Sister and me.

The "dead gallop" in my fortieth year pivoted my life, changing it forever. At age 41, alone, my uneasy world badly needing direction, I began riding. By the third lesson, I was jumping. I was making mistakes, but riding came naturally to me. From the time I started horse riding, free-floating nervousness plagued me no more. It simply disappeared. Riding competence sparked internal confidence, and fears receded into memory. Had it been eight years since my first lesson? Eight years leading me to the back of this gallant mare?

Sister stirred gently beneath me, nudging my thoughts toward the impending race. Still Willie had not returned from reconnoitering, and thoughts drifted again.

One year's riding, and I'm planning English riding holidays for college students, demanding—and getting, if you can believe it—the best riding instructors in England. By my second year, I knew I was great. That is no longer true, but in those days, I absolutely knew I was great. That second year, bent on impressing Maj. J.M.B. Birtwistle, trainer of English Olympians, I prepared to go over an indoor course of seven jumps.

"Ellie, the horse you're on stops at the fourth jump," warned an instructor.

"Not with me, he won't!" But, alas, the horse refused, while I, staying on course, cleared the jump with ease. Remounted, reluctant horse and red-faced rider cleared the jump in unison.

But something was wrong. Parts of that undergarment peculiar to women dangled near my wrists. What could I do? Heading for the next jump, I desperately tried to wiggle the offending garment into place.

"The hands," commented Maj. Birtwistle, "are very busy."

My antics undoubtedly fueled the cheeky American stereotype. Sister, I'm glad you didn't know me then.

Eight years in the saddle over hundreds of English and Irish miles and I became a weaver of dreams. My livelihood was accompanying riders to the British Isles. And to this windswept beach.

Today, Sister, the gods have blessed us, have granted us power to race the very wind. Confidence born of other lifetimes connects us. One in body, mind and spirit, we are invincible.

Suddenly, I understood that, as surely as we two were sisters and the race was ours, just as surely my life was mine, not to be lost to invading cancer. Weakened from chemotherapy, weary at the prospect of imminent surgery, I had arrived for this Connemara trek.

Willie, with uncanny Irish inkling, sensed the importance of this race, suspected the supernatural bond that would unite horse and rider. He felt it, and sent for Sister. Now joy coursed through my veins as her great body anticipated my thoughts.

The bets were in place, the markers laid, the spectators waiting, mounted in the shallow surf boundary. It was time. I licked salt spray from my lips, and we were off. I never felt her hooves cut into the sand; we were winged sisters racing our brother wind. It was no contest. The contender lagged 20 lengths when we flew across the finish line. We did it, Sister, we did it!

Later, I basked in adulation. Teenage girls braided my hair; fellow rides praised my skill. The race netted me 50 pounds, and Willie grinned, a knowing twinkle in his eye.

Still, the 50 pounds were a bit of an embarrassment. I had, after all, brought these riders to Ireland on holiday. Sister, the next day, continuing to read my thoughts, came up with the perfect solution. As we walked through a gap in a farmer's wall, a dry stone wall hundreds of years old, she cleverly arranged for me to bump my toe on a particular stone—the keystone of 14 feet of wall. Amid 30 stomping, wild-eyed, spooking horses, the wall, like so many dominoes, fell. When the dust settled, I handed my 50 pounds to the farmer.

And so the trek ended. I returned home and regained my health, as I knew I would. Two years have passed. We two remain sisters of spirit, often sharing misty green miles. Ireland shines as my special joy.

I have a horse in Ireland.

Permissions Acknowledgments

Bill Barich, "Dreaming" from *The Sporting Life*. Copyright © 1999 by Bill Barich. Reproduced with the permission of The Lyons Press.

Stephen Budiansky, "Tallyho and Tribulation" from *The Atlantic Monthly* (September 2000). Copyright © 2000 by Stephen Budiansky. Reprinted with the permission of the author.

Esther Forbes, "Breakneck Hill" from *Grinnell Review*. Copyright 1944 by Esther Forbes. Reprinted with the permission of Frances Collin Literary Agency.

Dick Francis, "A Royal Rip-Off at Kingdom Hill" from *Classic* (June/July 1976). Copyright © 1975 by Dick Francis. Reprinted with the permission of Sterling Lord Literistic, Inc.

Gilbert Frankau, "Mustard-Pot, Matchmaker" from *Men, Maids and Mustard-Pot* (New York: The Century Company, 1924). Copyright 1924 by Gilbert Frankau. Reprinted with the permission of Timothy d'Arch Smith.

Ben K. Green, "Sleeping Sickness" from *The Village Horse Doctor: West of the Pecos*. Copyright © 1971 by Ben K. Green, renewed 1999 by Jaime C. Taylor and Martha K. Taylor. Reprinted with the permission of Alfred A. Knopf, a division of Random House, Inc.

James Herriot, Chapter 19 from *All Things Bright and Beautiful*. Copyright © 1973, 1974 by James Herriot. Reprinted with the permission of St. Martin's Press, LLC and David Higham Associates, Ltd.

Nancy Jaffer, "Nona Garson" [editor's title, originally titled "Riding High on the Grand Prix Circuit"] from the New Jersey *Star-Ledger* (May 26, 1997). Copyright © 1997 by The Star-Ledger. Reprinted with permission. All rights reserved.

Maxine Kumin, "Why Is It That Girls Love Horses?" from *Ms.* (April 1983). Copyright © 1983 by Maxine Kumin. Reprinted with the permission of the author.

Ring Lardner, "Tips on Horses" from *The Ring Lardner Reader*, edited by Maxwell Geisman. Copyright © 1963 by Charles Scribner's Sons, renewed 1991 by Ring Lardner, Jr. Reprinted with the permission of Scribner, a division of Simon & Schuster, Inc.

Beryl Markham, "Was There a Horse with Wings?" from *West with the Night*. Copyright 1942, 1983 by Beryl Markham. Reprinted with the permission of North Point Press, a division of Farrar, Straus & Giroux, LLC., Laurence Pollinger, Ltd. and the Estate of Beryl Markham.

Cookie McClung, "From Sailboats to Snaffles in One Easy Marriage" from *Horsefolk Are Different: A Selection of Short Stories on Horse Experiences*. Copyright © 1987 by The Chronicle of the Horse, Inc. Reprinted with the permission of The Chronicle of the Horse, Inc.

Thomas McGuane, "Buster" from *Some Horses*. Copyright 1999 by Thomas McGuane. Reprinted with the permission of The Lyons Press.

Holly Menino, "The Ponies Are Talking" from *Forward Motion*. Copyright © 1996 by Holly Menino. Reproduced with the permission of The Lyons Press.

William Nack, "Pure Heart" from *Sports Illustrated* (1990). Copyright © 1990. Reprinted with the permission of the publishers. All rights reserved.

Ellie Phayer as told to Geraldine Mellon, "Two Sisters" from *Straight from the Heart*, compiled by the editors of *Equus*. Copyright © 1997 by Fleet Street Publishing Company. Reprinted with the permission of the Primedia Equine Group.

Melissa Holbrook Pierson, "Personals" from *Dark Horses and Black Beauties*. Copyright © 2000 by Melissa Holbrook Pierson. Reprinted with the permission of W. W. Norton & Company, Inc. and Granta Books.

Alois Podhajsky, "School Horses, the Most Important Assistants of the Instructor" from *My Horses, My Teachers* (New York: Doubleday, 1968). Copyright ©

1968 by Alois Podhajsky. Reprinted with the permission of Trafalgar Square Publishing and Buchberlage Ullstein Langen Muller.

Damon Runyon, "All Horse Players Die Broke" from *Guys and Dolls: The Stories of Damon Runyon*. Copyright © 1992 by Sheldon Abend. Reprinted with the permission of Viking Penguin, a division of Penguin Putnam Inc. and Penguin Books, Ltd.

Andy Russell, excerpt from "Horses and Horsemen" from *Trails of a Wilderness Wanderer*. Copyright 1970, 1988 by Andy Russell. Reprinted with the permission of The Lyons Press.

Felix Salten, "The Imperial Spanish Riding School" from *Florian, the Emperor's Stallion* (Indianapolis, Ind.: The Bobbs-Merrill Company, 1934). Copyright 1934 by Felix Salten. Reprinted with the permission of Sanford J. Greenburger Associates.

Jane Smiley, "Mr. T's Heart" from *Practical Horseman* (October 1999). Copyright © 1999 by Jane Smiley/Horse Heaven. Reprinted with the permission of the Aaron M. Priest Literary Agency, Inc.

Gene Smith, Chapter 10 from *The Champion*. Copyright © 1987 by Gene Smith. Reprinted with the permission of Scribner, a division Simon & Schuster, Inc. and Curtis Brown, Ltd.

Red Smith, "A Vote for Ta Wee" from *The Red Smith Reader*, edited by Dave Anderson. Copyright © 1970 by Red Smith. Reprinted with the permission of Phyllis W. Smith.

William Steinkraus, "On Winning" from *Reflections on Riding and Jumping*. Copyright © 1997 by William Steinkraus. Reprinted with the permission of Trafalgar Square Publishing.

Paul Trachtman, "The Horse Whisperer" from *Smithsonian* (May 1998). Copyright © 1998 by Paul Trachtman. Reprinted with the permission of the author.

Carey Winfrey, excerpt from "Tip on a Lost Race." Copyright © 1972 by Carey Winfrey. Reprinted with the permission of the author.

Paul Zarzyski, "Good Horsekeeping" from *Horse People*, edited by Michael J. Rosen. Copyright © 1998 by Michael J. Rosen. Reprinted with the permission of Artisan, a division of Workman Publishing Co., Inc., New York. All rights reserved.

Paul Zarzyski, "The Bucking Horse Moon," "Buck," and "I Am Not a Cowboy" from *All This Way for the Short Ride: Roughstock Sonnets 1971–1996* by Paul Zarzyski and Barbara Can Cleve. Copyright © 1996 by the Museum of New Mexico Press. Reprinted with the permission of the publishers.